supported by a community goal and grant
FIGURE FOUNDATION

BLEEDING GREEN

BLEEDING GREEN

GREEN

*A History of the
Hartford Whalers*

CHRISTOPHER PRICE

UNIVERSITY OF NEBRASKA PRESS   LINCOLN

The University of Nebraska Press is part
of a land-grant institution with campuses
and programs on the past, present, and
future homelands of the Pawnee, Ponca,
Otoe-Missouria, Omaha, Dakota, Lakota,
Kaw, Cheyenne, and Arapaho Peoples, as
well as those of the relocated Ho-Chunk,
Sac and Fox, and Iowa Peoples.

Library of Congress Cataloging-
in-Publication Data
Names: Price, Christopher, 1969– author.
Title: Bleeding green: a history of the
Hartford Whalers / Christopher Price.
Description: Lincoln: University
of Nebraska Press, 2022.
Identifiers: LCCN 2022005487
ISBN 9781496222008 (hardback)
ISBN 9781496234216 (epub)
ISBN 9781496234223 (pdf)
Subjects: LCSH: Hartford Whalers
(Hockey team)—History.
Classification: LCC GV848.H37 P75 2022 |
DDC 796.962/640973—dc23/eng/20220209
LC record available at https://
lccn.loc.gov/2022005487

Set in Adobe Garamond by Laura Buis.
Designed by N. Putens.

For Mom

CONTENTS

ACKNOWLEDGMENTS

Wait, you're *doing a hockey book?*

That was the reaction that a lot of friends and family had when I told them about this project. I loved all sports growing up, but if you told me when I was in my twenties I'd write a book about hockey before, say, one on basketball, I would have thought you were crazy. But the Whalers do crazy things to you, I guess.

I can say, "This is a hockey book." But really, this is a hockey book in the same way that *Field of Dreams* is a movie about baseball or *He Got Game* is about basketball. Hockey is the backdrop, sure. But you should think of this as a love story between a region and a team and a fan base that, for a relatively brief period, took them in as their own. I lived that relationship, and that's what is at the heart of this book. I wish you all could feel the same level of excitement I did when I picked up the phone one morning and heard the words *Hey, Chris, Ron Francis here.* I would love to have the fiftysomething version of me be able to reach the sixteen-year-old Christopher Price and let him know, "One day, you'll have Kevin Dineen's phone number . . . and he's going to call you back to tell you more stories about 'Brass Bonanza.'"

Honestly, this was a very weird book to write. A sizable chunk of this book was done during a worldwide pandemic. In many ways, writing it helped keep me sane, especially after we all went into lockdown. When I was out of balance mentally and worried I was going to tip over, this project was a great way to shut the door and tune out the rest of the world. Honestly, being able to put the blinders on and write about the 1986 Whalers was great escapist therapy. There were times where I absolutely needed this project.

Really, this book took a long freaking time—six years from the initial idea to final product. In that time, I changed agents and had three different full-time jobs. (In between the start and finish of this project, two other books—*Drive for Five* and *The Ultimate Football Trivia Book*—have come and gone. Both are still available—check your local bookstores!) But with all my heart, I believe it was worth it. *Oh, indeed.* Every writer should be lucky enough to have at least one story like this in him or her, whether a newspaper story, magazine piece, or book. I really love all my other books, but I have a unique sense of ownership when it comes to this story and this team. Not since *Baseball by the Beach* has a story hit me this personally. It makes me happy and proud to be able to bring it to the world.

So who gets the credit? This might be the first book where the acknowledgments are longer than the actual manuscript. There are roughly a half million people who had a hand in this project (trust me—I'm only mildly exaggerating), and they all deserve a shout-out for allowing this to see the light of day. So settle in.

Let's start at the beginning with superagent Alec Shane. When I was looking to jump-start the second phase of my career as an author a few years ago, after a conversation with my wife (more on that in a second), I ran a bunch of book ideas past him. Most were dismissed relatively quickly, but he thought there was some potential with a history of the Whalers. It wasn't a straight line from idea to book—there were a few stops along the way. *We* fought and scrapped and worked to make this thing a reality. Alec, this wouldn't have come to fruition without you. You are a warrior.

My wife, Kate, deserves kudos for so many reasons, but she was the one who had the idea for this project. We were sitting in our living room one summer afternoon and talking about dream books. She suggested something on the history of the Whalers. "You always get such a great response when you wear your Whalers cap or T-shirt. Why not a book on the Whalers?" After pondering that for about a half second, I said, "That's a great idea." She's really the one you want to thank here. And thanks go to my son, Noah, who kept asking me, "So, when are you going to finish the Whalers book?" *Done and done.*

Thank you to the former players, coaches, and fans, as well as owners and employees of the Whalers and those who covered the team through the years. (Facebook might be a soulless and evil corporation, but it proved fruitful for tracking down ex-Whalers.) In the end, I spoke with eighty-one people for this project, all of whom provided something worth including. Ex-players usually started first conversations cautiously: "You're doing a book on what? Where are you from? Why should I talk to you?" By the end, many of them were sharing stories and furnishing entries from their own address books. Thanks to all the ex-players I met who opened their memory banks to provide me with all sorts of fun stories. There are too many to count here, but I especially want to acknowledge Jordy Douglas, Stew Gavin, Brian Propp, Mike Liut, Kelly Chase, Cap Raeder, and Andrew Cassels for their time and for serving as references when I needed an in with other ex-players. Getting the stamp of approval from former Whalers play-by-play guys Chuck Kaiton, Rick Peckham, and John Forslund was like getting into the inner circle. Thanks to all of you for serving as my unofficial passport. Connecting with Ben Baskin and Iggy Monda of the *Lost in Sports* podcast also provided plenty of help and information. Former Whalers employees Mark Willand and Victor Masi provided a wealth of information. And Dean Zappalorti and Jeff Dooley of the Hartford

Yard Goats were extremely helpful in setting up introductions with Whalers alumni during the reunion weekend.

Dan, Jon, and Jeff Tapper, as well as Stephen Popper, are Whalers fans from way back and knew exactly what I was talking about when I would text them excitedly something like, "I know someone who has Mike Zuke's phone number!" Their wisdom and passion helped fuel this project—whenever I started wondering about the readability of this book, I asked myself if it was the sort of thing they'd enjoy. Thanks for everything, fellas.

An early plea on Twitter for Whalers information led to a package from Kirk Luedeke that was filled with Whalers memorabilia, media guides, and hockey cards. Thanks so much for that jump start, Kirk, and I hope we can work together some day. A few books on the history of the franchise proved to be extremely helpful. Jack Lautier put together two great books about the Whalers with *15 Years of Whalers Hockey* and *Forever Whalers*. Quite simply, I wouldn't have been able to put this book together without using his work as a reference. Former Whalers goaltender Bruce Landon's book, *The Puck Stops Here*, is also well worth your time. As a former owner, Howard Baldwin was a tremendous resource, but his bio, *Slim and None*, is a terrific read that provides plenty of insight into the world of hockey and entertainment. *The Rebel League: The Short and Unruly Life of the World Hockey Association* from Ed Willes was not only a blast to read but also invaluable when it came to this project. I loved the passion that inspired *Brass Bonanza Plays Again* from Bob Muldoon. And books written by Stu Grimson, Dave Semenko, Brian Burke, Mark Howe, and Gordie Howe all shed some more light on what it was like playing for (or leading) the Whalers.

Colleagues at the *Boston Globe* were awesome throughout the process. I'll always be indebted to Matt Pepin for taking a chance on a veteran free agent in the summer of 2019. The day in July that I got the phone call from him welcoming me to the paper is on the short list of the single greatest days of my life. Jim Hoban, Bob Fedas, John Carney, Jon

Couture, Andrew Mahoney, Katie McInerney, Scotty Thurston, Craig Larson, Jim Clark, Greg Lang, Michael Vega, Bonnie Foust, John Vitti, Marty Pantages, Terrance Harris, Amin Touri, and Tommy Piatchek are amazing colleagues.

Journalists Mike Giardi, Alex Speier, Charlie Pierce, Leigh Montville, Aaron Schatz, Mike Adams, Steve Buckley, and Gerry Brooks provided good thoughts and inspiration. Old bosses Saul Williams, Rob Bradford, and Greg Bedard deserve thanks for helping me reach my destination. At the start of this book, I was a stranger in a strange land, and many of the hockey writers (past and present) in my life helped out with a phone number, email address, or just some positive feedback.

Speaking of journalists, it was hard to write this book and not think about the late Alan Greenberg. I spent a lot of time with Alan when he covered the Patriots in the early days of the twenty-first century; he was one of the only guys on the beat who could make Bill Belichick smile on a regular basis. A sweet guy who always had time for a younger reporter, he wrote extensively about the Whalers for the *Hartford Courant* in the late 1980s and early 1990s. Throughout the course of writing this book, going back and finding a well-turned phrase of his to describe Kevin Dineen or Ronnie Francis always made me smile. He was a terrific writer and an even better guy. He's missed.

Friends are everything, and they all played a big role along the way: Mike Biglin, Heidi Witt, Dan Brem, Rachel Resnik, Amy Cantin-Kaye, Stephen Kaye, Dave Guarino, Heidi Guarino, Jason Lefferts, Jen Lefferts, Ian Lefferts, Greg Petronzio, Ann Kathleen Guy, Greg Levy, Gretchen Dietrich, Darren Levy, Ed MacLean, Julie Cornell, Sandra Torres, Georgia Churilla, Paul Howard, Maggie Pasquale, Jen Timmins, Mike Merriam, Seth Schwartz, Jim O'Sullivan, Gerry Brown, Bill Taylor, Chip Bergstrom, Christy Bergstrom, Vin Ferrara, Windsor Ferrara, Chris Riley, Maureen Jones, Glenn Meister, Liz Meister, the McMahon family, and Jo Evans. I salute you all.

And then, there's family: my dad, Kate, Noah, Kelly, Terrence, Jas, Christopher, Molly, Marc, Mina, Kari, and Paul all get a big thanks, not to mention the great four-legged friends past and present like Boots, Scout, Stretch, Trevor, Prince, Caroline, Maggie, and Hamish. They're the best home-field advantage a sportswriter could ever hope to have.

My mom passed in October 2021. I miss her every day. She drove me and my friends to Hartford, dropped us off at the mall, and gave me money for chili at Wendy's and a ticket in the nosebleeds. She encouraged me to be a writer. This book wouldn't have been *this book* without her.

In the end, it's Kate. The truth of the matter is that I'm married to a rock star and genius and am lucky enough to be in touch with just a little bit of her magic on a daily basis.

BLEEDING GREEN

Introduction

They were *our* team.

If you grew up as a snot-nosed sports fan in the suburbs of Connecticut, you were always forced to choose your allegiances—the Red Sox or the Yankees, the Patriots or the Jets and Giants. The Border War was fought between Boston and New York—if you lived north of Hartford, chances were pretty good you were a Boston guy. If you were south of Hartford, you probably owned a Yankees cap and rooted for the Knicks. When it came to professional sports in Connecticut, there was passion but no *possession* and almost no professional sporting identity. It was a neutral area carved up by the Boston and New York fan bases.

But when it came to hockey, it was a different deal. Starting in the 1970s, Connecticut had *professional hockey*. The Whalers started in Boston, but they soon moved south—we welcomed them quickly, even supporting the team when it had to return to Massachusetts for a spell after the roof fell in. What did we get back? Professional sports. The state of Connecticut was suddenly more than just a pit stop between Boston and New York.

The thing was, they weren't that great. Hell, they weren't even that *good* for large stretches of their twenty-plus years of existence. But in the end, that really didn't matter, because they were *ours*. From the early days in the mid-1970s when they first showed up as hockey vagabonds, booted from the Boston Garden, they were *our* team. (Shout-out to Rhode Island for that one—if Providence mayor Buddy Cianci didn't preside over the most corruption-infested city in New England in the 1970s, they might have been the Providence Whalers. But I'll have more on that shortly.) The only pro sports team ever to survive over an extended stretch in the state, the Whalers helped usher in an era of big-time sports to the state of Connecticut.

The Hartford Civic Center collapsed one winter night—thank God no one was inside—and the team had to move into what amounted to an oversized barn in Springfield for a stretch. But they remained *our* team. My parents made the fifty-mile round-trip drive from the Hartford suburbs to western Massachusetts. When they couldn't give us a ride, commuter buses provided transportation.

Why did we do it? The Whalers had one of the greatest logos in professional sports history and a cheesy theme song ("Brass Bonanza"), and most of the time, their season was done by the time Mother's Day rolled around. But they were *ours*.

"The Whalers were the only game in town," remembered Sam Kennedy, who was an intern with the Whalers in the 1990s before eventually becoming CEO and president of the Red Sox roughly twenty years later. "Hockey has such a diehard, passionate fan base, and the Whalers were it. It was a great relationship between the state and the team. It was such a huge point of pride that I worked for the Whalers when I was younger. I can't tell you how many people I've engaged in conversations with over the years, anyone with any type of connection to Connecticut or Hartford, and they always say, 'Oh, I was the biggest Whalers fan you'll ever meet.' You get that in all sports, of course, but at that time in Hartford, you really sensed it."

"They didn't leave a big footprint when it comes to hockey terms, but that intersection with people loving hockey and people really being proud that Connecticut had a team of their own was really something," said veteran journalist Bruce Schoenfeld, who grew up in southern Connecticut. "When you love somewhere and are proud of where you live—I mean, most of New England really probably disdains Connecticut; 'You guys are basically New York'—to have something like that is special.

"Look, you can't run through the streets and cheer on the library. 'We have great bookstores! I love our weather!' You do that with your teams. *This was my team.* They stood for me. Even though they haven't had the sort of lasting legacy from a hockey standpoint, once you energize a fan base, that feeling lingers. You feel a sense of validation. 'I live in a real place and this team represents proudly.' We had that with the Whalers."

"The Whalers and I grew up together," recalled longtime fan Jon Tapper, who, like many, can chart a sizable portion of his life through Hartford hockey milestones. "The franchise moved to Hartford when I was a toddler. They entered the big leagues when I was in fifth grade—an age when nothing is more important than sports to a boy in a sports-obsessed house. They babysat my brothers, my friends, and me on countless Saturday nights in middle school—our parents giving us eight dollars for tickets way up in the 300s and dropping us off in front of the Civic Center, with a few extra bucks for dinner at Wendy's. We saw Gretzky, Lemieux, Bourque, and every other NHL superstar of the era. That the Whalers weren't any good didn't matter. They provided us something to do with our first taste of independence."

I was a fan. I wasn't a colossal *hockey* fan, per se. But I was a Whalers fan, because they were from Connecticut, and I was a sports fan who came of age in the state, and I needed a team to call my own. I delivered the *Hartford Courant*, surviving the chilly mornings with an extra sweatshirt and a Whalers ski cap. I listened to the staccato call of Chuck Kaiton on my transistor radio on winter nights, falling asleep in my Farmington (and later, Suffield) bedroom to the heroics of the Howe family, Dave Keon, Blaine "Stash" Stoughton, and Rick Ley. I got a three-quarter-sleeve shirt with the new logo shortly after it came out in 1979 and wore it until the elbows needed patching. I had Whalers stickers on my Trapper Keeper binder. I taped their hockey cards to my bedpost. I cut pictures out of *Sports Illustrated* and the newspaper and taped them to my bedroom wall.

When I played street hockey, I was Mark Howe. I watched the team on SportsChannel and was there for the glory days of the mid-to-late 1980s, when the Civic Center (stuck smack dab in the middle of a mall in downtown Hartford) was rocking and there was the brief possibility of the Whalers becoming a perennial playoff contender. I got a ride with my friends' parents or my mom and dad, who dropped us off in downtown Hartford without a worry. We ate dinner at Wendy's in the mall, looked at the Whalers Gift Shop, and bought tickets in the nosebleeds for $10. We cheered the green and white, guys like Ronnie Francis, Kevin Dineen, Sly Turgeon, Ulf Samuelsson, Mike Liut. They were all heroes who made hockey matter in Hartford.

I was emotionally invested, totally and completely. I had a giant Ron Francis "Drink Milk" poster on my wall. We saw owner Howard Baldwin and his family outside the Civic Center once, and I dined out on that for a solid month with my friends. I was at the game where Doug Jarvis broke the NHL ironman record for most consecutive games played. I was there in 1987 with my friend Rob when the Whalers clinched the Adams Division. And I went over to my friend Pete's house to watch "Whalermania," the cheesiest sports music video ever, which commemorated that season, when they came within an overtime session of knocking off the eventual Stanley Cup champions.

There was very little payoff, of course—I mean, other than a couple of failed postseason runs. (They might have been the only team in the history of North American professional sports to get a parade after winning a *single playoff round*.) But they were *our team*.

Let me put this fandom in some sort of historical context: The Whalers were the only big-time sports in the state for *decades*. You have to remember that UConn basketball (men's and women's) was not the all-consuming sporting monolith it is now. That Huskies team made noise throughout the 1970s and into the 1980s, but as the Big East blew up, UConn almost always played second fiddle. The UConn men's team *didn't even make the NCAA tournament* from 1980 to 1989, while the women's team made the tournament for the first time in school history in 1991. The Whalers were able to hold the attention of a sizable part of the state's sporting populace because they were the closest thing Connecticut had to big-time sports.

Of course, when the pendulum swung in the other direction, it was dramatic. In a chain of events that ultimately doomed the Whalers, the UConn men started to ascend at roughly the same time as the hockey team started its slide. The Huskies won the NIT in 1988, and the unlikely run in 1990—fueled by Tate George's historic turnaround jumper to beat Clemson and boost the Huskies into the Elite Eight—really sealed things. Meanwhile, the women's team was building a dynasty and broke through with its first national championship in 1995.

Against that backdrop, a series of missteps ultimately doomed the franchise. The Whalers couldn't sustain the momentum they had created with dramatic playoff appearances in 1986 and 1987. After the trade of Ron Francis to Pittsburgh on March 4, 1991—less than a year after George's shot—there was a shift. While the Whalers continued to remain competitive through the early-to-mid-1990s, after almost two decades, Connecticut had become a basketball state.

Throughout the 1990s, they made a series of cosmetic changes designed to build buzz around the team. They tried to get rid of the song, and they changed their primary colors from green to dark blue, stupid gimmicks designed to jump-start a franchise, which didn't work. In hindsight, it wasn't much of a shock—after the 1997 season, when the franchise and the state couldn't agree on funding for a few building, the Whalers were moved to Carolina by a tech mogul from Michigan with a ponytail. He had purchased the team as an investment—not for his interest in the actual *team* but in *an investment*. Twenty years later, hockey fans throughout southern New England use the name Karmanos as an expletive.

Ultimately, the Whalers suffered the same fate as several other professional sports teams who were picked up and moved. Fans of the Expos, SuperSonics, and Rams can all tell you that in this day and age, it doesn't matter how *much* you support your team. The franchise can have deep and long-lasting roots in the community. The fans can establish a bond with the players. Teams can win and win and win. The simple fact is that if a long-haired tech mogul rides into town promising to rescue your franchise, *don't believe him.*

Now, it's my curse—and the curse of hockey fans throughout Connecticut—to root for a team that doesn't exist anymore. As the newly minted Carolina Hurricanes were making a run to the Stanley Cup in 2006, sports journalist Steve Rushin called us hockey's Miss Havishams, jilted by a team and an owner and doomed to decry the lack of hockey in Hartford for the rest of our days. "The Stanley Cup is tiered like a wedding cake, which is appropriate, as Whalers fans resemble Charles Dickens's Miss Havisham," he wrote. "Jilted on her wedding day, she sits forever in her faded wedding dress, pining in her ruined mansion, all the clocks stopped at 20 minutes to nine, the precise moment of betrayal."

The calendars didn't stop on 1997, but for many, the metaphor isn't too far removed. I still like hockey, but the depth of feeling for the Bruins isn't nearly what it was when I was thirteen and rooting for the Whalers. Part of that's because things simply can't stay the same as they were when you were teenager. But to have your team taken away like that, well . . . it's just like something died.

But twenty years after the team pulled up stakes and left for Carolina, it's more than just the sweet-ass logo, some 45s of "Brass Bonanza," a YouTube library of highlights, and a sudden market for throwback jerseys. Nostalgia is a powerful draw, and that means the Whalers have carved out a unique little niche in the sports landscape as the one team pretty much everyone would love to see return. The logo still resonates with celebs: Snoop Dogg appeared on *Jimmy Kimmel Live!* wearing a Whalers sweater, actress Megan Fox was seen sporting a "Property of

Hartford Whalers" T-shirt, and Adam Sandler wore a Whalers shirt in *Grown Ups.* The brand is stronger than just about any currently active franchise in the NHL; Keith Leach, director of NHL merchandise at Reebok, said that the first year Whalers products were reintroduced by the company, sales reached close to $1 million.

"Back in the eighties, the logo was a little unappreciated," said Bob Crawford, who played for Hartford from 1983 to 1986. "But now, they see celebrities wearing something with the logo on it, and all of a sudden, they realize Dad was cool, and being a Hartford Whaler was cool. Honestly, the fact that the logo and the gear is cool again has helped me with my kids."

Look, I'm not going to tell you that this is a hardcore hockey book. You're probably not going to learn a lot about the intricacies of Jack Evans's coaching style, Mike Liut's goaltending technique, or Andrew Cassels's setup skills. More than anything, this is a book about the power of a franchise to build a bond with a community, the love affair between a team and its fans, how a series of ill-timed events brought about the end of it all, and the legacy that remains.

"There was an intensity when it came to the love of the team with that fan base that was really something else," recalled former TV play-by-play man Rick Peckham. "It wasn't in the millions of people, but the community loved them. It faced a true uphill battle at the start, coming into the NHL. They were fighting established, Original Six teams like the Bruins and the Rangers, and those fan bases that had been in place for decades. Then, there were the Islanders, who won four straight Cups. It was a big challenge, one they nearly pulled off when you look at the success on the ice in the late eighties, combined with how the team was marketed locally, and the execution of those ideas.

"I still see Whalers fans today—the love of that franchise is still there. It's burning with those people. Every time, every building I walk into, I see someone with a Whalers jersey or a cap. It's an iconic logo. It's a shame that it didn't last, because for a couple of years there in the late eighties and early nineties, it all just clicked."

Today, the Whalers Booster Club numbers in the hundreds. A Whalers Fan Fest drew almost five thousand people a few years ago. A semiannual Fanniversary get-together marks the last Whalers game in Hartford. And Hartford's Minor League baseball team—the Yard Goats—happily embraces the Whalers' legacy by sponsoring an alumni weekend when ex-players are flown in from all over to spend some time with former teammates and connect with a new generation of fans.

Social media has stoked the fires: the official Facebook page and Twitter account of the team has a rabid following, all of which keeps the rest of the fan base rallying together. For me, there's a camaraderie with fellow snot-nosed kids who grew up in Connecticut and are now money-earning middle-agers who have the disposable income to buy the throwbacks and engage in the sort of sports nostaglia-gasms we could have only dreamed about as kids. *This is our team.*

1

You Say You Want a Revolution?
1970-72

Jesus saves . . . and Espo scores on the rebound.
—Popular bumper sticker of Boston hockey fans in the 1970s

I truly believe we'll give you a major-league product.
—Jack Kelley, after being introduced as the first coach and GM of
the New England Whalers

The National Hockey League was vulnerable. By the mid-1960s, the
most established professional hockey league in North America had
started to show some cracks. An antiquated labor agreement angered
players and agents. A league that had been a forerunner when it came
to TV—NHL games were broadcast on CBS as early as 1956—saw its
rights package end in 1960 when the owners refused to cut the players
in on a share of the profits. The cut-off-your-nose-to-spite-your-face
thinking meant that with only six teams—Boston, New York, Detroit,
Chicago, Montreal, and Toronto—and no national TV deal after 1960,
sizable portions of the country didn't know *anything* about professional
hockey by the middle of the decade, much less have a rooting interest
in one of the teams.

As is usually the case when it comes to professional sports, money—and the possibility of losing it—would catalyze change. The Western Hockey League was a rising threat, and having witnessed how the infusion of TV money helped legitimize the American Football League in the 1960s, the NHL wanted to prevent the same thing from occurring with the WHL. The league returned to TV in the middle of the decade and considered the idea of expansion. After all, professional baseball, basketball, and football all started expanding in earnest in the 1950s and '60s, moving west and south and finding lucrative new markets. Now, professional hockey would do the same.

Buoyed by the prospect of new money and new markets, the league expanded, with the Original Six becoming a dozen in 1967. For the first time, the NHL's imprint was coast to coast: the California Seals (which would ultimately land in Dallas and become the Stars), Los Angeles Kings, Minnesota North Stars, Philadelphia Flyers, Pittsburgh Penguins, and St. Louis Blues were all added. In the next seven years, the aggressive expansion continued, as teams landed in Buffalo, Vancouver, Atlanta, New York, Washington, and Kansas City.

But the NHL's labor agreement remained its Achilles' heel and would leave it vulnerable to a challenge. To keep its players in check, the NHL depended on the reserve clause—a statement in every player's contract that automatically extended a player's contract by one year when it expired, tying the player to his team for his career. It angered the players, along with the agents. *In the modern era, this was no way to treat the product.* But no one could do anything about it. The Western Hockey League was burgeoning, but by the late stages of the 1960s, no alternative league was competitive enough to keep pace with the NHL, and Europe wasn't a viable option.

Enter Gary Davidson and Dennis Murphy, two guys interested in pushing the pro sports envelope. As entrepreneurs who spearheaded the rise of the new American Basketball Association, they decided to take aim at the NHL. For Murphy, a friendship with Oakland Raiders renegade Al Davis nearly led to a franchise in the AFL, but the pending merger with the NFL threw up a roadblock. He ended up leading the way with the ABA, but he was also involved in World Team Tennis, Roller Hockey International, and the International Basketball Association, a league designed for players six feet four and under. He looked at everything as a possibility.

On a cross-country flight to Los Angeles in 1970, he thought, *What about hockey?* A new league would lighten up the occasionally stodgy, old-school world of the NHL and break its monopoly. After all, the freewheeling ABA was a fun league, and while it faced stability issues, it was able to push the NBA on a number of fronts while bringing some radical new ideas to professional basketball. Could they do the same with hockey?

He and Davidson had some juice with the ABA, which had recently gotten off the ground and was doing (relatively) well. And so, by July 1971, articles of incorporation were filed in Delaware for the World Hockey Association, and Davidson and Murphy began looking for investors. They found some Americans with deep pockets who were impressed by the suddenly rapid growth of the NHL, as well as some disgruntled Canadians who were angry the NHL had passed them over. One of the attractions? How cheap it was to land a team. When it came to early investors, Davidson and Murphy were charging just $25,000 as an entrance fee. The NHL's entrance fee was in the $5 million to $6 million range. The thinking was that the extra cash would be spent on players.

By October 1971 the WHA had ten teams, some in cities that already had NHL franchises and some that were looking to capitalize on the hockey market: Calgary, Chicago, Dayton, Edmonton, Los Angeles, Miami, New York, Saint Paul, San Francisco, and Winnipeg. That ten grew to a dozen a month later when Howard Baldwin's Boston group and a group from Ottawa were granted teams. Teams ended up shuffling a bit before the first puck was dropped—the San Francisco team ended up in Quebec, while Miami moved to Philadelphia and Dayton to Houston. But by the start of 1972, the new league was on the move and ready for its first season.

In New England, Baldwin and his contingent jumped in with both feet. After all, in the early 1970s there was an almost insatiable appetite for hockey in Boston, thanks in large part to the Bruins. Bobby Orr, Phil Esposito, Derek Sanderson, Gerry Cheevers, and the rest carved out a niche as a fun-loving band of stars, and the city had fallen hard for them. They won Stanley Cups in 1970 and 1972 and would reach the finals in 1974 before losing to the Flyers. In all, they played in five Stanley Cup finals between 1970 and 1978. As a result, kids from Charlestown to East Boston were all asking for a pair of skates for Christmas. And if they couldn't get those, they'd have to settle for a stick, an orange ball, and a game of street hockey.

"Living that close to the Garden at that time and having access to that team and the Red Sox a couple of years after 1967 and the ups and downs that came with it, you couldn't *not* be a fan," recalled Pro Football Hall of Famer Howie Long, who grew up in Charlestown loving the Bruins. "The 1972 Bruins winning a championship for me, at that age, was pretty big. There were a lot of big moments with the Celtics, but hockey was so big when I was that age. In many ways, I was a disappointment I think because I didn't play hockey. But skates were so expensive, and for a kid who was growing out of sneakers every four months, how do you afford a new pair of [skates] in that time?"

But it wasn't just the NHL. Boston was home to a thriving high school and college hockey community. The four major college programs—Northeastern University, Harvard University, Boston College, and Boston University—staged the Beanpot tournament every February, an event that packed the Garden and fueled the local mania. BU was a perennial national-title contender, thanks in no small part to the work of coach Jack Kelley. High school hockey stars would routinely reach the NHL a few years later.

Into this environment strode Baldwin, a twentysomething New Englander with a few dollars in his pocket and a dream of becoming the next great sportsman. Baldwin already had roots in the game; as the business manager for the Jersey Devils of the Eastern Hockey League in the late 1960s, he learned all the intricacies of what it took to run a team, including selling tickets, driving the team bus, and marketing and promotion. (According to reports, he even coached the team for a week.) That led to a promotion, and he joined the Flyers as a ticket manager, but after the brief stint in Philadelphia, he decided to move back to Massachusetts with his young family.

Baldwin had financial backing, but he certainly wasn't an ostentatious sort. Instead, he was looking to make his own path. He had tried to land a hockey arena for Cape Cod, but the McMahon wrestling family beat him to the punch, opening the Cape Cod Coliseum, which would eventually house an EHL team. Baldwin and his partner Johnny Coburn saw a story in the *Boston Globe* on Davidson's idea for a new hockey league. They found the number for Davidson and the WHA and gave him a call out of the blue.

"The landscape was perfect," remembered Baldwin. "You couldn't do it today. You also have to remember that new leagues were working back then. The AFL worked, and the ABA was working."

Baldwin and Coburn somehow talked Murphy and Davidson into flying into Boston for a meeting. Waiting on the tarmac at Logan Airport, Baldwin saw a short, stout man in the doorway of the plane, who subsequently fell down the steps. That was Murphy.

"If you were casting a movie, he'd be an Irish Danny DeVito," said Baldwin with a laugh.

New England's entry into the WHA would take a side trip to the emergency room for a look at Murphy's ankle, but soon after that, the four held a meeting. It was the first in a series of get-togethers that ended with Davidson and Murphy telling Baldwin and Coburn they were in. All they had to do? Come up with the $25,000 entry fee and another $10,000 for league rules.

"We *thought* we could come up with it," Baldwin later wrote. "But I'll emphasize this—at the time, we did not have it. That said, they didn't have a *league* yet, either."

Coburn and Baldwin were instructed to show up at the first league meeting in October 1971 in New York, and when they walked in, they were met by a group who were suitably unimpressed with their youthful exuberance. Three lions of Western Canadian hockey—Ben Hatskin of Winnipeg, Bill Hunter of Edmonton, and Scotty Munro of Calgary—sized them up when they walked in the door and didn't like the looks of things. For their part, Baldwin and Coburn weren't thrilled with them either. "Visualize *Goodfellas*, and you'll get what we saw when we walked in," Baldwin said.

But their pitch—when you have nothing to lose, you can achieve great success—was good enough to get them a second meeting with the league founders. Even though they didn't have an arena yet, the old-timers were ultimately impressed by the delivery of the kids from New England, the appearance that they had the money, and their commitment to creating a stable ownership group. They had passed the first test, so they were invited to a second round of meetings a few months later in Miami.

On the way to Florida, they connected with Phil David Fine, a friend of Baldwin's father who played a sizable role in the building of Schaefer Stadium in Foxborough, Massachusetts. They hit it off.

"I'll tell you what, son. You get the franchise, come back to me, and I'll get you a place to play," Fine told Baldwin.

Boom. While Baldwin later admitted he had exaggerated a connection with the Boston Garden a bit, they were in. The only hitch? The franchise fee was now $250,000, not $25,000.

Well, we're too far down the road to pull back now, they thought. *Let's agree to it.*

They offered $25,000 now and $225,000 at the first draft, set for February. The response? "Congratulations. You are now members of the World Hockey Association."

They weren't completely sure where they were going to get the other 225 grand. They had no coach, no players, and no place to play. *But they had a team.*

"Quite obviously, we would like the team to play in Boston. We will have further meetings with Garden officials, but we are prepared to seek some alternatives," Baldwin told reporters shortly after the group was approved. "We would be satisfied if we could play 20 of our [39 home] games next year in the Garden. We could play the remaining games in other New England rinks."

THE MORNING AFTER THE ANNOUNCEMENT, BALDWIN wandered into a New England diner for breakfast. Before he started eating, he opened up a Boston newspaper and saw the latest column from famed New England hockey writer D. Leo Monahan. Monahan had gotten wind of Baldwin's deal and wrote that New England's newest hockey team had two chances to survive: slim and none.

"Are you sure you know what the hell you're getting into?" asked the guy sitting next to Baldwin that morning.

"Used to go there every morning," Baldwin said when he was asked about what happened that day at the diner. "I'd sit with the carpenters and plumbers and talk. It was an iconic place. I looked up and saw a guy in the next booth holding up the tabloid. *Jesus, how do I get out of here without anyone realizing it's me?* I wondered."

He actually wasn't so sure he knew what he was getting into. Certainly, hockey in New England was wildly popular. But the hockey-mad market was also saturated at the time, and there was real concern about interest reaching a tipping point somewhere down the line.

The Whalers were not only going up against the Bruins, a successful, Original Six franchise with deep roots in the New England community. The AHL's Braves were also part of the hockey scene, as were the aforementioned numerous high school and college teams.

Throw in the fact that the Whalers had no building, no coach, and no players and had to get the whole thing off the ground quickly, and it looked like Monahan might have been onto something. *Other than that, no worries, right?*

"When I think back [to] it, it was overwhelming," wrote Baldwin later. "[We] had to raise money, find a place to play, get a hockey team put together, and *then* get a marketing and business group together. And you couldn't get numbers two, three, and four without getting number one. You had to have the capital. That would make the difference between 'none' and at least 'slim.'"

Enter Bob Schmertz, one of the wilder and more underrated figures in New England sports history. Schmertz had periodically ventured into the world of professional sports over the course of his adult life. He was an owner of the Portland Trail Blazers from 1970 to 1972 but jumped to New England when the Celtics became available, buying the team in 1972 for almost $4 million. The real estate executive didn't much seem to care about potentially losing a few bucks here or there along the way; instead, he enjoyed being the center of attention in the sports world.

"A friend of mine in Seattle called to say we had a chance to get a basketball team," he explained once to the *New York Times*. "He said he couldn't tell me more but send money. I wound up as part owner of the Portland [Trail Blazers]. But that was no fun because Portland is in Oregon and I live in New Jersey. So when I got a chance to buy the Celtics, I grabbed it.

"About the same time, the opportunity to get a percentage of the New England Whalers came along, and that seemed an attractive prospect, although I've never seen a hockey game. I guess I'm a collector. It's an ego trip. It is tremendously satisfying to own the best team in a league, to win championships, to excel. You could ask Red Auerbach with the Celtics, and [he will] tell you I don't get involved telling the coach or general manager how to do his job because I don't know. I just know it's great to win. There's real satisfaction in creating something.

"And as for making money, you give a lot of it away anyway. If I can make a buck, that's even better. But if you were primarily interested in profits, you wouldn't go into sports. And as for money, you can only eat three meals a day."

"He was just looking to have some fun," Baldwin said of Schmertz. "Those were days where sports were almost like just owning a race-horse. Things were very clubby. With the new leagues, that sort of just busted sports wide open as a viable option for anyone. . . . I think he just saw it as a good investment. He saw the ABA and NBA merge, and he thought we could do the same thing."

With that sort of philosophy, you can understand why Schmertz was interested in the WHA. After all, he had experience tilting at professional-sports windmills. (When Baldwin and his contingent reached out, he was in the process of trying to get a Canadian Football League team into Yankee Stadium.) Schmertz thought outside the box when it came to professional sports. For Baldwin and the Whalers, he could offer financial support, and his presence could open the door to the possibility of the Whalers playing in the Boston Garden—a win-win.

Schmertz did have his share of legal issues. He owned the Celtics from 1972 until 1974, when the previous owners Irv Levin and Harold Lipton took Schmertz to court, claiming Schmertz had reneged on a contract that had been set up between the three of them that stated Schmertz would sell them 50 percent of the team after they had divested themselves of the Seattle franchise. Levin and Lipton won their court battle, and in 1975, Schmertz was indicted on bribery charges. Five months later, he had a stroke and died at the age of forty-eight.

In hindsight, it seems a little surprising Schmertz didn't try to take over Baldwin's attempt. Maybe it was because, by his own admission, Schmertz didn't know anything about hockey.

"I once showed him a puck," said Baldwin. "All he said was, '*Oooohh.*'"

But the idea intrigued him nonetheless. Instead, after a meeting with Baldwin, Schmertz offered the Whalers a $1 million line of credit and $300,000 in working capital. Baldwin and Coburn quickly said yes. Schmertz's legal woes were still down the road, but in that moment the Whalers had some of the most stable ownership in the league. That helped them clear the next hurdle: at the next round of league meetings,

Schmertz let the rest of the WHA know in no uncertain terms that the Whalers were not going to be on the hook for $250,000.

"I'm glad to be in this room. I'm excited about the league," he said. "However, I want to make one thing clear—we aren't paying the 250 grand for dues. You'll find we will be great partners in the league, but just because we came in 30 days after the original 10 franchises doesn't mean we are going to pay 10 times more than what they paid. Particularly when three or four of them are no longer in the room. We'll pay the 25, but if you think we're paying the 250, throw us out right now."

The room was silent for a few seconds. No one moved. And when no objections were raised, they had their team. They were the youngest ownership group in the league, but they made the inexperience work in their favor. To hear Baldwin talk, they didn't know any better.

"We were twenty-eight years old. We had no fear, which is good," he recalled. "I mean, the upside was all in front of us. At that age, we hadn't had the fear of living on the edge. We only really felt it when we went to the first six months of meetings, where there was a lot of resentment toward us. I remember when Coburn and I walked into the first meeting at the Americana in New York, and these guys like Bill Hunter all looked like mean, one-hundred-year-old Canadians. They looked at these two spoiled brats with our family's money, and they sort of had that attitude of 'Who are these rich kids from Boston, and what are they doing in our league?' But we didn't use our family money—they didn't give it to us. We did our job and raised it. And once we had Schmertz, we quickly became—oh, who's kidding who here—we became the most well-run team in the league."

The Whalers had money and stable ownership. Now, all they needed were coaches, players, and a building—oh, and a name. Baldwin later remembered the ownership going through a bunch of different names, color schemes, and logos. But after a suggestion from Ginny Kelley, Jack's wife, they settled on Whalers. It had WHA in the title, and it paid homage to New England history.

When Kelley was inducted into the Connecticut Hockey Hall of Fame in 1989, he recalled the early days, telling the story of how the team was named with his tongue firmly in cheek: "This would-be team didn't even have a name until my wife Ginny came up with Whalers one night over dinner. The franchise picked that name. They picked me to be the general manager and coach. . . . They kept the name."

While Baldwin was building his team, the WHA was caught in a whirlwind. It was soon clear the new league would be a drain on the NHL talent pool. The WHA said it would not include the reserve clause in players' contracts, a landmark decision that changed the face of the game. As a result, the floodgates were open—the WHA went after all sorts of NHL stars, including Bobby Hull.

One of the preeminent stars of the game, Hull was criminally underpaid by the Blackhawks. Nicknamed the "Golden Jet," he was a two-time MVP and three-time winner of the Art Ross Trophy, and his slapshot routinely topped out at one-hundred-plus miles per hour. With his impressive résumé, mane of blonde hair, and dynamic playing style, he was a big-time, marketable star you could build a league around.

But Chicago was trying to hold the line when it came to salary. And so, in 1972, Hull, who was in his early thirties, was curious about the WHA and what it might have to offer—even though he would later say he thought he wasn't going anywhere because he "had the Blackhawks emblem tattooed on my chest." In a conversation with Winnipeg ownership, Hull half-jokingly tossed out the sum of $1 million, thinking there would be no way the team would accept.

It did. In June 1972 Hull signed a deal with the Jets that had the potential to climb as high as $2.5 million. The contract had an instant $1 million bonus (part of which was paid by the league, with the understanding that a rising tide lifts all boats), as well as a $200,000 annual salary over five years as player-coach. If he retired as a player after that time, he'd receive $100,000 for five additional years as either a coach or front-office official. However, if he played in any of those next five years, he would receive $100,000 extra for each season.

"If I told you that the big contract had nothing to do with my signing, I'd be lying," he told reporters when the deal went down. "It made the future secure for my family. Then there were some things that disenchanted me in the NHL, and the way the Hawks handled their attempts to sign me. They just didn't think I'd consider jumping."

Boom—*instant credibility*. "Bobby Hull would become the WHA," wrote Ed Willes in *The Rebel League*, a book that would become the definitive history of the WHA. "He was its star, its face, its drawing card, and its roving goodwill ambassador. His presence encouraged a wave of NHLers to sign with the rebels and ensured the league would be more than a glorified version of the AHL. Hull didn't just give the league instant credibility; without him, it is doubtful the league would have survived its first year, and the NHL would have gone about its business of printing money and exploiting players."

Although the NHL tried to prevent many of the defectors like Hull, it was the beginning of the end for old-school hockey. In November 1972 a federal judge placed an injunction against the NHL, preventing it from enforcing the reserve clause and freeing all players who had restraining orders against them, including Hull, to play with their WHA clubs. The decision effectively ended the NHL's monopoly. *It was a whole new game.*

As the new league started to take shape, it continued to take direct aim at the NHL, a group of old-school franchises who had been around since what seemed like the dawn of time. It had deep roots throughout Canada and into the United States. And by the early 1970s, if you were a young hockey player, the ultimate goal was to play for one of the dozen-plus franchises that now stretched from coast to coast throughout North America.

Of course, the flip side of all of that was that despite expansion having increased its coffers, the NHL remained a relatively intractable, old-money bunch fairly set in its ways. The NHL had no reason to change things before because it had never seriously been challenged.

But old-school owners were dinosaurs, and soon, they had to understand the meaning of "adapt or die." And the WHA didn't give a you-know-what about the unwritten rules of old-school hockey. The league talked openly of raiding NHL rosters, while NHL president Clarence Campbell warned the WHA that if it raided NHL players, "we will fight them from the ramparts."

As it turned out, it wasn't much of a fight. Hockey players were looking for a way around the reserve clause. The merger between the AFL and NFL showed that if things were done right—particularly when it came to money, player acquisition, and an ability to appeal to a younger demographic—an upstart league could really make an impact.

"The WHA was *the best thing* that happened to hockey," said Andre Lacroix, who would spend seven years in the league—including one with New England—and end up as the leading scorer in WHA history. "It ultimately gave a chance to a lot of players to play professional hockey that otherwise . . . would not have made it. It increased the salary for the players and coaches. It opened the door to so many people and exposed hockey in places that the NHL had no desire to go.

"We all took a chance to jump to the WHA, knowing it was not going to be easy," Lacroix added. "But I believe that all of us who made the initial move were committed to make the league work. There were a few moments where we had no idea if the next paycheck was going to be there, but I must say that I never missed a paycheck. I know some of the players did."

"All the guys who left the NHL—guys like Gerry Cheevers and Derek Sanderson and Bobby Hull and Gordie [Howe], all of them—when they left the NHL and stepped into the WHA, for them, it was stepping into an unknown minefield," said future Whaler Jordy Douglas, who was watching the whole thing play out as a teenager in western Canada at the time. "They had no idea what was going to happen by them taking the proverbial jump. But they did so much for hockey players then and now. For what they did, they don't get anywhere near the recognition or respect for being that brave to step into the unknown and put that pressure on the NHL to play fair. They broke the reserve clause and allowed players to have a little bit of freedom. [For] what they did for hockey players who came after them, everyone owes them a debt. They literally risked their careers to do what they did."

"I think people today don't realize how much the WHA really opened the doors when it came to professional hockey, for both new markets and players," Baldwin said. "Keep in mind, in 1967, there were six teams. By the end of the 1973 season, there were 28 teams, including the WHA. That's 22 new teams. They all carried somewhere around 40 guys under contract. Twenty-two times 40? The hockey world exploded. *It wasn't an evolution. It was a revolution.*"

As the new league started to look for personnel to fill its rosters, teams also started to fill out their front offices and coaching staffs. In New England, Baldwin and his team narrowed its GM search to two men: Boston University coach Jack Kelley and former Bruins GM Harry Sinden. Baldwin—who later confessed to being a little buzzed when he called Sinden to feel him out about the job—made a connection with Sinden.

While Kelley had lots of juice in college hockey circles, Sinden was by far the more intriguing choice. The former coach of the Bruins, he led Boston to the 1970 Stanley Cup, but there was apparently some lingering bitterness because he hadn't gotten a raise. At that point, he was working as an executive for Stirling Homex in New York but was clearly interested in getting back in the game—at one point in 1972, he told the *Boston Globe*, he had three NHL offers and six offers from the WHA.

"Some of the offers are very flattering," Sinden said to Will McDonough in February of that year. "It's nice to know that some people are still interested in you, even though you might not be interested in what they have to offer. With some of the money [the WHA teams are] talking about I sometimes wonder why I don't go back. It got so that after a while I told some of the people calling me: 'Listen, don't even talk money to me unless it's 'blank,'' and then I'd give them some outrageous figure that they couldn't possibly afford to pay me."

After a meeting in Toronto, he initially expressed interest but later backed out. Baldwin and his partners later believed that Sinden was using the Whalers' potential interest as a way to get back in with the Bruins. He ended up sticking around the Bruins for the rest of his hockey career.

The episode generated one of the greatest what-ifs in New England sports history: Sinden would go on to serve as a Bruins executive for several seasons, but who knows what would have happened if he could have made a connection with Baldwin and the Whalers? The snub also really jump-started one of the more underrated rivalries in local sports history, as he was never shy about sniping at the Whalers for the rest of his career in Boston. He was at the center of some memorable scraps in the 1970s: When the Bruins believed the Whalers stiffed them on a portion of the rent at the Garden, Boston ownership backed the Garden's Zamboni against the Whalers' equipment truck to prevent the club from moving to its temporary quarters in Springfield. In 1979 the Bruins were the only American club to vote against the Whalers and three other WHA teams entering the NHL. "Hartford? Albany?" Sinden told the media. "I didn't know the difference then." And in 1990 after a Hartford win over Boston, he told reporters, "I got a somewhat bush-league feeling about Hartford last weekend. What I saw out of Hartford was a real low-class situation. They have to do what they can to try to get rid of the second-class citizen image."

But in the early 1970s the Bruins had probably earned the right to be a little cocky at the prospect of more competition. After all, they had the New England hockey world in their grasp. In 1972 they won their second Cup in three years. Between 1972 and 1979, they finished second in their division only twice. Orr was the default Norris Trophy winner, winning it eight straight years from 1967 through 1975. Esposito was one of the most dominant scorers in the league, winning the Ross Trophy four straight years. In 1974–75, he tallied his fourth 60-plus-goal campaign. And the wild-haired Sanderson was one of the most charismatic athletes in Boston.

"Derek was to hockey what Joe Namath was to football," remembered Lacroix.

The Bruins felt they had little to worry about when it came to competing for the love of local pro hockey fans. *What's the name of your team? The Whalers? That's cute—good luck with that.*

And so, talks continued with Kelley. Reached by the *Globe* when his team was in Syracuse set to face Minnesota, he played it coy. "I have not signed or accepted anything yet. I was offered the job. . . . It's a fine job and I intend to give it every consideration," he told Bob Monahan. "I've met with them four or five times. What they offered . . . well . . . it was just an excellent offer."

Ultimately, the team landed on Kelley as the choice to lead the fledgling franchise. Baldwin said they made the move for two reasons: Kelley was a nontraditional choice, and he had deep local roots.

"We felt like for Boston, we had to make a splash and get ourselves on the front pages of the sports section. And we just thought that with our backgrounds—and I've kind of done this my whole life—we should go against the grain," recalled Baldwin.

To that point, Kelley had rebuffed multiple offers to coach professionally and carved out a niche as one of the best bench bosses in the recent history of the college game. The former BU star had built a powerhouse in Boston—in a six-year span, he would get the Terriers to three National Championship Games and bring home a pair of titles. He was as well ensconced a coach as any in all of college sports, but he decided to take a leap.

"Howard Baldwin, you better know what you're doing," Kelley's wife, Ginny, told Baldwin shortly after Baldwin convinced Kelley to take the job. "My husband is leaving a pretty stable gig here."

So much to her chagrin, Kelley was the guy. The Whalers signed him to a three-year deal worth roughly $30,000 a year, with bonuses for winning. The former BU coach went about building out his coaching staff—he added Ron Ryan out of Colgate University as his assistant GM; Bob Crocker, his assistant at BU, as an assistant coach; and Jack

Ferreira as his chief scout. The group started prep work for the WHA's first draft, set for February 12, 1972, in California.

Needless to say, it wasn't your usual draft. During the two-day exercise, teams got either a little punchy or a little boozy—or maybe both—and had some fun. Soviet premier Alexei Kosygin and Minnesota governor Wendell Anderson were drafted, as were a whole mess of foreign players whom the general public had never heard of before. In all, almost 1,200 names were included in that first go-round, most of whom were amateur, professional, or retired players. And teams didn't necessarily limit themselves. At one point late in the proceedings—more as a way to liven things up than anything—a Dayton rep announced that the team was drafting the rights to Bobby Orr. (It later did the same for Phil Esposito.) In all, there were seventy rounds, and the draft ended only when teams agreed to simply stop picking.

As for the Whalers, Kelley remained back in Boston, guiding the draft by phone. The franchise had a very clear plan—instead of chasing big stars, the Whalers actively sought out American college players for a few reasons, including Kelley's cache when it came to the college game and the fact that in most cases, they'd be able to play professionally close to home. New England took eighty-five players in all that day, and while not all of them ended up sticking around, the organizational emphasis on college and local talent was clear.

That talent included Larry Pleau, a Massachusetts native who was with the Canadiens but wanted out for a few reasons, not the least of which was that he was sitting behind Henri Richard, Jacques Lemaire, and Peter Mahovlich. He went to Montreal management but was told a trade was out of the question. "And there'll be no WHA, so you can forget about that too," Habs GM Sam Pollock told him.

Many members of the NHL establishment were similarly dubious. When *Boston Globe* writer Fran Rosa went around the Bruins locker room to ask the players what they thought of the WHA draft process, many of them scoffed. Esposito chuckled over the fact that no one took his brother Tony, who was coming to the end of his contract. Johnny

McKenzie was taken by Quebec but said, "No way. I don't want to leave Boston. I found a home here. But you've got to listen to them. How do they pay there, in dollars or francs?" And Sanderson laughed when he was informed he was drafted by Miami.

"The World Hockey Association, new rival to the NHL, is probably on its last legs, with Miami, Calgary, Winnipeg and Edmonton likely to withdraw, and BU's Jack Kelly may soon find himself as coach of the New England Whalers directing a team as ephemeral as anything in Moby Dick," wrote Harold Kaese in the *Globe* on April 12, 1972.

But not everyone shared Kaese's doom and gloom. Days after the draft, Pleau called Pollock to let him know he was signing with the New England Whalers.

"Like I said the other day, there will never be a WHA," Pollack told Pleau.

But Pleau became the first player to put his name on a Whalers contract. "I checked the WHA and the Whalers out thoroughly," Pleau told reporters when he signed on April 19, 1972. "My advisors and I are 100 percent convinced the new league's for real." Pleau signed a three-year deal worth $180,000.

Tim Sheehy, who played at Boston College and captained the 1972 U.S. Olympic team, was added soon after that. John Cunniff, an All-American from Boston College, and Jake Danby and Ric Jordan (two of Kelley's former players at BU) joined the roster. More players from Boston University and Boston College were added.

"Build a winning team, and try and give it as much local flavor as you could. That's what Jack did," Baldwin said. "BC kids, BU kids. I don't think we had any Harvard kids. But there were a ton of good local players, kids who could play."

Of course, not everyone was impressed with the idea of loading up on local talent. "We were in the room, basically, with a lot of Canadians who knew the game pretty well. Each pick he selected seemed to be a college person," recalled former New England executive Bill Barnes of the inaugural WHA draft. "There was a little laughter—a little tittering there for a little while. I remember one person saying to me, 'You not only have a college coach, but now you have a college team.' We did take some digs, but we knew Jack was a winner."

"What I loved about Jack was that to two young guys starting something new, he could appear to be very fierce. He was like a drill-instructor personality," said Baldwin of the reaction he and Coburn had to Kelley. "We were a little intimidated—make that more than a little—but we also knew he would take charge and put a competitive team on the ice."

In addition to the local flavor, Kelley stocked the roster with plenty of established talent but mostly stayed away from the high-end stars. Rick Ley and Brad Selwood of Toronto, former Bruins defenseman Ted Green, and ex-Bruins winger Tom "Hawkeye" Webster were among the NHLers added. And popular netminder Al Smith, who had stops with Pittsburgh, Detroit, and Toronto, signed as the first goaltender in franchise history on August 7.

In all, as the first season loomed, New England had ten players with NHL experience, as well as a plethora of former Boston-area college standouts. There weren't a lot of big names, which allowed the Whalers to retain some financial flexibility—Baldwin recalled that the entire payroll that first season came to $700,000. Green turned out to be the player with the priciest deal—depending on whom you talk with, his deal was somewhere between $60,000 and $80,000 annually, one that was ultimately a personal services contract. (Green's nonplaying duties included helping Kelley run a summer hockey camp in Norfolk.) In contrast, Bobby Hull's eight-figure contract with the Jets included a player-coach deal.

"When we got the NHL players, they were young studs," Baldwin said.

Green was one of the more remarkable hockey stories in New England sports. A hard-hitting defenseman for the Bruins, he was an All-Star in 1965 and 1969. But on September 21, 1969, he and St. Louis forward Wayne Maki were involved in a wild, stick-swinging brawl in which Green suffered a fractured skull and brain damage. (Maki and Green were both charged with assault as a result of the incident, the first time

NHL players faced charges as a result of on-ice violence; both were acquitted.) Green missed the remainder of the season, a year when the Bruins won the Cup. He worked his way back to become a part of the Boston team that won the 1972 Cup. But the Whalers swooped in and swiped him away from the Bruins, adding a sense of legitimacy to their roster and bolstering their blue line. Ultimately, the addition of Green and a bunch of familiar college names helped build the Whalers brand in Boston and made it easier for them to find a fan base.

But where to play? They weren't going to get into the Boston Garden. Boston Arena, located near Northeastern University, was an option, but it was considered old and too misshapen to host a professional hockey team on a regular basis. Maybe Providence? That city was on the verge of opening the Providence Civic Center, a building that would have suited the Whalers on a number of levels—they could have shared it with the Providence Reds of the American Hockey League, for example. But it was doomed from the start for a few reasons, not the least of which was the level of corruption that had sprung up around the building.

"It was everyone protecting the AHL and George Sage," explained Baldwin. "He owned the local bus company, and was a local guy who had put a lot of money into the hockey team there. He was a well-regarded guy, a businessman. And they were going to protect him and do what was best for him. Not the city. Not the WHA. But George.

"We started out with the best of intentions—we got a call from a business guy, and there were three guys who came to the first meeting, including someone named Ray Badway. Seeing him should have been enough of a warning for us, but we were fishing for a place to play. They said, 'Look, if you give us 10 or 15 grand, we'll see to it you'll have a place to play.'

"This quickly went south," he added. "We were really naïve, but we felt, 'Look, the less we ask, the better. As long as it all works.' Of course, it didn't. God knows where *that* money went."

Baldwin and the Whalers wanted no part of Providence. But the upshot of the whole thing? Rhode Island's assistant attorney general,

Buddy Cianci, used the corruption case—including what happened with the Whalers—to propel himself to the corner office in City Hall. Cianci, of course, would eventually end up behind bars because of a corruption case of his own.

But within months, the Whalers were able to sell roughly two thousand season tickets, while still needing a spot to play. With Providence out of the picture, they started thinking outside the box, eventually landing on a handful of dates at Boston Garden and another set of games at Boston Arena. The franchise made the grand announcement on June 7, 1972, that it would play between fifteen and nineteen games at the Garden the upcoming season, and the remaining twenty to twenty-four games would be played at a still-to-be-determined location that ended up being Boston Arena.

Because the Whalers were the fourth team in a four-team building— behind the Bruins, Celtics, and the AHL's Braves—they'd play most of their games in the Garden on Saturday afternoons and Monday evenings, in addition to other occasional weekend nights. Three season-ticket plans were offered—the A package was for all thirty-nine home games; the B package was for the Garden games only; C was for the still-to-be-determined location.

Even though the dates were less than optimal, playing in the Garden gave them some instant credibility in the eyes of the league, as many other teams were forced to settle for lesser-known venues. Old Boston Arena, just outside the campus of Northeastern University, had an ice sheet and seated roughly five thousand; it was used primarily for college hockey and boxing. Let's just say some didn't find it ideal.

"Dad, we've got a place to play," Baldwin told his father in a phone call. "The Boston Arena."

There was a silence on the other end of the phone.

"You're kidding, aren't you?" his father finally replied.

"No," said Baldwin.

"I played there in 1933 with Harvard, and it was a dump *then*. You can't play there."

The ice was shaped like a football, and the building—the first home of the Celtics and Bruins—was partially renovated. "If you shot the puck along the boards hard enough, it would have gone round and round all day, like a pinball," Baldwin recalled.

The Whalers got to work with some renovations: a new lighting system and a new floor that consisted of boards and glass, seven miles of piping, more than 250 gallons of paint, and a rounded-off rink (195 by 85 feet), which was moved seven feet down from the back end so that, at least from the first four rows of the balcony, a fan could see the near net. "I'm delighted with the way the arena looks," Baldwin proclaimed to the *Globe* when asked about the work, which cost $225,000.

The arena wasn't much, but it would be home for a sizable portion of the Whalers' first new season in the WHA. They had established a beachhead in a well-known hockey town and stocked their roster with a ton of local talent. While they hadn't managed to turn Monahan's proclamation completely on its head, they had done their part to help the hockey revolution. Now? All they needed to do was play—and win—some games.

2

Building a Champion
1972-74

I remember being in Boston and being part of the WHA, something brand new, and winning it all the first year with the Whalers. I remember all the people involved in bringing the Whalers to Hartford. I remember [Governor] Ella Grasso taking some charter flights with us. I remember her coming with us to Quebec City and sitting behind the bench. She heard some blue language. She just kept on smiling.
—Tom Webster, speaking with the *Hartford Courant*, March 29, 1997

The addition of established stars like Hull was paramount in helping make the WHA a legitimate league. One other thing—the WHA, in marked contrast to the NHL, tried to appeal to a younger demographic. It was going for cooler names and colorful uniforms. The ABA had the red, white, and blue ball and the three-point shot, both of which were attempts to liven up the game of pro basketball. The WHA wasn't thinking of anything along those lines, but it was clear by the marketing, promotion, and overall attitude that it was aiming to make the league a lot more fun—not to mention a lot more flexible—than the old-school NHL.

˙ "One thing I loved about the WHA was they *literally* made the rules up as they went along," said Jordy Douglas, who grew up watching the WHA before eventually signing with the New England Whalers in 1978.

"It was easy to take [the NHL] on because they were old and stodgy and we were young and likeable—at least, I thought we were!" Baldwin later wrote when comparing the two leagues.

In New England, the Whalers were more than willing to chip in to help bring Hull to the WHA—they were one of several teams who helped pay off Hull's deal. "We knew enough to know that you needed a star to make a new league work. A lot of owners think people want to look up at them in their private box, but I'm a great believer that the athletes are the stars, so we—the Whalers—immediately voted to chip in our share for Hull," Baldwin later wrote. "We trusted the people around the table and we assumed that when they said they were going to chip in, they were going to come up with the money. Hull was going to be great for the league."

Multiple stories exist as to whether every team paid its fair share of Hull's deal. Baldwin estimated "only three or four" franchises chipped in, while others remember six or seven teams. Regardless, the deal was done, and the WHA had its star.

While the legal drama surrounding Hull continued to play out, the start of the inaugural season loomed, and the Whalers continued to build out their roster. Baldwin and Kelley weren't going to be swinging for the fences like Winnipeg was. Instead, they kept the focus local, both on and off the ice. Kelley, who was not only coach but also general manager, drew some chuckles throughout the league for that decision.

But no one had more pull in college hockey circles than the ex-BU coach, who ended up inking several college-area stars. While much of the rest of the league was built on unsustainable flash, Kelley and the Whalers went mostly for substance, signing guys who weren't exactly top-shelf talent but the sort who were affordable and weren't going to bolt for the NHL at the first opportunity. Lynn native Pleau—who was with the Canadiens—was lured away from the NHL by Kelley, and he was followed by a cadre of homegrown talent, including former Boston College stars Tim Sheehy, John Cunniff, Paul Hurley, and Kevin Ahearn. In addition, Jake Danby, Bob Brown, and Ric Jordan, all of whom had played for Kelley at Boston University, signed with the Whalers.

Those former Terriers played a sizable role in helping smooth things over. They had played for the hard-nosed Kelley for several years and knew what to expect.

"The difference went back to freshman year at BU for me. We were loaded. That whole class of freshmen, we played three years of varsity, and by then, we were immune to his style of coaching," Danby said. "We heard the rants and raves and rah-rah all the time, time and again, and it just didn't faze us. By the time we were seniors at BU, we just kind of rolled our eyes to it while he did the rah-rah thing. We knew how good we were—we were able to motivate ourselves as players. So when we got to the Whalers, we knew what was coming."

"He was a tough coach, but he was fair," Pleau said. "You knew where you stood. He had a good feeling about the game. He was sharp, and he wanted you to work hard and stay disciplined. I'm sure it was a different world for him dealing with pro guys, having come from college. But we had a good group of players, and everything went well for the team."

For equipment manager Skip Cunningham and the rest of the support staff, Kelley's occasionally blunt approach made their lives easier. "He knew what he wanted. And when something wasn't right, he would say something," Cunningham recalled. "At the same time, he thanked me every day for *everything*. You know, pro sports is a tough job, and it takes somewhat of a good communicator. As a person, the coaches and players, they have good days and bad days. As an equipment guy, you can't bring your bad problems into work with you. Having been brought up in sports since I was a kid, I knew what to expect when it came to working for Jack."

Some of the veterans weren't crazy about Kelley and his coaching style. "That first training camp—for me—was a *scream*," said goaltender

Cap Raeder, a New England kid who shuttled between the minors and the parent club that season and who grew up idolizing Kelley, a college hockey legend. "I was so pumped to get there. I get there, and it was an eye opener. Kelley is talking about the curfew, and all these veterans are just making fun of him—Tommy Webster and Brad Selwood and Ricky Ley. All these guys [are] in their thirties, and I'm just twenty-one. This is Jack Kelley, and they're giving him shit. You have got to be kidding me. They called him 'beady eyes.' But he was a tough guy who was bringing his college coaching style to the pros."

Webster was one of several NHL vets who liked what the WHA, and the Whalers in particular, had to offer. He was stuck in a miserable situation with the California Golden Seals—Charlie Finley was going to cut his salary from $15,000 to $12,000. He went to see the owner, who used to cook hamburgers in his office. He cooked one for Webster while they talked about Webster's contract offer from the Whalers, a deal that would net him $50,000 a year guaranteed for the next three seasons.

"I think you should take it," Finley told Webster. "But remember, if this league doesn't go, you're coming back to me, and your contract might be much less."

"So my decision was very simple," Webster later recalled in an interview with the *Los Angeles Times*.

Webster indeed found a home in New England, but it wasn't without a few changes. The Golden Seals had white skates, and the Whalers went with the traditional black. That meant a quickie paint job.

"We had to paint the skates black, and the paint would occasionally flake off, so we had to paint them black *again and again*," said Cunningham.

Green, who was elected captain, was a public backer of Kelley, but he still knocked heads with the head coach. Danby recalled a story from that first preseason.

"Teddy couldn't have been a better pick as captain because of the different personalities on that team," Danby said. "He never really recovered from that skull fracture—he had some slurring in his speech, and his motor skills weren't like they were before. But he was still an incredible human being and a great player and leader. Seriously, what he did coming back from that stick-swinging incident was absolutely beyond amazing.

"Teddy was also a no-bullshit guy. And so, very early in that first season, even before the regular season began, the guys who didn't know Jack were kind of getting to know him and hearing what he had to say. For people who didn't know him, in some cases, it made them say, 'Oh God, this guy is a little *out there.*' For others like myself who had heard it time and again in college, I wasn't going to say anything. I was a rookie, just out of college. But it was a situation where [for] some of the NHL players—and Teddy was one—it was the opposite.

"One of the very first rah-rah speeches Jack tried to throw at the team was in preseason, during training camp. He started in prior to going out on the ice before practice. These NHL guys like Teddy hadn't ever heard anything like this before. Partway through getting dressed, Teddy stands up and looks right at him. 'Jack, shut the fuck up. This isn't college hockey. We don't need this bullshit. Just shut up.'"

Despite the fact that the players occasionally butted heads with the coach, it all came together nicely. The first game in franchise history was on the night of October 12, 1972, in the Boston Garden, and it was a sellout. Veteran Tommy Williams, a member of the legendary 1960 U.S. Olympic team that took home the gold medal, scored the first goal in franchise history, while hometown hero Pleau netted the game-winner with 2:11 left. In the end, the Whalers took home a 4–3 win. Under the headline "Whalers' Home Debut Win Has Fairy Tale Touch" in the *Boston Globe*, Tom Fitzgerald said things couldn't have gone any better for New England, from the exciting, well-played game to the dramatic game-winner coming from a local hero and the return of Hub favorite Green to the Boston Garden ice. (Williams, who was the oldest player on the roster at thirty-two, not only landed the first goal in franchise history but also became the first player to record a New England hockey hat trick, playing for the Whalers, Bruins, and Braves.)

The opener's big story, many believed, was the return of Green. "Teddy was absolutely immense," Kelley told reporters after the win. "From the time we got started he has been a big man for this team. And he was great in this game. The first impression was so important for us. Teddy said, 'Nobody knows better than me that Boston fans are the greatest anywhere but they can either love you or hate you.' I think they loved us tonight."

That opening win set the stage for a terrific start for Kelley and the Whalers, with nine wins in their first thirteen games. But league-wide drama—specifically, the future of Hull and the WHA—continued to churn in the background. Despite Hull jumping from the Blackhawks, the NHL wasn't going to give up the fight. Chicago got an injunction and effectively blocked Hull from moving to the Jets. That set the stage for *another* round of legal battles, and this time, the WHA would find a better outcome.

In early November 1972 a 124-page ruling by Judge A. Leon Higginbotham rendered the NHL's reserve clause invalid, freeing the players to change leagues. Higginbotham wrote that there is "a clear and substantial likelihood that at trial the interlocking agreements among N.H.L. teams, and the reserve clause . . . will be found to have given the N.H.L. the power of a monopoly."

It was a landmark decision. While there would be more court battles to come, the reserve clause in the NHL was now suspended, and players were free to sign wherever they wanted. Hull, who had been under an Illinois injunction not to play, was given the green light. As soon as Judge Higginbotham's decision was made, his lawyers flew the document to Chicago and presented it to Judge Francis Delaney of the Illinois Circuit Court. After reading the decision, Delaney concurred and lifted the Illinois injunction against Hull, making it possible for him to play that night against the Nordiques.

Of course, while players were now ultimately free to sign with the WHA, this was the worst possible news for some of the new franchises. When a group of hungry teams are given the green light to head to the buffet, they're going to stuff themselves, regardless of whether it's advisable. In hindsight, most of the WHA's failed franchises ended up part of some half-assed financial hellscape of their own doing. They either chased NHL stars, mortgaged their future on trying to play in a building they couldn't afford, or tossed the keys to coaches or GMs who had little long-term vision of success.

That doesn't even begin to include the ill-informed decision to try to make hockey work in parts of the country that had no interest at all in the game—those places had to spend more just to try and get people into the building. The bottom line was that many franchises believed they had to spend crazy dollars in hopes of building a fan base.

But in New England, it was a different story. It turned out that even with two other professional hockey teams in town, in the hockey-crazed region the market for the sport was bottomless, so attendance wasn't a problem. The Whalers drew the largest WHA crowd of the season for their home opener, as 14,552 witnessed the win over Philadelphia. On Hull's first visit to Boston as a member of the Jets, the Whalers drew 9,119. New England would end up leading the league in attendance that first season, drawing an average of 6,981 fans a game. That was just good enough to edge Quebec, which drew an average of 6,923 that season. For some context, on the other end of the spectrum, the Ottawa Nationals were last with an average of 3,226 per game.

Though the rest of the league snickered at the Whalers' idea of stacking their roster with local talent, it paid dividends on a few different levels: One, the local kids were pretty good and helped create a culture of winning right out of the gate. Two, as a fan, you were going to be more financially and emotionally invested in the success or failure of your team if it had players from your area. And three, the sight of local kids on the ice, playing professional hockey, inspired area youngsters. Chris Nilan, who was born in Boston and played in the NHL for fifteen seasons with the Canadiens, Bruins, and Rangers, remembers sneaking into games at Boston Arena and being inspired by the sight of Pleau.

"I remember Larry Pleau was playing, and I liked him because he was a local kid. I saw that, and I started to think that local kids could play pro hockey," said Nilan. "That wasn't the only reason, but that was one of the things that got me pointed in the direction of pro hockey, the fact that I saw a guy like Pleau doing it. I know it wasn't the NHL, but it was still pretty good hockey."

At the same time, things were crowded in the Garden. The Bruins, Whalers, and minor-league Braves all shared the ice. It wasn't always easy.

"We'd go to the game with church groups—you couldn't get Bruins tickets, because they were sold out," said Mark Willand, a young hockey fan who would eventually work for the Whalers as an adult years later. "The games were tough to get to—the Whalers were the third hockey team in the building, so they got all the bad times. They would play on Monday night against Monday Night Football, or Sunday at one o'clock—the worst days possible."

In addition, cranking up Boston Arena on game nights wasn't always easy. The evening of the home opener, Baldwin recalls walking into the arena an hour before the gates opened, and *poof!*—the lights went out. It was a blackout, with fans were milling around in the lobby. Baldwin was taken down to the electrical room by building manager Chuck Toomey, and the owner saw three or four fans cooling the red-hot fuses. Baldwin later remembered that during most of their nineteen home games in the venue, he'd sit there, silently praying the game would end before the lights went out.

But it was better than most of the rest of the league. New England had a robust home crowd, but the road was a different story. The Whalers' first away game was in Philly against the Blazers, and in the hours before the game, the arena crew in the old Philadelphia Convention Hall made a surprising discovery. "Our first game in the WHA in Philadelphia was cancelled because the Zamboni took a chunk of the playing surface when it was coming off the ice," recalled Lacroix.

Sanderson and Philadelphia mayor Frank Rizzo were sent out to tell the fans what happened. "Rizzo was beside me, and he had the mic,"

Sanderson later told author Ed Willes. "He said, 'Here Derek, take the mic. You learn in politics when things go bad, you get out.' And he jumped into a penalty box and down a hallway and he was gone. So now, I've got the mic and I say, 'On behalf of the team, I want to apologize' and *pow!*—the first puck hit the glass. So I kind of move, and it's *pow, pow, pow!* Now, I'm blocking them. I get the fuck out of there and head down the hallway. I can still hear the pucks bouncing everywhere."

One of the principals involved in making the decision was Bill Friday, the WHA's primary referee. He said he made the call after talking with James Cooper, president of the Blazers.

"I conferred with Mr. Cooper and both of the coaches. I don't know what the problem was, but the ice was very hard and it chipped in large chunks," Friday told reporters. "Even if it had been possible to repair all the spots, it would require two or three hours."

Boston wasn't immune to the occasional bump in the road. In November the Whalers' dressing room was looted by thieves who ransacked the place, taking custom-made skates, sticks, and large racks of uniforms. For an expansion team without a lot of financial flexibility, it was a serious blow—it was estimated that $10,000 worth of equipment was stolen. A team spokesman told reporters, "The people who took our gear don't understand what the consequences may be for the players. I'm certainly worried about what was taken."

How did the Whalers respond? Equipment manager Skip Cunningham says they got themselves some guard dogs.

"We had some attack dogs in the locker room, but some of them were low-budget, WHA attack dogs—attack pups," he said with a laugh. "Some of them also had a tendency to sleep. But we were still scared to death of the bigger ones, especially when it came to opening the doors. You never knew if they'd be asleep or not.

"One time, we got to the airport, and we forgot a bag of underwear. We were going to go back and get it, but we were wondering if it would work, because we were afraid of the dogs we had put in there while we were gone. We'd also be cutting it close, because we were on a commercial flight. But we took care of it."

In the end, the ice in New England, as well as the on-ice product, was sturdy and substantial—certainly better than what most WHA teams were running out there on a nightly basis. The Whalers enjoyed success that first season for several reasons, including netminder Al Smith, a journeyman who played with Toronto, Pittsburgh, and Detroit before he was selected by Whalers in 1972 WHA draft. A veteran who had been around pro hockey for many years, he went 31-19-1 and posted a goals-against average (GAA) of 3.18 in his first year in New England. But he distinguished himself as someone who was "a little to the left of the right side of the railroad tracks," recalled Pleau. Smith was a writer and free-thinker, and in the world of professional sports, that didn't always fly. But when it came to his time in New England, as long as he kept winning games, it was all good.

Smith was backed up by Bruce Landon, who initially made the leap to the WHA because—in part—he was didn't want to sit behind Ken Dryden in Montreal. Thing was, when he joined New England, he mostly backed up one of the most durable netminders in WHA history.

"Al was a warrior," Landon said. "He never wanted to come out of a game. When I was backing him up, you knew he was almost never going to want to come out of a game. He was never hurt and always wanted to finish every game."

Ultimately, that first year, the Whalers finished with league highs in wins (46), winning percentage (.602), points (94), and goals (318) as they took home the Eastern Division title, outdistancing their division rivals from Cleveland, Philadelphia, Ottawa, Quebec, and New York. Kelley was named the WHA Coach of the Year, while Terry Caffery, who finished with 100 points, was named Rookie of the Year.

"We were lucky with New England—we never missed a check, and we got playoff bonuses," Pleau said. "The Whalers did a great job. It was different, but a great experience. We were young and didn't know what the fuck we were doing—we were just hoping we could all make it work."

Of course, even though he was a local kid living the dream playing professional hockey in his home state, it wasn't always perfect for Pleau. He didn't always jibe with management, but he always managed to cover his bases. One day, he got a call from someone in the front office who said the team was trading him to Indy. Only thing was, he had a no-trade contract.

"I can hear in the background, 'What the fuck are you doing?'" Despite the confusion in the front office, Pleau remained with the Whalers. "I came here and wanted to stay here. That was important to me and my family. Between my time as a player, coach and GM, I had sixteen great years."

NEW ENGLAND STORMED INTO THE POSTSEASON ON A ROLL, winning eight straight at one point and cementing its status as the league's premier team that first season. The Whalers dumped Ottawa and Cleveland in five games each in the first two rounds, rolling over a Cleveland Crusaders team that finished with 89 points on the year, third-best in the WHA, thanks in large part to their defense.

"Our defense was outstanding," Kelley said after the Game Five win that wrapped up the series. "It has to be when these two teams play. You don't outscore a team like Cleveland by something like 7–6 with goalies like Al Smith and Gerry Cheevers. Defense has to be the key."

The finals against Winnipeg was a matchup of the two best teams in the WHA—the Whalers were at or near the top of the league in most major categories and ran away with the East Division crown, while the Jets did the same out west, largely due to the work of their top line of Hull, Chris Bordeleau, and Norm Beaudin, who all finished in the top seven in the league in points that season. Kelley knew his team had a sizable challenge ahead.

"Now we will have to think about Winnipeg," said the New England coach shortly after his team finished off Cleveland in the semis. "We will have to spend all our time figuring out a way to contain their big line of Bobby Hull, Chris Bordeleau and Norm Beaudin."

But if the semis were a tribute to the work of the New England defense, it was the Whalers' potent scoring attack that was on full display in the finals. Playing without Terry Caffery (39 regular-season goals, good for second on the team) and John Danby (14 regular-season goals)—both of whom were injured in the semis against Cleveland—New England scored a combined 14 goals in the first two games, overwhelming Hull and the Jets on the way to series leads of 2–0 and 3–1.

The Whalers were surprised at how easy things were. "I couldn't understand the way they played the game," New England veteran Tommy Williams told reporters after the first few games. "They tried to skate with us and they couldn't. We're a better skating team than they are."

Kelley took a different tone. "They've played much better against us this year. We just had some luck," he said.

Regardless, New England had the chance to close things out in Boston on May 6, 1973. Pleau, who had played a sizable role in helping the Whalers dominate much of the first four games, woke up early on the morning of Game Five.

"I couldn't sleep that morning," remembered Pleau. "I woke up at 5:00 a.m. and looked at the calendar. It was opening day for fishing in Lynn; I had a couple of rods in my car. I told my roommate Jimmy Dorey, 'Let's go fishing.' We were catching trout at 5:30, six o'clock in the morning, and I scored 3 goals, and we won the Avco Cup that afternoon."

Game Five was a wild, back-and-forth contest that saw New England take a 6–2 lead early in the second. Webster scored twice, and Pleau, Guy Smith, Rick Ley, and Tim Sheehy added tallies for the Whalers, who also got some stand-up work between the pipes from Smith. But the Jets staged a furious rally, scoring three times and pushing their way back into it early in the third period.

That's when Pleau—who finished the postseason with a whopping 12 goals—took command, scoring 2 more third-period goals to give New England an insurmountable lead. Hull, who was serving as Winnipeg's player-coach, pulled the goalie with roughly three and a half minutes to go, but Mike Byers added an empty-netter to make it 9–6, and the celebration was on.

Of course, this being the WHA, the trophy situation that first season was unclear. The one thing we do know? There are three Avco World Trophies currently in existence—one each at the Hockey Hall of Fame, the Nova Scotia Sport Hall of Fame, and the Manitoba Sports Hall of Fame and Museum. However, none of them were available the day the Whalers won the title, because the first trophy hadn't been finished yet. As a result, multiple stories exist when it comes to how the Whalers celebrated.

One story, via Baldwin, is that a PR guy went to a local sporting goods store and returned with a large, shiny trophy that cost twenty dollars, and by Baldwin's estimate "looked real good on 1973 television." Another story is that the Whalers simply skated their divisional trophy around the ice as part of the postgame festivities.

"I was at the very first Whalers championship game at the Garden in 1973," said New England–based hockey writer Mick Colageo. "I was gifted a ticket behind the penalty box, and after the game, I went on the ice, and Teddy Green was carrying around the Eastern Division Championship trophy. There were two stories—either the Avco Cup was too heavy, or it wasn't ready in time for the game. I don't know. I do remember being close enough where I think the edge of my head is in some of those pictures. And I was close enough to know that it was the Eastern Division trophy he was carrying."

Regardless of what happened, the Whalers were champions, and Baldwin immediately issued a challenge to the NHL for New England to meet the winner of the Stanley Cup for a one-game playoff on neutral ice. Although the NHL didn't take him up on the offer—some owners scoffed at the idea of facing the WHA—it was clear the rebel league had shaken up the hockey world.

AFTER THAT FIRST YEAR, THE WHALERS DECIDED TO MAKE some changes. Kelley became a full-time GM, and New England hired

Ron Ryan as its new head coach for the 1973–74 season. While the move caught some by surprise, the shift from Kelley to Ryan didn't bring about wholesale changes, at least as far as most of the players were concerned.

"Jack and Ron were pretty close in coaching style—I don't think Ron changed things very much from the way Jack did business," said goaltender Bruce Landon. "Ron wasn't nearly as intimidating as Jack could be at times. Jack had that look in his eye; when he set his gaze on you, sometimes it was like his eyes were boring right though you.

"But we continued to play well and respond—there really wasn't too much of a change in the locker room, at least as far as I could tell. Jack was certainly still involved in the day-to-day with the team, but Ron put his own stamp on things."

"There was some eventual moderation on Jack's part as the season went on, because I think Jack realized his personality wasn't going to be a good fit as head coach," said Danby. "I think that was one of the reasons why he made the decision to back off after that, and the next year, become the GM and let a different personality like Ron Ryan take over. Ron was more of a laid-back guy—a better fit for the various personalities in the early stages of the WHA. Ron was more of a players' coach and more laid-back."

A great sense of optimism welcomed the new season. There was greater depth at all three levels (forward, defense, and goalie) and some new faces from the NHL (namely Al Karlander and Don Blackburn), plus the group that had just won the WHA title now had a full year under their belts as champions.

"The Whalers are going to be an even better hockey team this year," Kelley promised in an interview with the *Lowell Sun* before the start of the 1973–74 season. "We have better overall balance upfront, and the mere fact that we played together as a team for one year will make us a stronger unit. It really wasn't until the playoffs last spring that we came of age, winning our last 11 home games and 23 of our final 28 games altogether.

"Over the summer we've helped ourselves where it was most needed. We were shallow at center and left wing but the addition of Al Karlander, Hugh Harris and Don Blackburn from the NHL has strengthened the club. Their presence in camp has added competition for positions. We didn't have that last year because we were struggling to put a team together and most of the second-liners were amateurs. This year, 95 percent of the team is comprised of second-year pros, and that has to help."

That faith was vindicated, as Ryan ended up guiding the Whalers to another first-place finish—New England ended the regular season with forty-three wins and 90 overall points and cruised into the playoffs as a prohibitive favorite to repeat.

However, as the Whalers continued to impress on the ice, a far more compelling drama was simmering off the ice, as the franchise was in final talks to move out of Boston permanently. The only thing was that their ultimate destination was a bit of a mystery.

"To say that the New England Whalers are going to Hartford is, at best, premature at this time," Baldwin told reporters in January. "I have said before we are contacted on a regular basis by cities that have existing facilities or have new buildings in the construction stages, which is the situation in Hartford."

It wasn't going to be easy to pick up and leave Boston. Baldwin tried to keep the news of the impending move a secret, but it got out, sooner rather than later. He suffered serious blowback from not only the Bay State fan base but also the Bruins. One afternoon, the Garden's legal counsel Charlie Mulch called the franchise and let them know in no uncertain terms that the Bruins were not going to let the Whalers' equipment out of the building unless they settled up financially. To stop the Whalers' equipment van from leaving, they had the Garden Zamboni block the entrance.

"To hell with them," Baldwin recalled saying. "They can keep the equipment. I'm going to torture them, because they've tortured us for two years."

For the next few hours, the van stayed put. So did the Zamboni. Then someone noticed that Bruins owner Weston Adams had his Corvette parked on the wrong side of the Zamboni. The Zamboni moved, and the Whalers' equipment van sped away. (The Whalers eventually paid the rent, but not before adding another chapter in the rivalry between the two franchises.)

"It wasn't that we didn't have the money," said Baldwin. "We just wanted to stick it up the Bruins' ass. We paid them back eventually."

"We were looking to get out of a negative situation in Boston," Baldwin later explained. "We sought a good market and good partners. There was really nothing scientific about it. We were going down slowly, and we needed to do something. We made a quick decision not to chase it in Boston. We won the championship, our dates at Boston Garden went up from twenty to forty in our second year, but we couldn't draw flies. Gordie Howe and his kids were selling out building after building. They came to Boston and drew eight thousand. We knew we had to get out of there."

The bottom line? If the Whalers wanted to reach firmer ground, they had to find new digs. The Bruins weren't making it easy to stick around Boston, hiking the rent, offering subpar home dates, and showing a general unwillingness to share the facility.

But the Whalers weren't the only dissatisfied tenant at the Garden— for years, the Celtics claimed they were losing money because of their lease with the Bruins. One *Boston Globe* report in June 1972 indicated that the Celtics paid $300,000 a year, the highest rental fee of any NBA or ABA team, and would welcome the opportunity to move into a new building. (Most teams paid one-third that cost.)

It wouldn't be financially feasible for them to move into their own building, but if they could pair with the Whalers on a new venue of their own—forty home dates each for both teams, plus potential playoff dates and other attractions like concerts—that would work for both teams. A new deal was floated, with the South Station area as a potential landing spot. That was contingent on Schmertz, who owned a piece of the Whalers, gaining at least a partial ownership stake in the Celtics.

However, in the summer of 1972 it became clear that wasn't going to happen, causing the Whalers to strike a deal with *the Bruins*, of all organizations, on a new building. In December, the teams jointly announced a new arena, a $16 million, eighteen-thousand-seat building slated to open in 1975. But that was eventually torpedoed, and after Schmertz suffered a stroke and passed away in 1975, any deal that would pair the Whalers with any other Boston team seemed finished.

So where to go? Other cities were in the mix, however briefly, including Providence. Baldwin again flirted with the idea of moving to Rhode Island and its new Civic Center. But as was the case with their initial series of meetings with Rhode Island officials when they were first looking for a place to play, there were some serious doubts about Providence for several reasons, including that, whenever they tried to get any sort of license, they were met with a "fee" or "surcharge" or were otherwise forced to grease the palm of some city officials. (Baldwin ended up testifying as part of a trial against some city officials found guilty of bribery.) That's when Hartford entered the picture.

ON APRIL 2, 1971, HARTFORD CITY OFFICIALS AND OTHER assorted dignitaries—as well as an elephant and a donkey, to symbolize a burgeoning political partnership—broke ground on a new downtown project that was dubbed the Hartford Civic Center, slated to ultimately cost $30.5 million, cover 7.5 acres, have ten thousand seats for hockey and twelve thousand for stage events, and include a seventeen-thousand-square-foot assembly hall. In addition, through a partnership with Aetna, the building would hold a shopping mall and office space and be connected to a four-hundred-room, twenty-story hotel via a bridge over Church Street. Mayor Ann Uccello optimistically said the new venture was "an act of faith, of hope and of love" and added that the joint venture between Aetna and the city would "infuse a new life—a new vitality into Central Hartford."

You can't tell the story of the Whalers in Hartford without Aetna. By this point, Hartford had become the insurance capital of the world, and the company had largely become the leader in the field. Founded in 1819 by local merchants and named the Aetna Fire Insurance Company, it distinguished itself through the years by evolving while offering insurance of all kinds. Aetna went from insuring farms against fires to investing in home mortgages to insuring factories to marketing war bonds to offering workmen's comp and the rest. In 1973 it created its first HMO, a lucrative venture that would set the table for a decade of profits that soared into the billions. At one point in the 1970s an Aetna ad boasted insurance that could "protect just about anyone, anywhere, against most anything."

Against this financial backdrop, the company decided to spread its wings a bit. Its aggressive approach, in part, helped pave the way for a building boom in downtown Hartford, and the Civic Center was going to be the crown jewel to help revitalize the city. The state didn't have any other sort of similar facility at the time—the only venue that was close in terms of size was the New Haven Coliseum, which was built in 1972 and had room for just over eleven thousand people. But if the city and Aetna could pull it off, the Hartford Civic Center would be far superior to New Haven Coliseum on several fronts.

It was a bold venture for a few reasons, not the least of which was that the city did not yet have a regular tenant lined up. There had been talk of building a sizable arena in the middle of the state since the 1940s, with *Courant* sports editor Bill Lee being one of the primary advocates. The first league to show interest in Hartford as a potential landing spot was the American Basketball Association. Jack Dolph, ABA commissioner and Greenwich resident, said in December 1971 that the ABA was investigating the possibility of a regional team that would cover New Haven, Hartford, and Springfield, Massachusetts. "With a regional team, you have three different 10,000-seat arenas in three different cities instead of having to sell tickets for 42 home games, a city has only 15 or so home games—one-third the number of the traditional pro basketball franchise," Dolph explained to reporters at the time. It was a concept that had proven to be successful with other ABA franchises in Virginia and Florida.

Nothing ever came of the regional-team idea, but as the ABA under-went a wave of ebbs and flows over the course of the next couple of seasons, plenty of franchises eyed Hartford as a potential landing spot. The New York Nets, Spirits of St. Louis, and Memphis Tams (owned by Charlie Finley) were all publicly linked to the new building at one time or another, but a deal didn't happen for a few reasons, including that the Celtics strongly opposed any move into their territory.

From a distance, Baldwin saw what happened and knew it was an opportunity he and his team couldn't pass up. A shiny new venue needs a tenant. After touring the city and meeting with business leaders and poli-ticians, he sensed their willingness to work with him and was able to make a connection. Baldwin later recalled it was an awful lot like the way they initially landed the franchise: by being in the right place at the right time.

Of course, Baldwin and his partners could have used a geography lesson. They decided to charter a plane from Boston to Hartford—a ninety-minute drive—in the middle of a snowstorm. ("We nearly crash landed on the runway in Hartford," Baldwin later remembered.) But Baldwin and his partners were about to walk into a marriage between a franchise and a city that would last for almost twenty-five years. Buoyed by an endorsement from Donald Conrad—the CFO of the Aetna Insurance Company—the two sides quickly came to an agreement.

"It was clear to us that the city was desperate to have a prime tenant for the Civic Center, which was being built to revitalize downtown Hartford," Baldwin said. "And we just got lucky."

Ultimately, the announcement of the move to Hartford was made in February 1974, and while Baldwin told reporters the team "regret[ed]" leaving Boston, Whalers fans should view the move "not as a retreat but as a giant step forward, not only for us but for professional hockey. The Whalers are a major-league team. Hartford is a major-league city; the marriage is a natural."

Of course, the financial bump helped as well. UPI reported that the move was accompanied by more than 30 percent of the team's stock going to Hartford-area businesses—according to reports, twelve businesses put up $1.5 million for the stock. The franchise needed the financial boost—Baldwin said club losses the first two seasons climbed to $2 million. "We were prepared to lose money," he told reporters, "but not that much."

Ultimately, the move was really one of the first examples of Baldwin being able to not only recognize the need for long-term capital but also get it by using bridge-building techniques with local corporations, as well as partnerships with area politicians who recognized the impact of having a local sports team.

"The reason we did well in Hartford, even when we had some weaker teams later on, was that the front office was solid. And the market was solid too," he would later write in his autobiography. "It was the perfect blend of the corporate and the political coming together in harmony. The key people in the early years were Don Conrad from the Aetna, Nick Carbone, the power broker on the City Council, and seven or eight business leaders from the insurance companies that owned the team who were going to make damn sure that this team succeeded. The city had built the arena in the corporate sector, had landed the team to make Hartford a better place, building civic pride, and they really threw themselves into it."

Baldwin quickly won over the city with a combination of charm and the promise of big-time professional sports. "I remember covering the initial news conference when the seed was planted," said longtime New England TV and radio news reporter Gerry Brooks. "This brash young guy came in and said, 'I'm the owner, Howard Baldwin, and I'm bringing big league hockey to town.' *Wow.* I'm sure at that point a lot of people thought there was going to be a merger down the road, and Hartford could eventually become an NHL city. He was the guy who did it, and he was still just in his twenties. I wish I had half his personality—George Frazier, the old sports columnist for the *Globe*, used to use the word *duende* to talk about charisma. I guess that's what Howard had—duende . . . and some big balls."

"Howard—he was right out of central casting, if you're looking for a guy who is a wannabe sports mogul," remembered sportswriter Dom Amore of the *Hartford Courant*. "The guy was launching a new league and bringing a new team to town. Sometimes, those type of guys turn out to be Harold Hill in *The Music Man*. And Howard did have plenty of that sort of show in him.

"But he also brought real hockey to town. And that gave him tremendous credibility with the fans and the fan base and the people of Hartford. People believed in him. For all his *Music Man* approach—and people in Hartford can be skeptical of those types of guys—he delivered the goods."

"He was just a guy who loved hockey and was willing to take a chance," said Upton Bell, a friend of Baldwin whose father, Bert, was commissioner of the NFL in the 1940s and '50s. "He started from just about nothing, and the next thing you know, he had a franchise and a league. Whatever you think about the WHA, they had a lot of new ideas and had a lot of fun. I said to myself, *This is a guy who I know is legit.*

"You *have* to have a little Harold Hill in you if you're going to do what Howard did. In any walk of life, if you can sell somebody on your product and you stay the course, good things are going to happen. That was the experience I had watching the growth of the NFL under my father, and Howard was one of the main reasons why that same sort of approach made the WHA a success."

Hartford was the new home of the Whalers, but the new building wasn't going to open until the midway point of the following season. And so, with the 1973–74 regular season at an end, the Whalers ended up ditching Boston for the postseason and playing their games at the Eastern States Exposition Center in Springfield.

An old-school barn that was located on the site of a fairground, it was for many years the rink with the biggest capacity in western Massachusetts. Built in 1916, it first hosted hockey in 1926, as well as agriculture events, circuses, and rodeos. It was the premier location for minor-league hockey in western Massachusetts through the early 1970s, when the Springfield Civic Center was constructed. The exposition center was initially the home to the Springfield Indians, which moved into the Civic Center in 1972 when that building opened, freeing up some short-term space for the Whalers.

Against this backdrop, the Whalers wrapped up the regular season, bidding an official farewell to Boston on April Fool's Day, 1974, in front of a record crowd of 14,711. In a game some expected would be a preview of the WHA finals, New England was waxed by Houston, 4–1, in a showdown of the East and West Division leaders. Don Grierson had a pair of goals fifty-five seconds apart in the second period to lift the Aeros to the win. It gave Houston a 4–2 lead in the season series between the two clubs and assured the Aeros of home-ice advantage when—not if—they met again in the finals.

"It'll go to seven," Houston coach Bill Dineen said of his prediction of a hypothetical Whalers-Aeros final.

However, to get to that point, New England had to get through Chicago first. The Whalers and Cougars split their regular-season series; in addition, the Cougars had finished in last place the year before, but under fiery player-coach Pat Stapleton had made enough personnel tweaks to reach the playoffs in 1974.

Ryan certainly sounded impressed. "The Cougars will be fighting tough. They were the worst team last year but the most improved this season," he told reporters before Game One. "They've made a believer out of me."

Ryan's words proved prophetic. The two teams split the first four games, and the Cougars took Game Five with a 4–2 win. Afterward, Stapleton seemed to hint the series was in the bag. "We have two games to win one, and I believe we will get that victory," Stapleton said.

New England won Game Six, but Chicago took the decisive Game Seven with a narrow 3–2 win over New England, a game that saw New England goaltender Al Smith buried by a wave of rubber—the Cougars put 43 shots on goal, including 24 in the third period. Chicago also seemed to get an emotional boost after Stapleton got a ten-minute misconduct after being the third man in on two separate fights and was later tossed when he gave referee Bill Friday the choke sign from the penalty box.

In the end, Ralph Backstrom tied the score at 2 in the final period, and Jan Popiel finished off the Whalers with the game-winner shortly after that.

"During the season, when we were going really good, I said that Ralph Backstrom might be all through as a hockey player," said Smith after the game. "That's what I get for opening my big mouth. He was really something in the third period."

The Whalers were ultimately dogged by too many penalties, which took a toll, according to Ryan. "Killing an awful lot of penalties tired my team and it couldn't overcome the situation in the final period," he said.

"No game was decided by more than 2 goals," he added, "which made it a heck of a series, and it came down to which team got the breaks."

The Cougars very nearly pulled off the sizable upset, as the fourth-place team made it all the way to the WHA finals. One thing that might have hampered them was that the owners of their building—the International Amphitheatre—didn't have a lot of faith in a deep playoff run. They had booked an extended run of the show *Peter Pan* in the arena, forcing the team to look elsewhere. Chicago Stadium was out because the Blackhawks also reached the NHL playoffs. The Cougars ended up using a public rink, the Randhurst Twin Ice Arena, which had only two thousand seats but was located next to a high-traffic mall. (*Pro hockey in a mall? That's crazy!*) Regardless, they were steamrolled in the finals by Gordie Howe and the Aeros—Chicago lost the finals in four straight by a combined score of 22–9.

FOR THE WHALERS, THE END OF THE SEASON MEANT THEIR first on-ice chapter in franchise history was coming to an end. While the Garden wasn't always the best host—and from a citywide perspective, they were always going to take a back seat to the Bruins—in many ways, the season provided a level of stability that many other WHA teams aspired to. A move to western Massachusetts followed by a splashy debut in Hartford would mark the start of an exciting big-time sports era in southern New England.

3

Welcome to Hartford
1974-77

This team just pushed all my buttons as being this cultish, cool team. They had a great logo. They played that great song. It was like this cool club—for a brief, shining moment my own state had a big-league team. I just remember it so fondly.
—Veteran journalist and Connecticut native Bruce Schoenfeld, who grew up as a Whalers fan

They never had the hold on Connecticut the way that UConn basketball has. But the people they had a hold of, they *really* had a hold of.
—Connecticut sportswriter Dom Amore

The Whalers fell short of going back-to-back in their first two years in the WHA, but in many ways they remained the very model of a team that was part of a start-up league. While others handed out ill-advised contracts to fading stars in hope of creating a bit of a buzz, the Whalers moved adroitly, signing New England–area talent—college and ex-NHLers—and adding a few savvy veterans to the mix as needed. There was stable ownership, a (mostly) full building, and a steady and consistent product on the ice that won more than it lost.

Other teams came and went—and owners ended up losing their shirts. The Whalers were at or near the top of the league on a consistent basis, thanks in large part to the work of Baldwin. While other franchises went for short-term gains and crazy promotional ideas, the Whalers were steady-as-she-goes. The second year, despite the upset at the hands of the Cougars, the feeling was that the Whalers had become one of the league's flagship franchises. Bolstered by consistent fan support and always competitive play, the Whalers were to become the only franchise in league history to never miss the WHA playoffs, winning three division championships along the way. And although there was some movement, they also became the only America-based team in the WHA to play in the same region over the life of the league.

"I was pretty naive at the time, but I could see guys on other teams complaining about things like not getting paychecks," said goaltender Cap Raeder, who was with the Whalers in the mid-1970s. "There seemed to be a lot of instability around the league at that time, but the Whalers never wavered. A lot of that credit goes to Howard Baldwin. Howard was a pretty neat guy—very classy and straightforward. I liked Howard—he seemed to be on top of things."

That stable ownership, steady front office, capable coaching, and on-ice talent combined to make them a fan favorite.

"Webster, Selwood, those guys, boy, they were good," said Tom Hine, the first Whalers beat writer for the *Hartford Courant*, told the paper in 1997. "Not only were they a threat to win it every year, they generated a lot of enthusiasm. It's one of the things I remember most: The thing to do in the city was go to Whalers games. They were social events. Everybody went. I just can't describe it. It was so much unlike what it became; I mean, there were no unfilled corporate seats in the lower concourse. The day after the games, everybody talked about the Whalers. Nick Fotiu could've run for mayor."

The pugnacious Fotiu, who surpassed 100 penalty minutes in seven of the first eight years of his career, became a fan favorite for his willingness to mix it up, as well as his tireless work with kids. He often visited children's hospital wards on his own time and handed out pucks to kids before games at his own cost. The Staten Island native originally spent two years in the WHA with the Whalers before a stint with his hometown Rangers. Fotiu returned to Hartford shortly after that, and in 1979–80, spent half a season centering a line that included Gordie Howe, scoring 10 goals. (It was the first time in his career he had more goals than fights.)

That same year, Fotiu became so fed up with what he perceived as a lack of playing time that he stalked off during the middle of game against the Canadiens in January 1980. While he and his wife were dining on Chinese food, the Hartford crowd chanted, "We want Nick!" He eventually apologized.

Fotiu would be remembered as one of the great characters in franchise history. Al Sims was a defenseman who made his bones with the Bruins before joining the Whalers for the 1979–80 season. That year, Whalers teammates became fed up with Sims going on and on about the Bruins, so one day during a layover in Chicago on the way to Detroit, Fotiu hatched a plan. He called ahead to the hotel in Detroit and left a message: "This is Al Sims' agent. Please have him call me when he checks in. He's been traded back to Boston."

"In Pittsburgh, where the ceiling of the visiting locker room went up at an angle, Nicky got a twenty-foot atrium ladder and a hot glue gun," recalled Mark Howe. "When someone who had been bothering him tried to get dressed after practice and wondered, *Where are my shoes?* they were found twenty feet overhead.

"If there was a Hall of Fame for pranksters, Nicky would have been on the first ballot. He's a great guy," added Howe. "I had the chance to play with him when we were together with the Whalers and later with Philadelphia. Anybody who knows Nick would call his personality . . . infectious. He's a fun-loving guy, a wonderful teammate, and a caring person, and that's how he came across to his teammates on a daily basis. He was quite the prankster, but teams need that sort of personality and character, and Nick delivered that on a regular basis."

Buoyed by fan favorites like Fotiu and kept alive by Baldwin off the ice, the Whalers were as steady as any team in the WHA in the early to mid-1970s. "The Whalers, for what they had to do, they always paid their players and took care of them," equipment manager Skip Cunningham said. "There were other teams that were folding or moving or trading guys, and all of a sudden, we would have one, three, five new guys on our team. Jack [Kelley] always did a great job with the new guys, bringing them in and getting a good mix of college guys and pros—a lot of professionalism.

"But across the league, it was a tough time," he added. "Anytime you're starting a new league, it's tough. I don't care how smart you are; I don't think anyone can really estimate the total cost of what it's going to take. You can juggle figures and all that, but all these things start to transpire, and it really adds up. You have a problem with your flight, you spend a day at the airport, you have to come up with meal money. Your practice is cancelled, and because you're flying commercial, you have to find another flight. For a lot of teams, every day was an adventure trying to make it work."

"When I played for the Jersey Knights, we played our home games at Cherry Hill Arena—probably the worst rink in hockey," said Lacroix of the team that spent the 1973–74 season as the WHA's representative in the Tri-State Area. "There was no locker room, so the visiting team got dressed at the hotel. It was a sight to see Bobby Hull or Gordie Howe coming off a school bus."

That wasn't the only issue in Cherry Hill. The ice surface was later found to have a slope, which caused pucks to shoot upward following a pass or shot and teams to skate uphill or downhill. It also had a chain link fence instead of Plexiglas surrounding the rink. "You'd fire a puck from one end of the ice to the other, and by the time it got there, it would hit the guy in the face," said Wayne "Swoop" Carleton, a WHA vet who played almost two full seasons with New England. "It was crazy."

Furthermore, there wasn't enough room for long, regular-sized benches. Instead, benches were three rows of five seats, like a choir.

One night, Winnipeg coach Nick Mickoski sat in the first row of the stands. But every time he stood up to talk to his players, the fans would complain so loudly he would have to sit down.

Cherry Hill wasn't the only arena with some quirks. At the Chicago International Amphitheatre—which also hosted livestock shows, in addition to the Chicago Cougars—the referee and linesmen had to walk through the stadium bar on the way to the ice.

One way to try and find some stability? Explore the possibility of a merger with the NHL. The expansion conversation dated all the way back to 1972, when the new league swiped Hull a full four months before the WHA's first regular-season game. But while the public perception was that the NHL would be the league operating from a position of strength, offering support to the fledgling World Hockey Association, WHA president Gary Davidson flipped that idea on its head.

"At this point, we aren't even thinking of a possible merger. I don't see how we could acquiesce to some of the rigid NHL practices," Davidson told reporters in June 1972. "The National Hockey League is controlled by the Big Six, the old established teams. We don't have a Big Six. Each of our 12 teams is starting out on an equal footing."

Despite Davidson's brash statement, some WHA teams were struggling right out of the gate. The league tried its best to minimize the disruptions by moving franchises instead of having them fold—the Dayton Arrows became the Houston Aeros and the San Francisco Sharks became the Quebec Nordiques even before the first puck was dropped.

The idea of two sports leagues merging wasn't as far-fetched then as it is now. The NFL and AFL combined forces at the start of the 1970 season, and while the WHA was just getting off the ground in 1972, the NBA and ABA were already discussing a way to pair up. (That deal would come to fruition in 1976.) But it would take a lot to make it happen, as there were several hard-liners among the NHL owners who wanted to do whatever it took to put down the WHA. NHL teams worked with local arenas to jack up the rates, give WHA teams bad dates on the calendar, consign teams to second-rate locker rooms, or just make things as hard as possible for the them. In Toronto, that meant Leafs owner Harold Ballard clearing the cushions off the team benches after games and telling the Toros they needed to get their own.

That said, moderates on both sides saw value in the two leagues joining forces. In 1973 NHL governors Bill Jennings of the Rangers and Ed Snider of the Flyers reportedly approached the WHA and offered to have all twelve WHA teams join the NHL—some reports had the sum at $4 million each, some had it at $2 million. That plan ultimately failed, but it showed that there was an appetite among some on both sides for a unification plan.

"It was a hell of a plan, creative and ballsy, and it would have solved everything and prevented the escalation of the war that had already started and was only going to get worse," Baldwin wrote in his autobiography. "The Whalers would have had to pay an additional indemnity to the Bruins to play in New England, and the Chicago Cougars would have had to do the same thing in the Blackhawks' territory. But when the NHL militants found out—with Bill Wirtz and Clarence Campbell leading them—they went crazy and the whole plan blew up."

So while it wasn't all the way back to square one—the merger conversation would continue in some fashion over the next five-plus years—the Whalers would try to make the best of the situation. Hartford seemed to embrace its new hockey team. Despite the fact that the Whalers were opening the regular season in Springfield, the *Courant* began to ramp up its coverage during training camp at Wesleyan University in anticipation of the team's eventual move. Under a banner headline "N.E. Whalers Open Camp Saturday," on September 17, 1974, were multiple stories to help readers understand the state's newest professional sports team, including a list of terms that read like Hockey 101 for new fans: "Body check—Making body contact on man in possession of the puck." Thirteen games were going to be broadcast on Connecticut's Channel 3. Big-time sports were coming to the state of Connecticut.

The 1974–75 WHA season dawned with thirteen teams in three divisions—the Eastern, Western, and Canadian. The Whalers headed up the Eastern Division, a group that included Chicago, Cleveland, and Indianapolis, in its first season. But right from the start, it didn't much matter who else might have been in the same division, as New England would run away and hide, winning eleven of their first thirteen in Springfield to start the season. The exposition center certainly wasn't ideal, but the Whalers still dominated. With an unbalanced slate that featured more road games than home contests at the start of the season (the better to maximize the new building), they put the capper on their Springfield stint with a 4–3 OT win over Vancouver. (Don Blackburn scored the game-winner for New England.)

The beautiful new Hartford Civic Center opened a week ahead of schedule, and on January 10, 1975, the team played its first game there in front of a sellout crowd. The arena footprint was relatively small compared to other professional venues—so the pitch of the upper deck had to be fairly steep. (Baldwin later said he was able to find other seats for those who might be squeamish in the upper reaches of the building.) Although the facility didn't have luxury suites—those were down the road—the 10,500-seat capacity was more than adequate for the WHA.

The distinguishing characteristic? *The mall.* Whereas the arena footprint was small, the Hartford Civic Center Veterans Memorial Coliseum plus the Exhibition Center took up a sizable chunk of real estate downtown. Flanked by two floors with plenty of retail space, the Veterans Memorial Coliseum, later rechristened the Civic Center, was surrounded by as many as nine different storefronts. Also, office space was on the third floor to accommodate the burgeoning insurance industry.

The Whalers were roundly mocked by many over the years for playing in a mall, but in many ways, the arrangement was forward-thinking. Mall culture in America was about to reach an apex—the new American retail space was warm, inviting, and family-friendly. It was considered safer than shopping out on the street; consequently, malls would often cater to high-end shoppers. In Hartford, that meant the new arena would share space with Luettgens, Ann Taylor, B. Dalton Booksellers, and other companies. It was no surprise that, despite featuring the neo-brutalist architecture of the time, it was an economic catalyst for downtown.

In addition, the Whalers' gift shop, which sold all sorts of team merchandise, soon became a mall fixture. Believed to be the first in-arena gift shop, its distinguishing characteristic was the store entrance, which was shaped like Pucky the Whale. "Take a Walk through the Whale!" shouted the ads, as the store sold everything from keychains to hats to posters and T-shirts in a storefront located next to one of the main entrances.

"We had three weeks to take an empty space and turn it into a gift shop," said George Ducharme, Baldwin's assistant. "We had to get merchandise and train people and get ready for the opening. And I'm pretty sure we sold out of just about everything that first day. People would bring in stuff that they made, that they'd knit, and it would sell out.

"People would come from all over the league just to see the gift shop," Ducharme added. "I told someone I wanted an entrance that would stop traffic. I want people to stop and look at it and say, 'Whoa, what's going on *there?*' I showed them the whale, and asked if they could make this into an entrance. We did it and put a record player on the landing when it opened, and we had 'Brass Bonanza' playing all day, from 10:00 a.m. to 9:00 p.m., on repeat."

The use of that song, the biggest memory off the ice that season, had its beginnings when Ducharme said he noticed something was missing when it came to the atmosphere in the building. "When we opened in Hartford, half the house had never seen a hockey game before," said Ducharme. "They just sat there. When the red light came on, they eventually understood what was going on—there was more polite applause. If the team won, more polite applause.

"I said to Howard, 'What would you say if I brought you a piece of music that was loud and brassy and got people out of their seats?'"

"What the fuck are you talking about?" Baldwin said, and walked away.

Well, he didn't say no, Ducharme thought to himself.

"So I went to bandleaders and asked them to write me a piece of music," he added, "but they all responded, 'You didn't give us enough to go on. You have to give us more.' The problem was, I didn't know really what I wanted. I mean, it was like pornography. I couldn't quite define it for them—when I heard it, I'd know it."

One afternoon, he was thunderstruck. "At the end of the first year, the marketing and PR department produced an LP of the highlights from that first year, and they gave everybody on the staff a copy. I lived that first year, so I didn't need to hear it," he said. "I brought it home and left in on the coffee table in the living room. On Sunday, some of my younger relatives came over and saw it and asked what the record was. I tell them it was highlights from that first year. I leave the room with the rest of the adults and hear the first three notes and scream out: 'That's it!' I come back in. 'What station are you listening to?'

"'We're playing your record!'"

The kids were listening to the flip side, which was a song by Belgian composer Jacques Ysaye called "Evening Beat."

"I shut my eyes and heard it," he said. "*This* is what I want. It was like a dream for a marketing person. When you can identify something or someone with just three notes from a song—*da da da*—that's what it's all about."

Ducharme went to D&K Sound in Wethersfield, introduced himself as the assistant to the president for the Whalers, and got five thousand copies printed. Meanwhile, he went to the arena's audio guy before the next game and handed him the record with a simple directive.

"Here's what I want you to do with this: I want you to play it when the team is introduced. I want you to play it when they score. And if they win, I want you to play it until every last person is out of the building. I want them going home with that goddamned song in their heads."

It was a hit. It was rechristened as the "Hartford Whalers Fight Song" and then "Brass Bonanza."

"Jack Kelley hated it," Ducharme said. "So we both went to see Howard. It was like we were two lawyers standing in front of a judge."

"Jack, you better hope you hear that song in your sleep, because when you do, that means something good is happening to your team," Ducharme told Kelley.

The coach was unmoved. The two stood in front of Baldwin, waiting for a decision. There was an extended silence before Baldwin rendered a verdict. "Well Jack, I think you lost this one," he told Kelley. Ducharme had his victory.

"It's a good thing you voted with me, because I have five thousand copies of that record in our stockroom, and we can't sell them if we don't play it," Ducharme told Baldwin.

"Son of a bitch," Baldwin muttered with a smile as he walked away.

However, the story isn't that simple. For many years, there was a dispute as to who was ultimately responsible for "Brass Bonanza" becoming one of the most iconic songs in New England sports history. Radio play-by-play man Bob Neumeier would contest Ducharme's claim of having discovered the song, saying that he found it one day while flipping through vinyl albums. Years later, Ducharme heard Neumeier discussing it on the air as a sports radio host in Boston and called in to upbraid the broadcaster. For what it's worth, Baldwin gives credit to Ducharme for coming up with the idea, but like all great sports legends, the truth of the matter has been lost to history.

Regardless of who was responsible, the Whalers' gift shop started selling 45s. Youth rinks all over Connecticut started playing it. As the years went on, Binghamton, the Whalers' AHL affiliate, played it—much to the consternation of Hartford's future play-by-play man, Rick Peckham.

"Rochester and Binghamton would go at it all the time—they were rivals for a good stretch. Ricky Ley was the coach in Binghamton, and Mike Keenan was our coach in Rochester," said Peckham, who started his career with the Rochester Americans before eventually joining the

Whalers. "We had some knockdown donnybrooks, and that song, it would just drive you crazy. One night, we got beat at their place 8–2, and I figured out on the two-and-a-half-hour bus ride home we must have heard that thing thirteen times. I had to listen to it before the game, when they started each period, after all 8 goals, and [at] the end of the game. I couldn't stand it," he said with a laugh, "but the fans went crazy for it."

And no street hockey game was complete until you could figure out a way to play it on your tape recorder after a goal. Throughout the 1970s, you couldn't play hockey in Connecticut without hearing the song at least once a week.

"We used to have it on the little tape recorder, and we'd play it in the locker room before we'd go out on the ice," Connecticut native and Hall of Famer Brian Leetch said in a 2011 interview with Versus.

"Whoever made that song didn't make enough money," said PA announcer Greg Gilmartin. "I thought, for us, it was iconic—a great song. I mean, it wasn't the sort of thing you play sitting around, but it really became the perfect song for the perfect moment. I don't think any other team had a song you can say that brings up those sorts of memories and is so instantly identifiable with a franchise."

The attempt to make the Whalers experience as family-friendly as possible was a conscious one, at least from Ducharme's perspective. The first logo had a harpoon, dramatically perched over a *W*. That ran counter to how he was trying to market the team.

"I thought that if you're a parent, you're not going to put a harpoon on a kid's body," he said. "They had made a little whale as an alternate logo, so we took that and expanded on it, added an *ers* at the end.

"The hockey people flipped out; they said it was too cute," he added. "They didn't understand. This wasn't for the hockey buff who knew all the stats and what happened every night to every player. This is for the people who come to the game to be entertained.

"We decided to give it a name, and so we held a contest. I knew what I wanted to name him, and so out of the fourteen thousand entries, I picked the one I began with: Pucky. I knew it would irritate the hockey department—'It's too damn cute'—but the mothers and the aunts and the sisters and the kids loved it. People were giving their babies onesies with Pucky the Whale on them. It created a new generation of fans."

Pucky was one way to reel in kids. There were also autograph sessions, visits to local schools, and promotional giveaways.

"We were sent these larger-than-life trading cards of the players," said longtime fan Stephen Popper, who started following the team in the 1970s as a kid. "I specifically recall listening to Kiss's *Destroyer* album and putting these up all over my room."

It all added up to the sort of place where parents had no qualms about dropping their kids off for a game. At least in part because of the mall, unlike a lot of other downtown stadiums, the environment was family-friendly and trusting. *It was a mall.* Parents could either swing back around in two-plus hours to pick up the kids or simply go to dinner or shopping in the mall during the game and meet the kids after things were done. For hockey fans in southern New England who couldn't get tickets to see the Bruins, it was a cheaper and safer alternative than braving Causeway Street and the ancient Boston Garden.

"It was so . . . *contrary* to the Boston Garden," said Mark Willand, a young fan who first started following the Whalers in elementary school and would go on to work for the team as an adult. "That was so smoke-filled, it had obstructed views. There was a beauty to the Boston Garden—don't get me wrong. But the Civic Center was so . . . civilized. The fans were relative neophytes, but the building was so clean and new. I loved being in that building. My mom would take me and my friend, and she'd sit outside and wait for us while the game was going on."

"My mother was ready at the drop of a hat to jump in the car and go to the Civic Center and see the Whalers," recalled journalist Bruce Schoenfeld, who grew up in southern Connecticut. "We were going to see New England's team. We were going to root for New England's team. And I'd go to school the next day and talk about this team, and people would say, 'Are you out of your mind? Why would you drive all the way to Hartford to see a minor-league hockey team?' But it became our little, cultish thing with our family and all sorts of other families."

The doors officially opened on January 9 with a Glen Campbell concert that kicked off a celebratory week. The following evening, Johnny Mathis and the Hartford Symphony Orchestra took the stage. And any fears about fan support were quickly quashed when, the day before the January 11, 1975, opener in Hartford, the team held an open practice. It was a full house, complete with cheering fans.

To say that the local populace was excited would be an understatement. Writing in the *Courant* on January 10, 1975, columnist Bill Lee could barely contain himself:

"If Hartford dawdled 30 years until it was beaten to the new coliseum punch by Springfield and New Haven, where old arenas had thrived for years, it is rewarding to know that, by waiting, Hartford now boosts a superior Civic Center to cities on either side of us. It is not too much to say that it is the finest new edifice in New England.

"The Civic Center will be, I'm confident, the greatest thing that has happened to Hartford. It will bring in hundreds of thousands of persons and millions of dollars into the city from cities and towns within an hour's drive.

"It will do big things for the downtown area, if downtown Hartford does a few things for itself. New Orleans visitors spent $60 million the last time the Super Bowl was played there. Much more than that will be spent by visitors to Hartford over a year's time—that is, if [off-track betting] doesn't take the money away from them before they can spend it elsewhere."

"The countdown is over," wrote Tom Hine in the *Courant*. "The many years of waiting have long since disappeared.

"It's now only a matter of hours.

"The City of Hartford is on the major-league sports map, and the New England Whalers have a home of their own. It culminates at 7:30 tonight when the first WHA hockey puck is dropped at center ice in the two-day old Hartford Civic Center."

"When I saw all those people at practice, I could have cried," Green told reporters after the open practice. "This is the way it's supposed to be. This is home."

This is home. The Whalers beat San Diego in the opener, taking a 4–3 overtime decision. Lacroix, who would play for New England later in his career, scored the first goal in the history of the building to give the visitors an early lead, but the Whalers answered, eventually winning when Garry Swain scored at 5:47 of overtime to send the sold-out crowd of 10,507 home happy.

"It wasn't a classic, but the guys worked hard. They really did, considering all the pressure. . . . The win was absolutely super before a super crowd," Ryan told the media after the game. "It was a hell of an opening win! It's especially nice when a guy like Swain wins it. Nobody deserves it more and gets less than he and Tommy Earl, our penalty killers."

From a logistical perspective, a few wrinkles needed to be ironed out. Everyone complained about how surprisingly warm it was in the building, and a few others things didn't work out as planned. But for the most part, hockey in Hartford was off to a bang-up start.

The Whalers quickly got used to their new digs, as they would go unbeaten in sixteen of their first eighteen games in Hartford and end the year with the best home record in the league at 28-8-3 to wrap up a third consecutive division championship. Two personnel moves were made down the stretch that provided a boost for New England: The team talked goaltender Bruce Landon—a member of the 1973 Avco Cup champs—out of retirement. And the team swapped Tim Sheehy to Edmonton for Ron Climic.

But as the season continued, the grind took a toll on Ryan, and he collapsed at Toronto International Airport after an overnight flight from Hartford in the last days of the regular season. The team, citing "fatigue," reassigned Ryan as a scout for the rest of the year, and Kelley returned to his old role behind the bench.

With the changes on the coaching staff, the Whalers opened the playoffs against a bruising Minnesota team that finished second in penalty minutes over the course of the regular season. New England finished the year with a nice balance on all three levels—Webster led the team with 40 goals scored, while Pleau and Carleton provided a nice bit of scoring depth. The penalty-killing unit was the best in the WHA. On defense, Rick Ley and Brad Selwood were a sizable reason the Whalers were fifth in the league in goals against, while Smith was steady in goal.

But the Fighting Saints had always been tough for the Whalers— New England had lost nine straight in Saint Paul. Through the first three seasons of the WHA, Minnesota had the best record against New England of any team, 11-6-1.

Ultimately, it shouldn't have been a surprise that it was a physical battle between two of the more rough-and-tumble teams in the league. From an on-ice perspective, the Game One highlight for the Whalers came in hosting their first-ever playoff game in Hartford, a 6–5 win for Minnesota. But then, things went to a whole new level: Saints coach Harry Neale booted Gord Gallant off the team that night after a late-night brawl between the two. Gallant, who had led the WHA in penalty minutes the last two years, socked Neale after the coach found out he had missed a bed check, and then the two exchanged more blows. The incident left Neale with ten stitches over his upper lip, a black eye, a bruised cheek, and ligament damage to his nose.

And then, things *really* went to the next level. Game Two of the series culminated with an epic donnybrook that was later nicknamed "The Brawl in the Mall." Although there are varying accounts as to how things started, on the surface it appears as though the thirty-two-minute scrap had its roots in a lineup change made before the start of the second period by Neale, who decided to put defenseman Bill Butters on a line with fellow bruisers Jack Carlson and Curt Brackenbury. An early hit from behind by Butters on Pleau touched off the fireworks, and Brackenbury and the Whalers' Brad Selwood went at it, but when Butters sucker-punched Pleau from behind, the benches emptied.

It all culminated with the main event—Fotiu going against Jack Carlson (who played one of the Hanson brothers on *Slapshot*), a scrap that continued off the ice and into the penalty boxes and the bench area. Even the two goalies, John Garrett and Al Smith, got into it, despite Garrett not taking off his mask.

"Butters hit Pleau with a sucker shot. It's a simple as that," Kelley said afterward. "The rest was spontaneous."

"It was one wild brawl, one of the wildest I had been in or would be in, no question about it," Fotiu later told hockey writer Liam McGuire. "One thing though that scared me more than anything else. If I could have, during that second fight with Jack Carslon, I would have killed him. I was that mad. We had gone through the door at the Minnesota players bench and I was fighting him in there and I wanted to kill him, seriously."

The hero for New England turned out to be Rick Ley, who collected a whopping 19 penalty minutes on the night but also connected for his first goal of the postseason with 6:46 gone in sudden death when he beat Minnesota's John Garrett with a low slapshot to win the game for the Whalers. "I just wanted to keep the shot low and on net," Ley told reporters after the game. "Al Karlander dug the puck out from behind the net and Gary Swain got it to me with a perfect pass."

The Whalers won, but the tone had been set for the rest of the series. "Our players were ecstatic after the game, figuring they had intimidated the Whalers," Neale later told McGuire. "We ended up winning the series in six games, so I guess they were right."

Remarkably, no video of the fight exists, but the battle was later commemorated via a recording of the radio broadcast for the B side of "Brass Bonanza," which was sold at the Whalers' gift shop. Neumeier and analyst Bill Rasmussen were on the call for what turned out to be a wild affair. At one point during the action, Rasmussen—the man who would go on to start ESPN—can be heard telling Neumeier, "You watch the left-hand boards, I'll watch the right, and we'll just kind of override each other."

The two teams would split the next two in Minnesota, but the Saints would finish off the series with victories in Games Five and Six (by a combined 10–1 margin) to advance to the Avco Cup final.

But while the Whalers fell short of their ultimate goal, the fans didn't consider the season a disappointment. After the Game Six loss in Minnesota, hundreds of fans turned out to welcome the team home, with Connecticut governor Ella Grasso among those showing up. Another indication of their popularity came when Connecticut Public Television announced it had raised $6,600 as part of a pledge night when it aired the Game Six contest.

After three years, the Whalers had established themselves as one of the WHA's premier franchises, and now, with a new building to call home, they had become a flagship professional franchise for the state of Connecticut. They were consistently drawing crowds in excess of 10,000 to the Civic Center, including an average of 10,174 for their home playoff dates.

The Whalers set their course for the 1975–76 season, and the offseason work began almost immediately when Baldwin named Kelley the head coach "for as long as he wants." For his part, Kelley seemed to indicate the Whalers wanted to tweak their overall philosophy, saying shortly after the 1974–75 season ended that speed and aggressiveness were two things he wanted in abundance the following year and hinting that he wanted to go after some European talent to augment the roster.

That came to fruition via a number of ways, including a WHA dispersal draft made up of players from the Baltimore and Chicago franchises, which had to fold following the season. New England plucked three from the old Baltimore Blades roster: goaltender Paul Hoganson and forwards Dave Birch and Bob Goodenow. The Whalers parted ways with Al Smith, Teddy Green, and Don Blackburn (who would eventually find his way back later in the season) but added highly touted youngster Danny Arndt (a second-round pick), as well as forward Rosaire Paiment, a former NHLer who could provide some scoring punch, and goaltender Christer Abrahamsson.

But the biggest news was the addition of seventeen-year-old Gordie Roberts, whose signing had drawn the ire of the rest of the hockey world. Underage players were believed to be off-limits, and Roberts wasn't going to turn eighteen until October 22. Baldwin and the Whalers were threatened on all sides with fines and the loss of draft picks for going after underage talent. (Houston and Toronto had signed eighteen-year-old players, but this was the first time a team had signed a seventeen-year-old.)

"I had only played one year of major junior—I was the only American in the Western Junior League at the time, and I didn't really expect at eighteen to sign a pro contract," said Roberts. "They thought I was holding out, but I was just happy being in Victoria in the junior league where I was playing. They ended up enticing me, thinking they needed to raise the contract offer.

"Another big part of it was my brother Doug, who played pro hockey with the Red Wings at the time, and he was getting ready to sign with the Whalers. It was kind of a package deal they were getting ready to do."

Roberts was believed to be worth it. The high-scoring forward, who played in fifty-three games and had 64 points for Victoria of the Western Canadian Hockey League (WCHL) the previous year, was pegged as the best junior player in Canada. After a protracted legal skirmish, Roberts eventually joined the team in October following his eighteenth birthday.

"The thing I'd like to be remembered for is the signing of Gordie Roberts," Kelley told reporters. "We signed Gordie for longer than you would believe and at a bargain price considering what he would have gone for in the future. I don't think he will be sorry about his decision. Whaler fans are going to see just how great he is in a short time."

"It wasn't easy coming in and playing with a bunch of older guys, trying to fit in and so on. For me, it was a bit of a struggle," Roberts recalled. "And there was definitely a lot of hype and extra pressure that the WHA—with Howard Baldwin and Hartford in a sense—trying to create as much buzz. 'We got one more young player over the NHL,' even though I probably wouldn't have played in the NHL for two more years. But once I got to the WHA, it was great experience."

The novelty of Roberts as a teenage star eventually wore off, and he became a vital part of the Whalers' offense in his four years with the team, finishing with a career-high 61 points in his third season with New England.

"When I was nineteen, my second year, I started playing a bigger role and producing offense and so on; it definitely gave me more confidence," said Roberts, who would go on to play almost twenty seasons of professional hockey between the WHA and NHL. "There were definitely a lot of seasoned veterans and young players and a good balance of everything, but I got a lot of ice time to improve. I've got nothing but good memories of my four years there."

THE 1975–76 SEASON WAS ONE OF THE MOST UP AND DOWN in franchise history. Where to start?

First, the team employed three different head coaches—Kelley opened the season behind the bench but, citing "family considerations," resigned in late December. He ended up returning to Colby College, where he had coached before coaching Boston University, while Ryan assumed the role of GM, and Don Blackburn took over as player-coach. That lasted until late in the season, when the Whalers, looking for a jump start, shifted course again, naming Neale as the new head coach to replace Blackburn.

For a team that had enjoyed relatively steady leadership over the previous four years, it was a tumultuous run. Neale was a Runyonesque character, a lifelong hockey man who could spin a yarn with the best of them. He was also aware of the situation he was walking into—Blackburn, who was less of a disciplinarian than Kelley or Neale, had become a popular figure with the players.

"I'm really hurt inside. I just can't believe that this actually happened to us," Webster told reporters. "I respect Harry Neale as a coach, but I feel it was the wrong time of the season to make a change."

Ley called the switch "unfortunate" and added that this was Kelley's team, and "when you step into a team that's already made, I don't know how you can fire someone."

"I realize I am replacing a popular man," Neale said after taking over for Blackburn, who had spurred the Whalers on to some of the finest hockey of the season. "All that I ask for is the fans to judge me on the job I do. I don't possess any magic solution for success. But the key to winning is working hard, and believing in the system you use. Don was respected and liked by the players and I'm sure some of them are justifiably upset that he has to take the blame. But I have to prove to these players that I can be an asset to this team. It will be a learning process for me, a learning process for them."

The wild ride started in November when Neale and the Whalers were celebrating at the end of a hard-fought 5–3 win over the Bulls in Birmingham. Neale stood on the bench to cheer a late empty-net goal from Mike Rogers and was beaned by a cup of ice. Soon, it was followed by beer, popcorn, and programs. Neale grabbed a hockey stick and swung it at a Birmingham fan who attempted to jump over the glass. The stick splintered and ended up cutting two fans, which caused the police to intervene.

"I only stood up because I was happy with the empty-net goal," Neale told reporters after the game. "We won a hockey game, and I guess that's not supposed to happen in Birmingham.

"One of those rent-a-cops handed a fan his billy [club]. What kind of crowd control is that? He had a gun too. I guess he would have given him that next," he added. "We shouldn't have to put up with that, and we won't." Neale was charged but not convicted.

After an inconsistent regular season, the team turned it on in the play-offs. Perhaps buoyed by "Brass Bonanza," the Whalers swept Cleveland in the first round and were set to face the Indianapolis Racers in the quarterfinals, where an unlikely hero—youngster Cap Raeder—would await.

"Bobby McManama, he came to me the morning we opened the series against Indianapolis," Raeder recalls. "I'm eating my pregame meal—I'm in seventh heaven. This is great, I'm with a professional team, we're in the playoffs. Life is good, right? He looks at me really seriously and says, 'You know you're just one injury away from playing, right?'

"'Oh, sure,' I say.

"'Are you ready, or are you just happy to be here?' he asks.

"Of course, I tell him I'm ready, but I wasn't. That night, Bruce Landon gets hurt four or five minutes into the game, and away we go. I'm facing the No. 1 team in the league in the playoffs.

"Just before I went in, I thought, *Holy shit*. Bobby just looked at me and said, 'There you go.'"

Thanks at least in part to the work of Raeder, the Whalers captured a wild seven-game series with Indy. Raeder pitched a shutout in two of the games, including a 6–0 win in Game Seven in Indianapolis.

"That was the most fun I've ever had," Raeder told reporters after the game.

It was on to the finals—after the Game Seven victory, Raeder was asked who he would rather face, Houston or San Diego. "I don't care," he replied. "I've never been to either place."

It turned out to be Houston and the mighty Aeros. The two teams split the first six games of the series, which included a dramatic Game Six win for the Whalers at home that was fueled by a sellout crowd (an overflow crowd watched the game on closed-circuit television in the assembly hall next door) and another masterful performance by the unemotional Raeder, who allowed just 1 goal in the 6–1 shellacking of Houston. "I wish we could start right now," crowed Neale when asked about Game Seven following the New England win.

As Whalers fans partied in the streets around the Civic Center and mechanics came in to try to fix the broken-down Houston team bus, both teams shared a charter back to Houston for Game Seven, with the Whalers getting into their Houston hotels at just after 6:00 a.m.

The stage was set for a dramatic Game Seven. Raeder was equal to the challenge against the powerful Aeros most of the night, stopping 35 shots and only allowing a single tally until the late stages of the third period. The trouble was that the Houston defense was just as stifling—the Whalers had three power-play chances but couldn't get one past Aeros goaltender Ron Grahame. A goal from Mark Howe at 18:21 of the final period clinched it for Houston and sent New England home for the summer. It also ended Raeder's unlikely playoff ride.

"We had a dozen, maybe fifteen chances when we could have iced it, and he wouldn't let us," Grahame said of Raeder after the game. "He was brilliant. He deserved a better fate. He was just fantastic."

"That kid in your net was fantastic," Gordie Howe told New England writers after the game. "My God. Isn't it funny how a kid can come out of nowhere and play so well?"

Despite the Whalers losing in seven games, many looked at the season as a positive. Given the turmoil that accompanied the year— three different coaches, some weak numbers overall (out of the fourteen teams, they were eleventh in the league in goals scored and ninth in goals against), and just barely making the postseason—stretching Houston to seven games before losing could certainly be counted as a feather in their cap.

"Really, nobody expected us to go anywhere," Mike Rogers said of that team. "Then we did kind of squeeze into the playoffs. You can call it timing—everything just fell into place for our team. It really wasn't unexpected, because we had a veteran hockey club and we knew we didn't perform well in the regular season. But we knew when it came to push and shove, we knew we could perform in the playoffs.

"To win those first two series and then to play the Howes and Aeros—one of the top teams in the league, if not the top team—and do what we did against them, it was just a great run. A lot of fun. I remember coming back to Hartford after we lost to Houston, and they had a parade for us. The people came out in droves. It was just an exciting time."

Small wonder there was a lot of anticipation heading into the 1976– 77 season.

THE BIGGEST GAMES OF THE 1976–77 SEASON? IN ALL likelihood, they had nothing to do with the usual WHA slate. The Whalers hosted a pair of exhibition games in December against some international competition: the Czech National Team, followed by the Soviets.

Things started on a down note, as New England was dominated by the Czechs, 4–1. Marian Stastny scored a pair in the win over the Whalers, a contest where the speedier Czechs always seemed to be a step ahead of a New England team that was looking to play a more physical brand of hockey.

"I was disappointed we didn't give it a better effort. Some did, but not enough in my judgment. Maybe it was my fault," groused Neale after the game. "Maybe we should've spent more time in preparation. But no system in place is worth a damn if the guys who were trying to make it work don't work."

The loss dampened expectations for the matchup with the Soviets a week later, at least as far as New England players and fans were concerned. "The biggest thing was we just didn't want to get embarrassed," recalled Rogers of the sentiment among the team leading up to the second game. "I think that was kind of the talk in the dressing room before the game. Let's just go out and play the game we know we can—let's just play Canadian hockey. Let's be physical, but not go too much. Just kind of go out and play as hard as we possibly can and see what happens."

As it turned out, the Whalers beat the Soviets, 5–2, as Lyle scored a pair of goals and Raeder finished with 31 saves.

"We received a great emotional effort from all our players," Neale told reporters after the win. "It was an 18-man triumph. I told the players I expected more effort from them than they showed last week when the Czech team beat us easily. Still, I don't think we can play at this peak very often."

The win was taken with a sizable grain of salt, as the Soviets were suffering from jet lag and the game was played at 4:00 a.m. their time.

But a win over the Russians—who were just 1-for-8 on the power play—was something to be acknowledged.

OVERALL, FROM A WINS-AND-LOSSES STANDPOINT, THE 1976–77 season would be remembered as the worst for the WHA Whalers. They lost their first three of the season, suffered a nine-game winless streak, and had to put together a furious rally down the stretch just to assure themselves of a fourth-place finish and a spot in the postseason ahead of Birmingham. It made little difference, as New England was hammered by Quebec in the first round, 4–1. For a team that had done well to set the standard in the WHA over the previous few years, it was nothing less than a disappointment, pure and simple.

"We were the underdogs and we should have made a better showing. I guess you can sum it up by saying we didn't challenge Quebec enough," Neale said after the Whalers were shut out, 3–0, in Game Five in Quebec. "We never got started in the series, but we did better than what some people predicted—by winning one game."

Baldwin was not as kind. The usually optimistic owner had some stern words for his team a few days after the playoff elimination at the hands of the Nordiques, saying the year as a whole was "the most disappointing ever" in the team's five-year existence. "I've got no alibis. But apparently, the decisions we made in the last year or two were not the right ones," he told the media less than a week after the Whalers were eliminated from the postseason. "Our caliber of play did not improve and the players never did come together as a unit.

"No one is untouchable, including myself. We cannot and will not be intimidated. If players do not play up to their abilities, they will be suspended and fined. And if a player is not happy, we'll see to it that he's given gainful employment elsewhere, or give him an unconditional release."

Less than a month after the postseason ended, Baldwin announced he was bringing back Kelley to run the hockey operations. And he also continued to hint that the Whalers would be inclined to land at least one member of the legendary Howe family for the following season. "They're still about 50 percent in the picture," he said.

THE WHALERS HAD THEIR OFFICIAL SONG. THEY HAD A NEW city and new building to call their own. They had a fan base that was willing to back them. Simply put, they were among the most stable franchises in a fledgling league that continued to gain momentum and threaten the established hockey hierarchy. But they were about to enter a transformational era that would set the stage for bigger and better things to come.

4

Next Stop: NHL
1977-79

I'll just be thanking the Lord that no one died. That day when I got to the site and I saw it, I just thanked the Lord that it didn't happen five hours earlier.

—Hartford deputy mayor Nicholas R. Carbone, after the collapse of the Hartford Civic Center

Out of adversity comes greatness.

—Howard Baldwin, days after the collapse

Gordie Howe. *The Gordie Howe?* Yep, *the* Gordie Howe.

To their credit, the Whalers had never done gimmicky stuff in an attempt to get people into the building. They had never succumbed to dopey, minor-league promotions in the same way that other WHA teams had done over the years. Attendance had gone up and down since their inception, and there were giveaways and the like from time to time, but never some of the stuff that took place in other cities. Instead, for the most part, it was simple, straightforward hockey.

But the prospect of landing Gordie Howe? Well, that changed things a bit.

Of course, none of it would have happened if George Bolin hadn't gotten fed up with Colleen Howe. To hear people in the Aeros organization tell it, Colleen, the wife of Gordie and mother of Mark and Marty, spent the better part of two years driving the Houston ownership crazy. She and the Houston owner clashed over all sorts of things. Of course, it was easy to see why: Bolin, who was the second owner of the team (he took over after original owner Paul Deneau had to sell after one year), was old-school Texas. Baldwin once described him as looking like Rock Hudson in the movie *Giant*: "blue jeans, big belt buckle, Stetson, cowboy boots." And Colleen, who had fundamentally become the family's agent (one of the first women in hockey to take on such a title), was a woman in a world filled with middle-aged, white guys who weren't all that fired up about dealing with *any* agent, much less a female one.

The thing was, Bolin needed the Howes. They were the best part of a hockey team that was hemorrhaging money. (Some members of the 1975–76 Houston team didn't get a $10,000 bonus that was promised to them for winning the Avco Cup.) The Aeros were one of the best teams in the WHA: After the Whalers won it all that first year, Howe and his sons helped lead Houston to back-to-back titles the next two seasons. Gordie scored 31 goals and added 69 assists to finish third in the WHA in scoring and win league MVP honors in 1974, and he had at least 99 points a year in two of his first three seasons in Houston. (Of course, the occasionally irascible Howe also had 84 penalty minutes in his second season—*at the age of forty-six.*) Meanwhile, Mark was a WHA All-Star at the age of eighteen, and Marty quickly impressed as a top-level defenseman.

Hockey in Houston? It was working, albeit barely, *because* of the Howes.

But it just never clicked between the powerful woman and the new Houston ownership. Once, after a dispute, she walked out of a negotiating session. Bolin then announced they had an offer ready. The sons, who were still in the room at the time, didn't take kindly to Bolin belittling their mother.

"Why don't you write [the offer] down on real soft paper," Marty told Bolin, according to Mark's book, "and then, shove it up your ass."

An enraged Bolin refused to hand over Marty's next paycheck until he apologized, and he later removed a LeRoy Neiman painting of Gordie that had been hanging in the front office. Bolin had had it. So one day in the fall of 1976, he called up Baldwin and dumped all three of the Howes right into Baldwin's lap. The Howe experiment was done in Houston.

"She could drive you nuts at times, but I loved her," recalled Baldwin of Colleen. "She worked hard for her children and for her family. She was a good person, and she had a terrific sense of humor, which helped."

Of course, it wasn't so simple. Gordie had never been traded in his career, and the Howe family wasn't planning on breaking precedent. Instead, the family would play out the final year of their four-year deal—keeping your word was a big thing with the Howe family, and they honored the contract. But by the time the following offseason rolled around, the Howe family was listening to offers, as all three were free agents. Boston held the NHL rights to Mark, and the Whalers and Bruins had gone around and around on several things over the years, which led many in the New England organization to feel as if the Bruins weren't going to give up easily on this one. From Sinden using the Whalers to set the stage for his return to Boston, to rent at the Garden, to the simple act of the Whalers existing (and swiping fans from the NHL), the Bruins were in no mood to do much of anything to help Baldwin and the Whalers. And they certainly weren't going to budge when it came to giving up Mark's rights.

But at the same time, there wasn't the same depth of feeling there for Marty or Gordie. The Bruins were certainly lukewarm on Marty, and they wanted no part of adding Gordie to the mix, other than as an unofficial club advisor. A planned return to Detroit for Gordie and the rest of the family never got off the ground for a few reasons, not the least of which was that the Bruins were unlikely to release or trade Mark's rights.

Bottom line? New England had the only playing offer for Gordie. It wasn't the NHL—which Mark desperately wanted—but it was a chance at fully guaranteed money for all three members of the family.

Sinden made a pitch for the brothers, but if Mark had jumped to the NHL, it would have meant the end of Gordie's career. Gordie wanted to play with his sons or wasn't interested in playing at all. And even though Mark burned for a shot at the NHL, he didn't want the idea that he drove his legendary father into retirement on his conscience.

"Initially, our first priority was to try and stay in Houston," Mark said. "We all liked it there; we had a great coach, and we loved being in the city. It was a good locker room and a good team. But financially, they were struggling, and it looked like the team wouldn't survive much longer. With me, personally, it didn't make sense for me to stay in Houston without a new contract. The contract offer I got was about 40 percent of what my offer was to go to New England or Boston. I mean, it was just a massive, *massive* difference. The financials were pretty straight—I mean, they had retained our playoff bonuses at one point. So the way things were looking, we had to make a choice."

Mark put his professional future in the hands of his mother, Colleen. "I knew my mom. I just put my total trust in her. I mean, I was just turning twenty-two. I was out golfing and other stuff," he said. "It's your mom; you don't have to worry when she's looking out for the bottom line. In the end, Howard Baldwin pursued my mom and dad and Marty and [me] pretty heavily. There was a deal in place where I could have ended up with the Bruins, a better individual offer than the one from the Whalers. If I had been a selfish person, I could have split for Boston. But I think Mom did the best thing for us for a few reasons; namely, if I had left, Dad would have had to retire. I don't think Dad would have kept playing if Marty and I weren't there. Really, I wouldn't have it any other way. It came down to going to Hartford as a group, and that was the decision that was made so Dad could keep playing and I could continue my career."

So in 1977 Mark put family ahead of cash and signed with New England. The Howes signed ten-year contracts—according to Mark, his total was $200,000 per year—deferred over fifteen. Marty's total was $1.2 million and Gordie's was $250,000 as a player. That was reduced to $100,000 when he retired and moved into the front office. According to multiple people connected to the organization, the deal also *eventually* included an office for Colleen, which rankled some. "[She] had so much influence that they gave her an office," Lacroix wrote of Colleen Howe. "That's why people would get upset sometimes because Colleen would let the scoop come out, like if somebody got traded."

Regardless, Baldwin was so spooked that the Howe family would change their mind, he called a press conference the next day. "The announcement caught the Bruins completely off guard," Baldwin said later. "A lot of people wonder if there's animosity between us and the Bruins, and there isn't any longer, at least as far as I know. Whatever tension there was, it was because of catching them off guard. There had been some problems with the old Bruins ownership, but I have nothing but the highest regard for the Jacobs family, Jerry and Charlie. They've been huge assets to the National Hockey League, and Harry Sinden has become a terrific friend. In fairness, the Bruins competed like hell, and we competed like hell, and this one we happened to get."

Aside from some early trepidation on the part of Neale, things seemed to work. Gordie loved the work and built up trust with his new coach in hard-earned sweat equity. While Mark didn't always agree with the idea of the team working his dad as hard as it did, Gordie appeared to enjoy things, at least in the early going.

The idea of having the Howes all together on the ice was great. The feature stories wrote themselves. And when the Whalers started a white-hot 15-1-1, it was like some fever dream for New England ownership. The building was packed. The team was the best in the WHA. The decision to sign the Howe family paved the way for its early-season success. *Come see the Howe family carry the Whalers to the top of the* WHA*!*

But for whatever reason, according to some associated with the team, the rest of the Whalers made it their mission to make life as miserable as possible for the Howe sons. Mark recalled that once, on a road trip, captain Rick Ley and teammate Brad Selwood hopped into a cab, only to shut the door on Marty and say, "Ride by yourself."

To this day, Mark remains puzzled as to why things were frosty between much of the rest of the team and his family. "I don't know. I mean, there was nothing to be jealous of," he said. "Making too much money? If I was making more money, that's the sort of thing that can help you out—you can go in and demand that kind of money for yourself if you see a teammate making that sort of money. We weren't there to steal publicity or credit or anything. We were just there to accomplish a goal, and that was winning as many games as possible through team play and hard, consistent effort. But yeah, it was pretty evident that there were a few people who weren't happy with us being on the team."

From the beginning, it wasn't easy at times for the younger Howes when it came to assimilating to life in Hartford. "As soon as the ink was dry on the contract, they took us out to dinner in Farmington," Mark said. "As soon as we walked away from dinner, the way things went, Marty and I looked at each other and said, 'Well, I guess it's back to business.'

"It was strange. When we went to Houston as a family, we had players come out and welcome us to the team, and a whole thing. We didn't get that when we came to Hartford. We grew up with Bill Dineen as a head coach, the sort of guy who would pat you on the back. There was a tight locker room with a close-knit group of guys. Hartford was all brand new. I was taught by my dad that when you go into a new team, you keep your eyes and ears open and your mouth shut and prove that you belonged. And that's what Marty and I tried to do.

"There were more benchings for mistakes, a lot of screaming by an often-red-faced Jack Kelley, and about as much togetherness on the ice as there was off it."

As Marty later said, a Whalers way of communicating was saying, "I had *my* man" after a goal was scored against Hartford.

The saving grace for the Howe family may have come in the form of veteran Dave Keon, who was part of a group from the old Minnesota Fighting Saints, which had just folded and essentially merged with the Whalers. Keon managed to forge a bond with the Howe family and became a legend-in-residence for some of the younger players who worshipped him back in his halcyon days with Toronto.

One really interesting aspect to the Whalers' business model in the late 1970s was that they had a roster with Howe and Keon, two hockey legends. Although it's unclear if the pairing was purposeful, younger players would later remark that the opportunity to play with Hall of Famers like Howe and Keon was a powerful lure, one that other franchises couldn't match.

"I had both New England and Winnipeg bidding," remembered Jordy Douglas, a prized prospect who came out of Alberta. "This is two weeks or three weeks before the NHL draft. Once you start talking about Gordie Howe and Dave Keon and Johnny McKenzie and Ricky Ley and Brad Selwood and Al Smith, John Garrett, Andre Lacroix—I just started thinking, *Why* wouldn't *I consider this?* That was the mitigating issue—just going there and making the team and being in that company. I guess I was little . . . not tainted, but I snuck in and saw the Jets any time I wanted. It was like they weren't new to me anymore."

In his first year, the team paired him with Keon, and Douglas quickly recognized what life was going to be like living with a Hall of Famer. "I'm in my room, and I'm watching TV, and I'm sitting on the edge of the bed. And the key fumbles in the door a little bit, and I'm thinking, *Here we go*. Dave Keon walks in," he said. "I have the utmost respect for Dave Keon, the consummate professional. He's also a quiet man. He's kind of the pay-attention-when-he-speaks-because-he-doesn't-do-that-very-often sort of guy. I totally love the man—respect him to death.

"He kind of nodded. I was like, 'Hi, Mr. Keon.' When I get nervous, I start talking a lot. And I wanted to break the ice. What am I going to say? And he's kind of fumbling around a little bit, getting organized, putting his stuff away, putting his shaving kit away.

"I finally look at him and say, 'I'm a graduate of your hockey school.'

"'What?'

"'The Bill Harris–Dave Keon Hockey School. You guys came to Winnipeg, and I went and met you there.'

"He's looking at me like, 'I only met about a thousand kids that day.' He said, 'Well, that's good. I'm gone, see you later on.' And he left, and I never saw him again until bedtime."

One issue with having too many veterans? Occasionally, the older players got time on the ice ahead of younger players, impacting the development of some of the better prospects on the roster.

When it comes to team building, players don't necessarily need to like each other to have a winning team. And thanks in large part to their hot start, the Whalers finished the 1977–78 season in second place with 93 points, trailing only Winnipeg, which pulled away from the rest of the pack with 102 points.

"For me, *playing* in Hartford was great," Mark said. "I was on a line with my dad and Tommy Webster, a wonderful, wonderful guy. Our whole line, we were in the top ten in scoring for the first fifteen or twenty games of that first season. Then, Tommy went down with an injury that basically ended his career. That was unfortunate—he was just great player. He was a hell of a sniper—that was one of the best lines I was ever a part of. It just didn't last long enough because of what happened to Tommy. But I think I continued to improve as a player and mature as a person that year."

That season, New England had seven players score 20 or more goals, led by the old guys: forty-nine-year-old Gordie led the team with 34 goals and 96 points. But it was a challenge for Neale to manage Gordie's workload. He was more than just a hockey sideshow; Gordie was a key figure on a playoff-caliber team. That meant finding a way to keep him fresh for the long haul. In *The Rebel League*, Neale recalled a stretch when the Whalers had three games in four days. The coach was firm in his belief the elder statesman needed a day off at the end of the trip, a contest in Edmonton, and so he told Howe in no uncertain terms that he didn't want to see him at the morning skate. He knew just telling Howe he didn't want him on the ice that morning wouldn't be enough, so he secretly told the trainers to hide Howe's equipment. Neale showed up that morning to find six or seven skaters on the ice . . . one of which was Howe in someone else's gear.

Howe did take advantage of Neale's goodwill from time to time—in camp, he was excused from a two-mile run. How did Neale explain things to the rest of the roster? "Gordie isn't going to run today, and I'm going to make you guys a deal. If any of you play for me until you're fifty, you won't have to run either."

That year, Howe wasn't the only veteran who played a big role in the success of the Whalers. Forty-year-old Johnny McKenzie had 27 goals and 56 points, and thirty-seven-year-old Keon had 24 goals and 62 points. But that Jets team was pretty well stacked, with five 30-goal scorers, including a thirty-nine-year-old Hull, who finished the year with 117 points. In the end, Winnipeg crushed the Whalers in the Avco Cup final, sweeping New England, 4–0.

The year Howe turned fifty, he played in seventy-six games and finished ninth in the league in scoring, all while remaining a physical presence on the ice.

"You didn't fuck with him," Bill Bennett said plainly, recalling a night against the Kings in that first NHL year where Howe got into a scrap with youngster named John Paul Kelly. The two got mixed up along the boards near the penalty box, and Kelley was later yanked—Bennett believed it was the player who pulled himself out the game because he didn't want to face the wrath of Howe later that night.

Bennett recalled another night when Howe and another player went into the corner, and Howe got tripped up. "They get up for the faceoff, and the next thing you know, there was blood all over the ice, and their trainer was rushing out with a towel," Bennett said with a snort. "Like I said, you didn't fuck with Gordie."

"We were playing the Winnipeg Jets. And that's when they had the great Hedberg, Nilsson, and Hull line," remembered Rogers. "We were in Hartford, and they were beating us quite decisively. I'm sitting on the bench beside Gordie, and he kind of looks at me says, 'Well, I've had enough.' I kind of look back at him like, 'So have I, but what are we going to do about it?' Gordie steps on the ice, and Hedberg and Nilsson leave the ice to get stitched, and Bobby is bleeding. And Gordie finally gets a penalty after he's clipped Bobby, and he complains about getting a penalty, so he also gets a two-minute unsportsmanlike after he's cut three guys in a row. So he comes back to the bench, and I'm sitting beside Gordie, and I just kind of look at him.

"'Gordie, that was unbelievable.'

"He says, 'Well, it could have been worse.'

"'Worse? What do you mean worse?'

"He says, 'I only clipped Bobby a little bit because I like him.'"

"I remember my first year in the WHA, and we were playing Gordie and Houston," said Dave Debol, whose first season was with the Cincinnati Stingers before joining the Whalers later in his career. "My teammates were telling me, 'Watch out for Gordie.' I was thinking, *Watch out for Gordie? What have I ever done to that old guy?*

"And sure as shit, in the third period, I fell behind a play and was the last guy back, and he just stepped in front of me and gave me an elbow to the face, just enough to stun me and draw some water in my eyes. He snarled, 'Welcome to the league, rookie.'

"I was like, 'Uh, excuse me, Mr. Howe, what did I do to you?'"

Woe to the opposing player who decided to take out one of his sons: One night, Cincinnati's Robbie Ftorek nailed Marty Howe with his stick, which caused a concussion, a broken cheekbone, and a scratched cornea. While visiting Marty in the hospital, Gordie asked if there was anything Marty needed.

"Dad, I was hoping—" Marty started to say.

"You don't even have to ask," Gordie replied.

A few weeks later, in a game with playoff implications for both teams, Ftorek grabbed a missed shot, and it looked like he had a breakaway opportunity. As Ftorek eyed a scoring chance, Gordie turned his stick over so the blade was facing up and delivered a one-hander across Ftorek's face.

"If somebody did that today, he would be kicked out of the league for two years," Mark later said. "Dad got just five minutes for the worst thing I ever saw him do. We killed a penalty, won the game, and beat Cincinnati in both home games of the best-of-three preliminary series to move on."

Many younger Whalers recalled the impact Howe had on them and their careers. Douglas got a helper from Howe on his first career tally. "They had me on the power play," Douglas recalled. "My very first shift and my very first shot was a goal. And it was assisted by Gordie Howe. I get the puck. Literally, this all happened very quickly in the first period. I have this puck. I can remember walking out the arena, and I'm still trying to figure out how I fit in with all of this, and he kind of snuggles up and says, 'Hey, you got your first goal. Good for you. You know that was my 2,500th assist?' I was gobsmacked. I pulled the puck out of my pocket, and I go, 'Do you want the puck?' He couldn't stop laughing."

Still, Howe didn't try to position himself as being better than his teammates. "Whether you knew him or not, he was your teammate— period. He was no Mr. Hockey—he just wanted to be treated like everybody else," Douglas said. "The first time I met him, I had just signed my contract, and the Whalers flew me and my family in and gave me my first signing bonus. We came in and stayed at the Hilton, right next to the rink. We went over to sign the contract the next morning at ten or eleven. I go upstairs to the office, and Gordie Howe walks in. My mom and dad were there, and I'm just gobsmacked. He walks over and shakes my hand and says, 'So you're the one we're all here to see. I'm your teammate, Gordie.' I'll never forget that.

"My parents never got over that. They were falling all over themselves—they were just giggling," he added. "He was the consummate people person, someone who made everybody feel comfortable. That was my introduction to Gordie Howe. I remember thinking, *Well, if he's my teammate, things are going to be all right.*"

"There would be nights where after the first or second period, we were getting blown out," Debol said. "I sat next to Gordie in the room, and our coach, Don Blackburn would come down the line and be like, 'Antonovich, you suck,' and, 'Debol, you suck.' He'd get to Gordie, Gordie would look up, and he'd just skip right past him.

"When the coach would get out of earshot, he'd lean in and tell me, 'Never listen to the fucking coach, kid. They never know what they're talking about.'"

The arrival of the Howe family helped put Hartford on the hockey map. The team was a legitimate presence in the professional game. To that point in the season, the 1977–78 Whalers had managed to distinguish themselves as the best team in the WHA with the finest start in franchise history. That blazing 15-1-1 start to the regular season, on the heels of a 7-1-1 preseason mark, was fueled by an impressive defensive performance; New England outscored its opponents 80–45 through the first seventeen games. The Whalers had an extraordinary mix of youth and experience, a balanced scoring attack, and solid and steady defense and goaltending. They sent six players to the WHA All-Star Game, including Gordie and Mark Howe, as well as Ley.

But they were hotly pursued by a Winnipeg team that was every bit their equal. Hull, Ulf Nilsson, and Anders Hedberg formed the most potent line in the league, as the Jets went 11-6-1 in their first seventeen games to stay within striking distance. (Winnipeg lost its first three games against New England that season.)

Things started to flip in November, when the Whalers lost top scorer Tommy Webster to a back injury in practice. Webster's scoring punch—15 goals and 20 points—was a big reason for New England's early-season success, and without him in the lineup, the pesky Jets would end up making it a battle all season long.

However, others would step up as scorers in Webster's absence, and while it wasn't a game-winner, the biggest regular-season tally for New England that year likely came on December 7 in Birmingham when Howe scored the 1,000th goal of his professional career in a 6–3 win over the Bulls. After the game, the forty-nine-year-old said his tally came on a sequence that was similar to his first of his career on October 6, 1946, against Toronto and Turk Broda.

That December, the Whalers were riding high. They were anchored by the Howe family, led by one of the biggest names in the history of hockey. They were more than ten games over .500 and seemingly cruising to another WHA title. And that month, they had back-to-back wins over a team of Russian All-Stars and Czechoslovakia, victories that made the international hockey community take notice. But as 1977 gave way to 1978, the biggest event in Hartford's pro sports history very nearly brought about the end of the franchise.

THE MOST IMPORTANT THING TO REMEMBER WAS THAT IT could have worse. It could have been *so much worse*.

The night of January 17, 1978, the Whalers were out of town. Following the WHA All-Star Game in Quebec City, they were scheduled to open a three-game road trip the next evening in Edmonton, followed by stops in Winnipeg and Quebec. It was going to be an evening of college basketball at the Civic Center, as UConn and UMass were set to tip off. For the second year, the Connecticut men's basketball program played at least a portion of its games at the Civic Center—the prospect of playing in a new, downtown facility would, it was hoped, be a recruiting draw for coach Dom Perno. Regardless, the Huskies seemed to enjoy playing in Hartford—the year before, they were 11-3 in games downtown.

That evening, the Huskies captured a 56–49 decision over UMass in front of roughly five thousand fans. It was a relatively uneventful affair that gave the Huskies their third win in four games, lifting them to 8-6 on the year. The game wrapped up without incident, and the five thousand people and change—including players, fans, media, support staff, and others—filed out of the Civic Center into a nasty January snowstorm. With the Whalers on the road, the building was to have a three-day run of basketball games—a high school contest was set for the next evening. As a result, the crew that would usually change the floor from basketball to hockey didn't have to work its usual late hours.

Early the next morning—roughly 4:15 a.m., by all accounts—with the building almost completely vacated, it collapsed. Two guards and two maintenance men were reportedly inside but not under the coliseum roof when the collapse occurred. No injuries were reported. There was no video of the incident, and only a few people even heard what happened when it all came crashing down.

It's hard to fathom just how destructive it must have been in the moment. Later, city manager James B. Daken said the preliminary evidence showed one corner of the roof fell in first, and the resulting compression of air inside the building apparently ripped loose the rest of the roof. Pieces of the metal wall—as well as pieces of insulation—landed on the roof of the mall and on Church and Ann Streets below.

The Civic Center was one of four major downtown projects the city undertook in the late 1960s to bring urban renewal to the capital city and help revitalize downtown. (Constitution Plaza, the area around Windsor Street, and Bushnell Plaza were the other three.) A major hotel, shops, and a sports arena could theoretically help provide a boost to the downtown area. In particular, the roof of the Civic Center was going to be a cutting-edge innovation. A complex computer program was used to come up with the "space truss" formula that included a series of unusual pyramidal trusses supported by just four columns, to provide an unobstructed view for fans. It was hailed as nothing less than a huge success, destined to be the model for stadiums for years to come.

But that morning, the building lay in ruins. Approximately 1,400 tons of steel and concrete fell almost evenly onto the roughly ten thousand empty seats below. It was nothing but twisted metal and wreckage, smack dab in the middle of the city.

"I did the UConn-UMass game on radio the night before. We were there at the game," said Gerry Brooks. "I got up the next morning to go to work at WTOP Radio, and we started getting word on the police scanners—the roof of the Civic Center had fallen in. *What?* Once the enormity of what had happened had sunk in, I called and woke up [team executive] Bill Barnes:

"'Bill, this is Gerry Brooks at WTOP Radio.'

"'What do you want?'

"'Well, the roof at the Civic Center fell in.'

"There was dead silence for about ten seconds. I got some sort of mostly unintelligible reaction, and we moved on," Brooks remembered. "It was so difficult to wrap your brain around. I didn't blame him for reacting the way he did."

In Edmonton that night to play the Oilers, the Whalers got the news when they turned on their TVs that morning. Barnes later told the Associated Press that after he found out, he sought out Baldwin.

"Howard was just sitting on the end of his bed, shaking his head in disbelief. We were all shocked," Barnes said.

The owner immediately reassured the city that as long as they could find a way to make it work, the Whalers would be sticking around. "Hartford is a great city for hockey, and will continue to be," Baldwin told the *Hartford Courant* hours after the collapse. "We plan to be in Hartford for many years to come. This is our home. We'd play in a swimming pool in my backyard before we'd ever leave here."

"I remember my roommate and [I] turned on the news in the morning," recalled Mike Rogers. "We had an adjoining room—I don't remember who the other two players were. But we had the door open, and I won't use the language we screamed when we saw this. But the four of us got in front of the TV and saw the Civic Center and saw these girders bent and the roof caved in, and we all looked at each other. 'What do we do now, boys?' We maybe thought our hockey careers were over, because the World Hockey Association didn't have a lot of money. There was a lot of talk about the merger."

"I got this call first thing in the morning from my wife," Neale told journalist Ed Willes. "She said, 'The roof fell in.'

"I said, 'Will they be able to fix it by the weekend?'"

Back home, people were stunned. "I remember waking up and my mom telling me that it was a bad storm and the roof had collapsed," said Howard Baldwin Jr. "My biggest fear at the time was if my dad was in the building, but it turned out when it collapsed, he was in Quebec. The snow just never ended that night—it was amazing."

In addition to putting the Whalers in a dicey spot, the collapse would be difficult for downtown Hartford, which looked to the Civic Center as the heart of a potential business resurgence. "It's a serious blow to the downtown," Mayor George Athanson told the *New York Times* the next day. "The Civic Center was the focal point of the new beat of Hartford."

That morning, the accident drew a fair share of gawkers, as reports indicated that a steady stream of people rode the elevator to the twenty-second floor of the Sheraton Hartford Hotel across the street to stare at the wreckage.

The official investigation didn't blame the ice and snow, but instead the construction of the building. The report indicated the roof began progressive failure as soon as it had been installed. Contributing factors included design errors, an underestimation of the weight of the roof, and differences between the design and the actual built structure.

In a weird bit of happenstance, Baldwin had some familiarity with this sort of situation: in 1968 when he was with the Flyers team, high winds ripped off part of the roof of the Spectrum. That damage, however, paled in comparison to what happened in Hartford. The Flyers that year played most of their final seven "home" games of the season in Quebec, home of their AHL team, or New York, while the 76ers made do with the Palestra or the Philadelphia Convention Hall. But the Flyers were back home within a month to open the playoffs. The

Hartford incident was clearly going to require a multiyear road trip; Baldwin later said it looked like Godzilla had stomped on the roof of the Civic Center.

And so Baldwin and the rest of the franchise had to scramble to put together a deal. Step one was to secure the Springfield Civic Center, just thirty minutes north of Hartford. Less than twelve hours after the roof collapsed, the Whalers were putting the finishing touches on a temporary move to Springfield. Baldwin reassured people he was "99.9 percent sure all of [their] games would be played" at the Springfield Civic Center while Hartford Civic Center was being rebuilt. And less than a week after the collapse, there was already talk of what the new building would look like. "It's going to be bigger and better—and have a different roof," Daken told reporters who asked about possible plans for a new building the day after the collapse.

The ramifications were felt throughout the hockey world. The WHA pledged to do whatever it took to support the team, but you had to wonder just how much other franchises might extend themselves. Things were already a little tenuous. Jordy Douglas, who had just signed with the Whalers, heard the following from a friend: "You just agreed to a contract with a team that doesn't even have a fucking rink, dummy." How would something like this impact their ability to land players? If players were already taking a chance on signing with the WHA instead of the NHL, would they also be willing to roll the dice to play for a team that currently had no permanent building, and the temporary place it was going to play in—Springfield—had five thousand fewer seats?

"Hey, what happened to your rink?" Oilers winger Brett Callighen, a former Whaler, asked some of his old teammates that night in Edmonton; Alan Hangsleben responded by using his gloved hand to demonstrate how the roof of the coliseum had met the floor.

Whereas the Whalers were not necessarily the flagship franchise for the WHA at that point, they might have been as close to the model for stability for the rest of the league as any team. Leaguewide, that consistency for an important team was key on a number of levels, including the possibility of a merger with the NHL. The WHA was in a delicate spot, and the loss of a franchise like the Whalers could be a sizable step toward ruin.

But Baldwin was relentless in rallying people to his cause. The team was quickly set up to play in Springfield, but Baldwin—who had assumed the role of president of the WHA by this point—kept a base of operations in Connecticut and preached the gospel of Hartford hockey to everyone and anyone who would listen. Comparing the collapse of the Civic Center to the Hartford Circus Fire of 1944, he said the event would have a galvanizing effect.

"Hartford's people are coming back from the roof collapse just as they did for that circus fire back in the [forties]," he told the *New York Times*. "People still refer to that bloody fire, how it got everyone united and working together for the good of the city.

"The roof collapse cost us what would have been our first profit for the season, by forcing us to play the rest of our home games in Springfield, Mass. I don't think there are many organizations in sports that could have withstood what we went through. Most teams would have folded. That says something for the ownership. We're not making any money out there in Springfield, with 5,000 fewer seats."

That spirit carried throughout the community, as local leaders and the media made a push to rebuild. "Come on Hartford. Suck it up. Let's get tall. Let's show 'em something," wrote *Courant* columnist Owen Canfield. "We had a hockey team, best in the WHA. Let's keep it. We had big league basketball in our town. It went. We'll have it again. We had UConn in the Civic Center, and good boxing and high school basketball. We had ice shows, circuses, figure skating championships. We'll get every damn one of them back."

"The Whalers do represent a financial commitment and it is one the partners expect will be repaid," wrote Aetna Life and Casualty executive Donald G. Conrad in an editorial in the *Courant*. "The real investment, however, is the health of the city of Hartford and its downtown businesses.

"The Whalers can't alone rebuild Hartford but we believe this attraction adds vitality to the effort of municipal government, the business community, and all the others who are creating a new downtown area. The well-being of the city is, after all, our well-being too."

The setback, however, enabled the franchise to broaden its horizons a bit. It built a significant bond with Springfield and expanded its fan base—the fans who commuted from Hartford to Springfield took I-91 to the Springfield Civic Center, and they were known as members of the 91 Club. The brainchild of Bill Barnes, it was a way to celebrate the fan base, rewarding them if they were going to make the twenty-six-mile trek north to Springfield while the Civic Center was being rebuilt. The franchise offered "official" membership, with a certificate that read as follows:

BE IT KNOWN TO ALL GENUINE HOCKEY FANS THAT [insert name here] is a Charter Member of the 91 Club, and as such, is entitled to all the rights, honors and privileges accorded the same. This 91 Club member is allowed at all times to wear the official Club insignia, shall be entitled to first choice of seating in the new Coliseum, and [is] generally recognized by all hockey fans as an individual dedicated to maintaining Hockey Night in Hartford. Further, this individual should be allowed unobstructed driving on Route 91 when attending Whaler games, and if ever stopped by a State Highway Patrol Officer should immediately give that officer the 91 Club handshake and victory sign. He should be allowed first perusal of the newspaper sports section, due respect at the Coliseum, the right to frenzied cheering upon victory and uncontrollable sobbing upon unlikely defeat. When meeting a fan from another city, this member should receive the deference and reverence to which a charter member of the official 91 Club is naturally entitled.

The document was signed by Gordie Howe (as the 91 Club Chairman of the Board) and Baldwin.

For fans who didn't want to drive, shuttle service was offered—$3 would get them a round-trip bus fare between Wethersfield or East Hartford and the Springfield Civic Center.

The local politicians, ownership, players, and fans all rallied to make the best of a bad situation. In a dizzying sequence of events, the region, team, and local business leaders worked together to move the base of operations, where the team spent the next few years, all while looking at plans to rebuild.

"Another franchise might have folded then and there," Brooks said. "Much to their credit, they had a plan. It was amazing how everybody came together almost seamlessly and set up a situation where they were going to be in Springfield until they were able to come home. The attitude and spirit . . . there's been nothing like it in Hartford since. I mean, it's not what you want to happen in order to have a renaissance, but it was a great time to be a Whalers fan or a part of the organization or someone who covered the team because of the can-do spirit everyone displayed."

"The community moved together quickly and in a positive manner because there was this big hole in the middle of the city," Barbara Kennelly, a former Hartford City Council member, told the Associated Press in 1988. "God was good, I guess, but at times we wondered."

While a rebuild could also deliver a jolt to downtown Hartford, a new building could also have other consequences. If the city and team could secure the requisite funding, it also represented an opportunity: if the talk of a merger with the NHL was serious, the Whalers were going to have to expand their building. A rebuild gave them that chance.

From a players' perspective, not a whole lot changed, at least when it came to the action on the ice. As a handful of players were coming from Quebec to Edmonton after the WHA All-Star Game, Neale held a team meeting in Edmonton the morning of the collapse with the players who were already there, and he tried to put everyone at ease.

"Harry said for us not to get excited about the news and just play hockey," center Greg Carroll told reporters who asked about the meeting.

"We'll just have to play the games somewhere else. Something will work out. We'll just have to wait and see."

That night in Edmonton, the team lost 1–0, kicking off an eleven-game stretch during which the Whalers ended up going winless in seven contests. For the best team in the WHA, it felt like possibly the beginning of the end. But it was able to right the ship briefly and, ultimately, finish the season on a strong note. The morning of the collapse—January 18, 1978—the Whalers were fourteen games over .500 at 26-12-3. When the season ended in mid-April, they were thirteen games over .500 (44-31-5), second in the league to the Jets. Four Whalers finished with 30-plus goals, with Gordie Howe (34 goals, 62 assists) ending the year with a team-high 96 points.

A lot of the stability came from the top in the form of the steady hands of Baldwin and Neale, but it was also because of an increased level of camaraderie among the players, veterans (Howe and Keon in particular) and youngsters alike. They pledged to get through it as a group, and they did it together, fueled at least in part by a unique sense of team-building.

"I liked living in Connecticut a lot more than I ever enjoyed playing for the Whalers," Mark Howe wrote in his autobiography. "We had a place in Avon, down the street from a great golf course, Bell Compo, and there was excellent fishing nearby on the Farmington River. After Detroit and Houston, I enjoyed a smaller city. But for as long as we were going to be playing in Springfield, I was on the wrong side of Hartford, a good 75 minutes away from our home rink, a pain in the ass when you had to go to the morning skate, then home, then back to the game.

"One time, in a snowstorm strong enough to cancel the morning skate, I left my house at 2:30 p.m. and didn't get to the arena until 7:45—15 minutes late for the start. Turns out only about eight players were there and the game had been pushed back to 9 o'clock."

"I lived in Manchester," Douglas recalled. "Everyone kind of lived in and around Hartford, whether it was Avon or whatever. And we'd commute [to Springfield] every day—pretty much every day—to games and some practices. What I do remember is that when we'd practice up there, there would be a caravan of us coming back down I-91. I remember we would all stop at the Wendy's about halfway down the highway. We'd pull in there, and it would be, 'Here come the New England Whalers'—Gordie Howe and everyone, ordering our Frostys. The fun we had without knowing it at the time, it was wonderful. It really was."

Springfield quickly rolled out the red carpet, recognizing a financial opportunity when it saw one. The collapse of the Hartford Civic Center provided a boost for the New Haven Coliseum (for concerts and other events) and the Springfield Civic Center, and while the Whalers thought initially about New Haven, Springfield quickly distinguished itself as a more-than-adequate temporary home.

The first Whalers game in Springfield was played just days after the roof collapse. The Springfield Civic Center staff had twenty-four hours to make ice for the game using ice-making equipment that had not been operated for more than a year. But everything went off without a hitch. The city added new street signs around the venue to help new fans find their way around Springfield. Parking regulations were changed downtown to provide more accessibility to fans. A "Welcome to Whalers Fans" sign was installed outside the Civic Center. Inside, booths were set up inside to distribute newly printed brochures on restaurants, hotels, and other attractions in the Springfield area.

"The spinoff effect on downtown restaurants and bars has been incredible," Joseph Montori, an aide to Springfield mayor Theodore Dimauro, told the *Boston Globe* shortly after the move was made. "We don't have any way we can measure the impact empirically, but I've been downtown on nights when the Whalers were playing, and you can't get a drink."

"It gave us a golden opportunity to show a big market from greater Hartford what we have here," added Harold Phillips, executive director of the Springfield Convention and Visitors Bureau.

The rest of the season wasn't ideal by any stretch, but everyone persevered. A 10-4-1 finish in its last fifteen regular-season games was partly the reason for the team's second-place finish in the WHA. The Whalers beat Edmonton and Quebec in the quarterfinals and semis, setting up a showdown with Winnipeg.

And while the Whalers were feeling good about themselves heading into the finals—they were unbeaten in six of their last seven in the regular season—they were wholly unprepared for the Jets. Arguably the best team in WHA history, Winnipeg won the first two games by a combined score of 9–3, and then blew out New England in Game 3, 10–2. By that point, Neale was out of strategy. Before the game, he gave his team one simple directive. "Boys, this is your one chance to fuck up a parade," he said. That wasn't exactly "Win one for the Gipper."

The homestanding Jets finished off the sweep with a 5–3 win, garnering another Avco Cup. "We died like rats," said one player afterward.

At one point, the Whalers' coach used a line of Gordie Howe, Johnny McKenzie, and Dave Keon, explaining that if this was going to be Howe's last game, he wanted to give Canada a chance to say goodbye. That 1977–78 team didn't win a title, but Neale, Howe, and the rest of the organization managed to keep everything together through an incredibly tenuous time. That accomplishment was enough to make the team one of the more memorable ones in the history of the franchise, and the season helped set up the success that the Whalers were about to enjoy.

The 1977–78 playoff finale wouldn't be the last game for Howe in a Whalers uniform, but it *would* be the last game in New England for Neale, who was being courted by several NHL teams. He received permission from ownership to interview with other franchises, eventually landing a three-year deal to become the new head coach of the Canucks on May 26, 1978.

It was a bittersweet decision. "There are two ways a coach can move; on his own or by getting fired. This is certainly the most desirable way," Neale told reporters. "My heart tells me to stay in Hartford but my head tells me to take advantage of this opportunity. That Howard Baldwin and Jack Kelley permitted me to buy [out] my contract shows what a class organization the New England Whalers are."

It was just one step in a wild off-season for the Whalers, as well as the rest of the WHA. The shifting sands of professional hockey forced the upstart league to become more aggressive in signing teenage prospects—the NHL had spurned the initial talk of a merger, so the WHA took the feud to the next level by again going after younger players who weren't yet considered draft-eligible by the NHL. That included a struggling Indianapolis team adding seventeen-year-old Wayne Gretzky and Birmingham signing seven underage players for the relatively paltry sum of $50,000 each, including future stars Michel Goulet, Rick Vaive, and Gaston Gingras. (They were rechristened the "Baby Bulls.")

Besides signing Douglas, New England landed Jeff Brubaker, traded for goaltender John Garrett, and signed WHA scoring leader Andre Lacroix. Douglas was an ebullient youngster from western Canada who jumped in with both feet.

"People . . . ask me, 'You played for ten years, where did you have the most fun? What was the best part?' Here's the ironic thing. The most fun I ever had was my first year in the WHA with the New England Whalers," Douglas said. "I just didn't know it. It was my first year. I was the proverbial wet behind the ears, trying to fit in and figure it out. But when I look back, I go, 'What a wonderful experience.'"

As for Lacroix, he would go on to set a unique milestone—in his seven seasons in the WHA, he played for teams in six cities. In each case, the team either folded or moved, and Lacroix ended up with what was perceived to be a steadier team. (Lacroix, who was his own agent, always included a clause in his contract that stipulated he could choose where he ended up if the team folded.) The lack of consistency wore on him, but he wouldn't have to worry about that in New England.

"I came to New England with the same attitude I had when I played in the other cities in the WHA—I was hoping this would be my last stop," said Lacroix. He had already carved out a niche as a terrific scorer—he had six consecutive years with 100-plus points—when he signed with the Whalers prior to the start of the 1978–79 season. "Every team I played with as a free agent, I thought I would finish my career with that particular team, and every team folded. I was fortunate to have a contract where I could choose where I was going to play, and I thought that each team that I chose would be my last team.

"What I liked about New England was the fact that Bill Dineen was the new coach and the owner Howard Baldwin worked for the Flyers when I played with them and [the Whalers] had a lot of success in the WHA."

With Dineen at the helm, the 1978–79 season started optimistically enough. After an impressive 4-1-3 preseason mark that saw the team compete successfully against NHL clubs, the regular season began October 15 in Quebec with a 6–5 win over the Nordiques, the first of a six-game unbeaten streak. The Whalers rolled through the early stages of the season, and after a 7–2 win over the powerful Jets on February 10—when Keon had 3 goals and an assist to push New England into first place—they were a season-high ten games over .500.

"We got goals from every line, and of course Keon had a great night," Dineen told reporters after the game. "We got great goaltending and the defense played well. We're playing well now and hopefully, we will continue to play well."

But that win would represent the high-water mark of the season. A stretch of nine games in twelve days ground them down a bit; they lost six of those nine games to slip back behind Winnipeg. More losses would follow throughout March, and on April 1, 1979, Dineen was let go in favor of former player and scout Don Blackburn. Baldwin took great pains to note that Dineen wasn't fired but, instead, had been reassigned within the organization, with an eye toward drafting and developing talent.

"It's just another area of my job. It's part of my job to try to help the Whalers any way I can," said Blackburn, who was stepping into the role of New England coach for the second time in his career.

It was a surprise to players for a number of reasons, including that the team decided to make the move with only nine games left in the regular season. "I can't realistically agree with it, but by the same token, there's nothing I can do about it," Dineen told the *Courant* the next day.

Dineen took a shot at the Whalers for still playing their home games in the tiny Springfield Civic Center. "I guess you could say, in my defense, we had the best road record in the entire league, but we couldn't win at home," he said. "Of course, it's tough for *anyone* to win in Springfield."

The Howe family wasn't happy with the news. They had played for Dineen in Houston, and some believed they were instrumental him getting the job in New England. "I'm going to miss him. I was surprised. I don't know if it will help," Mark Howe said after Dineen was let go. "We weren't playing that well for Dineen, and I think we let him down."

"He said and did all the things that a coach should say and do, but the players didn't respond," said Lacroix. "It was just a situation where, as a team, we didn't put out for him. All of us have to take the blame."

"This was a very difficult decision to make," Kelley said. "Bill Dineen is a fine person. He has worked very hard at making this club a winner. I just felt the club was losing its poise and direction. Don is experienced in handling players under situation[s] like this, and he has the respect of the New England players. I am hopeful that he'll get us headed in the right direction for the playoffs."

The difference was relatively negligible, at least from a wins-and-losses perspective. The Whalers went 4-4 over their final eight games and finished fourth overall.

An up-and-down stretch to the conclusion of the 1978–79 regular season for New England gave way to a wild start to the playoffs. The Whalers beat Cincinnati in a best-of-three first-round matchup and said farewell to the WHA with a rollicking seven-game playoff series against the Oilers that was chock full of wide-open hockey. A total of 64 goals were scored across the length of the series, including a Game

Two in Edmonton that saw a 9–5 win for the Oilers. Edmonton ended up closing out the series in Game Seven at the Northlands Coliseum with a 6–3 win that wasn't nearly as close as the final score would indicate. The Oilers took a 6–1 lead out the gate and coasted over much of the last period.

The series provided a preview for NHL teams that might have anticipated the arrival of Gretzky. The eighteen-year-old was the leading scorer in the playoffs, and his line—which included Brett Callighen and Blair MacDonald—scored a whopping 18 goals against the Whalers in the seven-game set.

"To our credit, we played to the end," Blackburn said after it was all done. "I'm proud of them. We have nothing to be ashamed of. We played a decent third. Went down 6–1 and didn't quit. Edmonton is a good hockey team. They beat us fair and square. Our power play died on us in this series. You have to get goals when you get the opportunity. They did. We didn't."

Blackburn also made sure Gordie Howe was part of the last shift, leaving him on the ice for much of the final minute in anticipation of him perhaps saying goodbye. "Nobody knows what his plans are," confessed Blackburn. "We're in Canada tonight, and I thought it appropriate if he played the last shift."

Against the backdrop of the Whalers' up-and-down 1978–79 season, the WHA and NHL continued to talk merger. When it came to New England, the Bruins weren't crazy about the possibility of some competition for the local market. In late March 1979 they threatened an antimerger lawsuit. With the merger looming, Bruins president Paul Mooney hinted that things were a little fishy because his franchise had yet to see a copy of the paperwork. "The way it stands now, we will bring suit, and we have grounds to do it. To me, it's all very interesting that all of the other teams getting ready for the meeting in Chicago have copies of the agenda and we don't," Mooney told reporters. "It's curious to me the way this whole thing is being conducted."

Mooney also noted the Bruins' territoriality rights. "So you draw a 50-mile circle out from their building, and you do the same for ours, and you find that they will be encroaching on our territory," he added.

The Bruins weren't the only ones sweating the idea of the Whalers—and three other WHA teams—joining the NHL. "Let me ask you something. Why does everybody want to get out of that league?" Toronto owner Harold Ballard chortled to the *Hartford Courant* in 1978. "If everybody's having fun and making money, why do they all want to get out? I don't know anything about the Whalers except that their roof fell in. I read that in the paper. I can't understand why everybody wants to get out of that league if it's such a great league."

But after several fits and starts—and the protestations from old-school owners like Ballard—it was clear that a merger was on the horizon. And after plenty of negotiations, the WHA finally came to an agreement with the NHL in early 1979, and on March 31, the vote passed the NHL Board of Governors by a 14–3 margin. Boston, Toronto, and Los Angeles all voted against the plan. Ballard was reportedly the first to bolt from the meeting when things wrapped up. Asked by reporters for his feelings on what happened, he was brief. "I don't feel very well," he replied.

Obviously, other owners felt differently. For Baldwin and the rest of the WHA, the merger was sweet vindication.

"I am very, very happy. I gave three years of my life for this and it's done," said Quebec owner Marcel Aubut, referencing the merger struggle. "We'll have our place in this league, and we've got security for many, many years."

The official announcement that four WHA teams would become part of the NHL came at the Loews Warwick Hotel in New York. The Oilers, Whalers, Nordiques, and Jets were joining the NHL—*probably.* Because a merger between the NHL and WHA had been discussed ever since the WHA came into existence, some trepidation existed across the league about the possibility of it going through, at least for a few months. Given the wild history between the two leagues, a last-minute change of heart was always possible. And some of the players knew it.

"When I left Hartford at the end of the [1978–79] season, I was told to take everything home with me because there was not a 100 percent commitment that any teams would go to the NHL," Douglas said. "I left Hartford and went back to Winnipeg to train; it was pretty much—from my point of view—it was still up in the air."

But eventually, all the t's were crossed, and i's were dotted. The merger was official.

"After some 35 different WHA ownerships in some 21 cities, it's hard to believe that, here we are, with four teams about to enter the NHL," said Baldwin, who joked he was glad to surrender his job as WHA commissioner. "This is a big moment. A very exciting moment.

"You're getting four good partners," he told NHL commissioner John Ziegler. "We'll do the NHL proud."

"The expansion of the National Hockey League to include a Hartford-New England Whalers and three other World Hockey Association teams will bring big-time professional athletics to a New England city of 140,000, a remarkable feat and a tribute to the perseverance that made it possible," trumpeted the op-ed page of the *Courant*.

"There is special pleasure in the Whaler set-up," continued the op-ed. "The team is more than one entertainment division among many. The coming of the Whalers and the opening of the Civic Center Coliseum were symbols of downtown growth that brought new spirit to the city. As the Civic Center rebuilds, the hockey team prepares for a new level of competition and excitement to match its new home."

For all the fuss the Bruins made over the Whalers, after the merger was approved Sinden said they'd support the addition of the WHA teams. "The Bruins will do whatever they can to make the new 21-team league as strong as possible," he said. "We are not taking a 'sour grapes' attitude and we won't let the league down. I've always been a big NHL man, and the Bruins are part of the NHL, one of the charter members. We lost and that's fact. We'll do our part."

According to Sinden, his beef boiled down to retaining talent. "They took something away from us in Chicago (last week). The [NHL Board of Governors] formalized a draft under which we would lose four players without our consent. If you have property rights, no one can take them away from you without your consent."

Sinden added that he felt "obliged to criticize" the new balanced schedule that had to be implemented with the addition of the new teams because, in his eyes, it took something away from established divisional rivalries. He also made sure to add that the Bruins owned the NHL rights to Whalers' Mark Howe and Ron Plumb.

But the deal was done. The wild roller-coaster ride that was the WHA would come to a stop.

Three Canadian teams completed all seven WHA seasons based in the same city and were the same three Canadian teams that ultimately joined the NHL. The other WHA team to enter the NHL, the Whalers, was the only other WHA team to play all of its home games over seven seasons within a relatively small geographical area. Of the original twelve WHA franchises, only the Winnipeg Jets remained for all seven seasons in the same building without relocating, changing team names, or folding.

In the end, the WHA left a unique legacy. There was wild instability, enough stories to fill a thousand books, and some great hockey. It paved the way for a new generation of stars: Wayne Gretzky and the amazing Oilers, the Stastny brothers (Anton, Peter, and Marian), and many others. It brought the game to corners of the country where people couldn't tell the difference between the blue line and red line and where ice was something used to keep a drink cold.

But ultimately, the WHA helped shape the financial future of the professional game, giving power to a generation of players in a way they had never enjoyed before. Stars like Hull benefitted, sure, but the real beneficiaries were the "middle class" players, the ones who had to deal with the reserve clause and the uncertainties that came with it. While it could be dismissed by some as a gimmicky league, the WHA had an undeniable impact on the sport, both on and off the ice.

As for Hartford, there was more than just a new league to get excited about. On May 23, 1979, the franchise made it official—the team would be renamed the Hartford Whalers. To go along with the move, the franchise unveiled a new logo, a dynamic new rendering courtesy of designer Peter Good.

Throughout the WHA days, the team had a simple *W* with a harpoon through it in a circle. The circle was surrounded by the words *New England Whalers* and a green outline. It was a perfectly adequate logo, instantly identifiable and unique to the region. But by WHA standards, it was a little stodgy. Many of the other WHA logos were flashier and splashier: the Indianapolis Racers, for example, had a red, white, and blue color scheme and a design that reflected the city's association with the legendary auto race. The Miami Screaming Eagles had a menacing bird with an impossibly large wingspan and a hockey stick in its talons. The Winnipeg Jets had a hockey stick and an airplane juxtaposed in a dynamic circular logo. And the Philadelphia Blazers had a hockey stick with a flame attached. When it came to the Whalers, the logo was good, but no one was necessarily buying the merchandise because of the logo.

Good wasn't a hardcore hockey fan, but he recognized that the franchise needed a new look to complete its makeover. "I played backlot hockey on ponds and things, and I knew the basic principles of the game, but that was about it," he recalled. "I followed baseball and football and basketball—hockey was sort of off to the side for me. I really didn't know a lot about the game when I started this."

Good came up with a handful of alternatives that he showed to Baldwin and the rest of the ownership. Baldwin recalled being impressed by one drawing that had a trident pointing upward with spikes coming off the three lines in the *W*.

"A harpoon is used to *kill* whales, but the whale was the team's mascot. So, there was something not quite right about that, some cognitive dissonance—you don't want to kill your own mascot," Good remembered. "And they agreed with that when I explained it to them. So that's when I came up with the whale's tail. I had done some other whale-based designs in that first presentation, but nothing that just had the tail. And I discovered that it worked really well with the 'W.' It didn't happen right away—it took a while to get there."

Good settled on a *W* that dropped the *H* into the negative space, creating an innovative look. Unlike most logo work—a painstaking process designed to appeal to as broad a fan base as possible—this was a one-man show. The Whalers gave him carte blanche, and he ran with it.

"This would *never* happen today," Good said. "You'd have to do it over and over, and market research would be involved, and there would be testing with teenagers and focus groups and all that stuff. It would be given to a team of designers, and there would be departments. It would be a nightmare. This one, this was a really lucky opportunity. They were wonderful in accepting it as quickly as they did, and they saw the potential right away."

Good got $2,000 for his work but still laments that he didn't keep the merchandising rights—twenty years after the team moved, it's still one of the hottest selling logos in the NHL. "There was no contract, which later became very complicated," lamented Good in an interview in 2016. "It's now a very popular logo, and the NHL makes a lot of money off of it, and so the question becomes, who owns it? We talked to some lawyers, and they agreed that I probably have the rights, but it got very complicated on the legal front, so I've given up on that."

Bill Barnes, the Whalers' director of marketing, explained the new look at the introductory press conference. "It's the state animal, first off," he told reporters. "And the tail is the most powerful part of the whale, which propels and protects him."

THE CIVIC CENTER WAS BEING REBUILT. BIG-TIME SPORTS were coming to Hartford. It was an exciting time for the city and the players on the roster. Youngsters were going to get their first taste of professional hockey, sure, but former NHLers who ended up making their bones in the WHA couldn't wait for a chance to show the NHL what it had been missing out on. Lacroix was part of a group of players who had jumped to the WHA at the start of the decade.

But he didn't get the opportunity he was hoping for. "I worked hard all the summer to make sure I was in the best shape possible for my return to the NHL," recalled Lacroix. "However, I believe management and coaching staff had a different idea. I did not dress for some of the preseason games because they said they wanted to look at the younger players and they knew what I could do. I didn't think they gave me the chance that I deserved after what I had done previously. I had two years left on my contract that was guaranteed and we finally came to an agreement before Christmas that we would work out a settlement. I felt bad because I knew that I still has something left, but they felt differently."

Lacroix wasn't the only player who felt like he got the short end of the hockey stick. When the merger went through, the Whalers landed a handful of players in the expansion draft, including New England native Bill Bennett, a big, rangy winger with a physical streak who had 71 points in seventy-two games the previous year in the AHL.

But he feuded constantly with Kelley, and years later, remained bitter about his experience. "If I saw him right now, I'd punch him in the mouth," Bennett said of Kelley. "I never thought he gave me a good shake. I look back at my career—it took me a little while to get established, but I did well for them. I knew I wasn't their golden boy, but I tried. They sent me down, and I scored 20 goals in twenty games. What did he say? 'Well, he's good in the small rinks.' If he had given me a chance, I would have done okay."

Lacroix would end up finding a new gig—in the broadcast booth. He was paired with Chuck Kaiton, a midwesterner who had carved out a niche as one of the best play-by-play men in college hockey while with the University of Wisconsin. Kaiton would go on to become the definitive voice of the franchise, as identifiable with the Whalers as Vin Scully with the Dodgers or Johnny Most with the Celtics.

But it took him a while to land the job. He first got a call about the Whalers in the summer of 1978, an inquiry that he remembers coming out of the blue. "Still, to this day, I'm not 100 percent sure of how they got ahold of me," Kaiton said with a laugh. "I had done an NCAA game in Providence that March when the Badgers lost to Boston University, a team with Dave Silk, and ended up playing in the consolation game against Bowling Green. I was broadcasting the game against BU, and the assistant GM of the Whalers, Bob Crocker, was sitting near me, and he must have been listening."

But he was wary of joining the WHA. Why jump to a league that looked to have a tenuous future at the expense of what could very well be a long and successful career doing play-by-play for one of the best college hockey programs in the nation? "They gave me a call in July of 1978, and I kind of brashly told them that I wasn't really interested in coming to the WHA. Some of my friends, including Dave McNab, were telling me that the WHA would fold. 'They won't be around much more.' They didn't tell me that they had one more year to go, and they'd end up merging with the NHL."

"Well, I guess I blew that chance," Kaiton said to his wife.

But that wasn't the end of it. In August of 1979, he got another call from the Whalers. "This is crazy, I'm thinking," Kaiton said, laughing. "Bill Barnes was on the other end of the line, and he offered me the chance to come out and interview for the job. I was perplexed. What happened? But it was soon clear I was going to be offered the job. I had a really good feeling about it, but I wanted to know what happened. Did you hire someone who only worked out for one year?

"They hired Bob Neumeier, and what happened was that he apparently got on thin ice with the Howe family—he supposedly hated Marty. And Colleen, being the mother that she was, she went into the front office and said they had to get rid of him. She felt that Marty was just a whipping boy on the air for Neumy. He eventually went to Channel 3 in Hartford, but that was the backstory on how I got a second chance to get the radio job."

Kaiton would be paired with Lacroix on WTIC for the next decade. "It was a dream come true working with Chuck," Lacroix said. "He was such a professional in his work. The time he put in before every game to be ready was unbelievable. He knew everything about each player without even looking at his notes. The most difficult part of doing color is that I had to listen to everything Chuck was saying, so when he turned it to me I did not repeat what he had just said. We were a very good team, and we had so much respect for each other. Chuck is one of the top broadcasters in hockey, if not *the* best."

The two become friends away from the rink. Their relationship was cemented when Kaiton arrived from Wisconsin; he leaned on Lacroix for help in getting acclimated to New England.

"I met Andre when I first came to training camp in the fall of 1979, and I really liked him," Kaiton said. "He was a nice guy—we hadn't moved yet, and my wife was back in Madison because we hadn't sold the house. He was just the nicest guy in the world to me, just helping with logistical things when I first got to town. He did things like find a car-repair person who was reliable and just introducing me to a lot of people in town who could help me out. He was just particularly helpful to me even before I knew I was going to work with him. A great person—I really enjoyed my time with him.

"On the broadcast, he was terrific. A natural," he added. "I just had so much respect for him as a player and his knowledge of the game. I helped him on the broadcast side of things. But having a rapport, I really didn't have to do a lot of work with that. He was a natural at broadcasting. That rapport and familiarity and ability to mesh, that started early. He's a hockey guy, but he was also down to earth. That mutual respect came across on the air."

WTIC had always been the standard bearer for radio broadcasting in New England, so having the Whalers games broadcast on the 50,000-watt station that could reach the Midwest on clear nights was a natural fit for a franchise looking to project a professional, stable image. (WTIC had the local broadcast rights to the Whalers but was also the prime Connecticut carrier for the Red Sox. Toss in the presence of sports-talk legend Arnold Dean, and it was the go-to station for Connecticut sports fans.)

WTIC's evolution would be a small part of the expansion of team coverage. The *Hartford Courant* was changing as well. America's oldest daily newspaper was purchased by the Times Mirror Company in 1979, and the new owners wanted to modernize things, including the sports page. The arrival of the NHL in Hartford provided them with an opportunity to shake things up.

"One of the things that dovetailed with rise of Whalers—maybe not a connection people make—was the fact that the Times Mirror Company took over the *Courant* in 1979," *Courant* sportswriter Dom Amore said. "That's when it made the move from an old-time 1960s paper that covered, like, Trinity College baseball, and they built it into this big-time, ambitious, national sports section. They brought in people from all over the country to cover the Yankees and Mets and Red Sox and Celtics. They wanted to upgrade the *Courant* to a big-time sports section across the board. The Whalers' move into the NHL coincided with that, and that became our thing. We probably covered the Whalers about as well as any NHL team was covered in those days. We had ambition to be big time."

Everyone—the team, the building, the newspaper, the city—was headed for the big time.

5

The Merger
1979-81

I was a true New Englander. I hated, hated, hated when they changed
the name to Hartford. I mean, I was born in Massachusetts, played
for the Whalers in Boston, went to college in New Hampshire, lived
in Maine, and played in Rhode Island for the Providence Reds. I'm
New England hockey, through and through.
—Former Whalers goaltender Cap Raeder (1975–77)

Why should we salvage them? They were our rivals. Let them die
on the vine.
—NHL president Clarence Campbell, June 1977, on the possibility
of a merger between the WHA and NHL

The NHL was coming to Hartford. *This was fun.* The state had a few
relatively brief stints when it came to professional sports, but nothing
ever really seemed to stick. Most notably, the Celtics played a few
"home" games in Hartford every year until the mid-1990s. The Red
Sox's Double A team—the Bristol Red Sox—played at nearby Muzzy
Field for a decade (1973–82). And the Hartford Charter Oaks (of the
Continental Football League) and Hartford Knights (of the Atlantic

Coast Football League) played at Dillon Stadium in the late 1960s and early 1970s.

But this was unique. Professional sports in the late 1970s was a different landscape than it is today. The year before the merger between the NHL and WHA, ninety-three teams were in the big-four leagues (NHL, NBA, MLB, and NFL). It *meant something* to have a professional sports team in town, especially in a city like Hartford that had been viewed as a professional sports off-ramp between Boston and New York. The fans responded with deposits for 1,379 new season tickets in the first five days following the announcement of the merger. The ticket office was busy. The franchise was moving into a new era.

One guy who had a slightly less eventful offseason than usual was Baldwin. He had gone from helping guide the WHA for several years, as well as serving as one of the conductors in the merger, to simply worrying about his own team. It was a radical change.

"When the phone rang," Baldwin would later remember, "no one ever called to say, 'Hey, Howard, things are great.' It was always something like, 'Hey, Howard. The Internal Revenue guys just padlocked the Indianapolis dressing room.'

"It's sort of a unique situation for me, not having to worry about Cincinnati or Indianapolis folding or something like that," he said. "It will be nice to just have to worry about the Whalers. Now we can concentrate on the product. People are tired of hearing about Indianapolis."

The Whalers had made their bones in the WHA as one of the most important franchises on a consistent basis, a stable and serious playoff contender. Now, the team was ready to make the leap into the NHL.

"It's a new era. Call it the Second Coming of the Whale," coach Don Blackburn joked.

It was an intriguing group poised to make the bold leap forward. In addition to Gordie Howe, the roster featured no fewer than ten players who had previously been part of the NHL, including Keon (Leafs), Ley (Leafs), Lacroix (Flyers and Blackhawks), and Bennett (Bruins).

Antonovich, Fotiu, and Stoughton were also among those who had collected an NHL paycheck at some point in their careers.

For his part, Stoughton was an intriguing prospect who had relatively brief stints with the Leafs and Penguins. A good-looking winger with a Tom Selleck–style mustache and a full head of wild hair, he brought a dash of glamour to the franchise; his wife, Cindy, a former *Playboy* bunny, also broadened the team's appeal.

"Why?" longtime Whalers fan Jeff Bamberger said when asked for one of the reasons why Blaine Stoughton was his favorite player. "It was 1980, and I was a fourteen-year-old boy. Could anyone have expected differently?"

On the ice, Stoughton had already had a measure of success, having scored 23 goals with Toronto in 1974–75 and 52 goals with the Stingers in the 1976–77 season. After being injured for the past two seasons, he was now healthy and seemed ticketed for plenty of ice time with the expansion Whalers.

"In terms of my career, it was just a good situation for me at that time," Stoughton recalled in an interview with the *Pro Hockey Alumni* podcast. "I was twenty-five or twenty-six. I had just gotten married. I just started a family. Although Hartford isn't Boston or New York, at that juncture of my career, I was starting to settle down a bit. So it was a good fit for me. When I was younger in my career—single—it probably wouldn't have been the best fit, Hartford, Connecticut. But at that time in my life, it was good for me."

"Stoughton didn't like the rough going and wasn't much into back-checking, but if you needed a goal, he was lethal," recalled Mark Howe. "When we were getting ready to pull our goalie, he would say, 'You know where to find me.' That meant at the red line, and when you got it to him, he scored."

Also, two types of players were jumping to the new league with the Whalers: guys like Mark Howe who grew up as WHA players but were finally getting the acknowledgment as NHL players, and those who were set to rejoin the NHL, like Keon. Among that second group, the biggest name was undoubtedly Gordie Howe. The holder of eleven NHL all-time records at that point—including goals (786), assists (1,023), and total points (1,809), he was excited to be back in the league. Gordie had been bothered early in camp by brief but recurring dizzy spells, but as the opener loomed it appeared that he was good to go, according to Jack Kelley.

"A big key will be if he can remain injury free," Kelley said of hockey's elder statesman. "The length of the season is also a concern but that is a concern for a lot of players. One advantage for Gordie, but not for the team, is that we do a lot of traveling earlier in the season when he should be stronger. That will work in his favor."

Hartford was assigned to the Norris Division with Los Angeles, Montreal, Pittsburgh, and Detroit, but the divisional alignment was largely seen as a moot point—with balanced schedule, each team would play every other team in the NHL four times, with two games at home and two on the road. In all, it would make for an eighty-game slate, with the top sixteen teams advancing to the postseason. (The teams would face each other according to overall point finish, with number one meeting number sixteen in the opening round, and so on.)

Little was expected of the Whalers in their maiden voyage in the NHL. "They have picked us for dead last, and that gives us something to shoot for this year," Mark Howe told reporters. "We may not be as good as we think we are, but we have to show that we are not as bad as everybody else thinks we are."

Hartford finished 4-1-3 in the preseason, which did spark some optimism that the team wouldn't be *absolutely* awful. "The pressure is on the NHL," Lacroix told the *Courant* on the eve of the new season. "We're the underdogs. They're the ones who are supposed to run us out of the building every night."

The team did make some news shortly before the start of the season, as the Whalers sent Marty Howe down to Springfield, their AHL affiliate. It would mark the first time since the start of the 1973–74 season in Houston that hockey's royal family would not open the season on the same roster. Gordie and Mark weren't thrilled at the idea—part of the reason behind Gordie coming out of retirement was the opportunity to play alongside his sons—but Kelley added that it was possible Marty could be recalled sooner rather than later.

"They're absolutely professional," Kelley said when asked about the reaction of Gordie and Mark to the news that Marty would open the season in the minors. "They know it's part of the game. It is a decision that was made in the best interests of the team. I know it's a unique situation, but Marty wouldn't want to be kept just because he is a Howe."

"As a father, Gordie was very disappointed and upset. Naturally, he would like to have Marty with the club."

"It was funny. Sometimes Marty wouldn't have a practice or game, so he would come down to one of our practices and talk to us," wrote Andre Lacroix. "He would mention to his Dad that they weren't going to have a game the next day, and he didn't know what to do. He would say he needed to find a good place to go fishing. Gordie would get so mad! 'Why don't you concentrate on coming back *here* instead?'"

"Marty's conditioning couldn't have been an issue," Mark Howe said later. "He had been running five miles a day to get ready."

Mark, who had started to transition to defenseman, was complimentary of his teammates, but lamented the loss of his brother. "Although we were a decent pairing," Mark said of Al Sims, "I would have been better off with a stay-at-home partner. I knew one very well, and he had been banished to Springfield without a real look because the Whalers were convinced Marty had a bad attitude. My brother is an easygoing guy, a fisherman whose nickname was 'Foggy.' But when he stepped on the ice, he was always competitive. There was no way Marty wasn't at least a third-pair defenseman on that team. 'Half my reason for playing is gone,' Dad told reporters sadly."

Regardless, with the roster set, the Whalers played their first-ever NHL game against the North Stars in Minnesota the night of October 11, 1979. Before the game, several players said the excitement in the room was palpable, but they were admittedly tight in the first period, fell into a 3–0 hole in the first twenty minutes, and never recovered. Minnesota scored a pair of power-play goals late after a Fotiu double-minor penalty. They played well in the second and third periods, and Gordie Roberts tallied Hartford's first-ever NHL goal on a slapper at the 14:15 mark of the third. But it wasn't enough.

"What I was concerned about all day happened," said Blackburn. "We were looking forward to it so much we were uptight."

Hartford had to wait until the fifth game of the season—its home opener in Springfield—for its first NHL victory, a 6–3 victory over the Kings. That contest was punctuated by a pair of goals from Mark Howe, as well as single goals from Allison, Stoughton, Sims, and Bennett.

"The lighting in Springfield wasn't the best, making it look smaller than its eight-thousand-seat capacity," remembered Mark Howe. "The building didn't have much character, but the ice was good, and the boards were fast, so I guess it served its purpose, even though there were more Bruins fans in Springfield than there had been in Hartford. I remember beating Boston—after we moved to the NHL—and the fans booing us."

Playing in Springfield had its issues, and not just on the ice. The arena was perfectly adequate for a WHA team, but these were the big leagues. When you stacked it against the likes of the Forum in Montreal or Madison Square Garden, the facilities came up woefully short. Some players indicated that the weight room and the workout equipment was lacking compared with other NHL teams, while others found the commute from the Hartford area north and back again for practices and games a pain.

But armed with the knowledge that a return to Hartford—and a brand-new building—was looming, the players kept their eyes on the prize. The Whalers stayed around .500 for much of the first two-plus months, a stretch that included an impressive 4–0 win over Gretzky, Messier, and the Oilers, the first time they played a game against Edmonton in the NHL, which made for a three-game winning streak.

For a lot of the guys who had the chance to return to the NHL, their joy was palpable. For the rookies who were getting their first taste of life in professional hockey, it was something even greater. "I remember the first game we were playing was in the Springfield Civic Center, and I scored on my first shift," said Dave Debol. "I was like, *This is great. This is great.*

"There were times where it was a rough year, and people would say, 'Don't you wish you were on a better team?' But it didn't matter to me. You make it to the NHL, you've achieved your dream. It doesn't matter if it was for one game, one year, five years, ten years, twenty years. I was just excited—my goal was to be able to play in the NHL, and I got that chance."

As for Gordie Howe, he was proving to be much more than just a sideshow. That season, he would finish sixth on the team in goals scored (15) and eighth in assists (26).

"It would be absurd to suggest that now, in 1980, Gordie Howe is the player he used to be. He will be 52 in March, and is the grandfather of two. To compare a 51-year-old man with the greatest player of all time is silly," wrote E. M. Swift in *Sports Illustrated* in 1980. "But it is not silly to compare him with the players coming into the NHL, the 20-year-olds who can skate and shoot and throw their bodies around but who cannot beat this man out of a job, or keep him from scoring. Howe has earned his position on the Whalers. He is not a continuing publicity stunt. The man can play."

Howe's contributions to the 1979–80 Whalers went beyond the ice. Roughly two-thirds of the roster was twenty-five or younger, and the Hall of Famer looked out for his younger teammates both on and off the ice, according to Debol: "One time, he said, 'I'll tell you this one time: Be a man at night and a man in the morning.' Basically, he was saying there was a time and a place for everything. 'After the game, you can go out and have a beer, but don't come to the rink the next day hammered. Be smart about it. You're a professional. In the summer, when the season is done, go out and do what you have to do. But when the season starts, you owe it to your teammates.'

"After games, a lot of times, we'd all go out to eat together, and that's the way Gordie was. I mean, he could have had a case of beer in his room for all we knew. But he watched himself in public. I can never remember him having more than two beers in a sitting."

When it came to the old guys, it wasn't just Howe who was getting it done early in the 1979–80 season. Like Howe, Keon was more of a set-up guy (he ended that season with 52 assists, third-best on the team), creating scoring chances for his younger teammates. Early on, his finest hour came on Halloween, 1979. With Hartford in Toronto to face the Leafs, Keon had a chance to exact a measure of revenge on the Leafs and their owner Harold Ballard.

By 1975 Keon had distinguished himself as one of the greatest Leafs of all time, but after fifteen years and four Stanley Cups, Ballard believed him to be washed up. Keon was still interested in playing, but Ballard set a return compensation price so absurdly high, it was impossible for Keon to go anywhere else in the NHL. So Keon jumped to the WHA, first with the Fighting Saints before joining the Whalers after Minnesota folded.

Five years later, that October night was his first time facing Ballard and his old team, and he came through with flying colors, scoring a second-period goal (which drew a big cheer) and setting up another on the way to a 4–2 win over Ballard and the Leafs. It was sweet revenge for Keon.

"You always hope it will come out this way, but it usually doesn't," he told reporters after the game. "I'm just happy it did."

The victory jump-started a three-game win streak for Hartford, which would hang around the .500 mark for much of the first two months of the year. But Ley suffered a broken bone in his foot in December, and while it wasn't the only reason the Whalers started to skid, it wasn't completely coincidental they stumbled with Ley on the sidelines. Hartford was 8-11-8 when Ley got hurt. Over the eleven games he was sidelined, the Whalers won just one, falling to 9-19-10.

"We were going along pretty good that year until Ricky Ley broke his foot," said left winger Bill Bennett. "Man, Ricky Ley . . . what a great defenseman. What a leader. But we had a good start for an expansion club, and the shit just hit the fan. We went on a skid, and I don't know if we ever really recovered."

"I don't think any of the guys that first year thought we were overmatched," recalled Jordy Douglas. "A lot of us were *occasionally* overwhelmed by it all—it was a step up—but I personally never felt we were overmatched or in over our heads. The bulk of the guys had played in the NHL before, and a lot of them—like Mikey Rogers—didn't get a fair shake. For a lot of those guys, there was more of an attitude that 'I will prove them wrong.' That was the driving factor for a lot of the guys. And you also have to remember we didn't get raked over the coals in the expansion draft like Winnipeg did."

"We had a pretty good hockey team at the time, but Winnipeg could have given any one of the NHL teams a run for their money, with Hedberg and Hull and the rest of them," said equipment manager Skip Cunningham. "They had just an outstanding team. The WHA wanted to play them, but NHL wanted no part of them."

Indeed, any time the Whalers might have started to feel sorry for themselves, all they had to do was look west to the Jets, who were decimated in the expansion draft. The most successful franchise in WHA history with three Avco Cups, Winnipeg suffered through some truly horrendous years when it first arrived in the NHL, including the 1980–81 season, when the Jets ended with a 9-57-14 record—a whopping 44 points out of a playoff spot.

But to Bennett's point, the Whalers spent the month or so after Ley's return trying to make up ground on the rest of the field. They were able to do just that, winning four in a row at one point in January. The highlight of that stretch was January 12, 1980, the return of Gordie Howe to Detroit for the first time since his retirement as a Red Wing following the 1970–71 season. Teammates recall the pregame was an awkward situation for the legend.

"I grew up forty-five minutes north of Detroit, and I always told my family that if I'm lucky enough to make it to the NHL, when I played the Red Wings, I'll buy everyone tickets," remembered Debol. "And I had a big-ass family, but I got tickets for everyone. The whole thing cost me around $750. I get everyone their tickets.

"So we're there in the room before the game, and I'm looking at Gordie, and he's pacing around. He's nervous. He would usually sit there and read the paper, but this time was different, you know?"

Howe's return was met with loud and sustained cheers from the Detroit faithful. "John Bell, the PA announcer, got only as far as 'Number 9' before he was drowned out," Mark later wrote. "The ovation had to last five minutes, long enough to embarrass Dad, who just kind of skated in small circles as it went on and on."

"When it came time for warmups, it's packed, and there's a standing ovation. I mean, I'm yelling at Mark about something a few feet away, and he can't hear me," Debol said. "I look over and see my family, and then, warmups are done, and we come off the ice and go back to the room. I look over at Gordie and say, 'Power, what are you so nervous about? This is my first time back in Detroit, and they gave me a standing ovation. I don't think it had anything to do with you, though.' He looked back with a smile and said, 'Thanks, kid.'"

Ultimately, Howe didn't score on any one of his three shots on goal, but as Keon got his revenge on the Leafs earlier that season, Howe would get a similar sweet feeling that day in Detroit, as the Red Wings' fans provided him with a memorable return to the Motor City.

When it came to a proposed plan to celebrate the Howe family in the return to Detroit, accounts are varied, with one person saying the Whalers were poised to call Marty up for the game but a hand injury he had sustained earlier in the season made it a moot point. Regardless, Marty was recalled near the end of the season, and the three Howe family members were all part of the same line in a 4–4 tie with the Wings on March 12, 1980, at Joe Louis Arena.

The Whalers got a sizable boost the night of February 6, 1980, when hockey had its second coming in Hartford. The Civic Center reopened, two years and nineteen days after the collapse of the old building. For the new venue, the price tag was $31.5 million—it would seat 14,682 for hockey, 15,700 for basketball, and 16,000-plus for concerts.

"It's really nice," said Nick Fotiu, who was part of the team that opened the first building in 1975. "This is the second time I've opened this place up. I hope I don't have to do it anymore."

"The Phoenix did rise from the ashes," proclaimed Connecticut governor Ella Grasso. "Hartford did move on. It's a great day."

"I think the crowd will be a factor," Blackburn said before the game. "They've got a hell of a treat in getting back in their building. It's been two years of frustration for players and fans alike."

"Going from Springfield to Hartford was night and day, night and day," said Debol. "Hey, Springfield, I get it. It sat about five thousand people, and it was okay. For a minor-league team, it was a beautiful place to play. But it wasn't Hartford."

Despite some early struggles that night, Hartford enjoyed a thunderous 7–3 win over the Kings, a victory that would start a nine-game stretch that would see the Whalers go unbeaten in seven of those contests. A home win over the Oilers that was part of that stretch featured Keon smothering Gretzky—the young star got off only two shots because of the work of the wily veteran—and Mark Howe figuring in 4 of the 6 goals in the 6–2 victory. (It was part of a crazy hot streak for Mark, who had 5 assists in an 8–2 win over the Bruins a few weeks before.) The victory over Edmonton lifted Hartford into third place in the Norris Division, and thirteenth overall in the league.

Being back in the Civic Center gave the team an acknowledged boost, and the feeling of winning games in their own shiny new building sparked a sense of pride among Hartford hockey fans. "To be able to have that joy *in Hartford*, that was cool. I mean, you were living the life as a sports fan. You were living it," recalled PA announcer Greg Gilmartin, who started with the team in its first year in the NHL. "I remember there was one game where Blaine Stoughton scored in overtime to beat the Rangers and I was down in the walkways and the crowd was still coming out, and the energy was at its peak. Cindy Stoughton is leading the cheers. In moments like that, there was a feeling like, 'Hey, we're here. We belong in the NHL. We can beat anybody.' Those are the sort of momentary highlights that every sports fan lives for: *This is our team. We are winning.*"

In the end, it wasn't always a smooth ride, but the Whalers made the postseason that first year in the NHL. (That team remained the most recent first-year expansion franchise to make the playoffs in its inaugural season, along with the Oilers that same season, until the 2017–18 Vegas Golden Knights.) They finished 27-34-19, the best record of any of the four ex-WHA teams, and set an NHL record for most home wins by an expansion team (22).

"We were [one of two] expansion teams that made the playoffs that year," said Debol, "and a lot of it was because we had that experience on the roster, guys like Gordie and Dave Keon and Bobby Hull. We had the old guys with that experience to help guide us."

They were back in Hartford, in one of the newest venues in the league, and they were getting solid support from their fan base. They had a legendary—if aging—core of players: Gordie Howe and Keon provided plenty of veteran leadership that season, and the Whalers got a late-season jolt with the acquisition of Bobby Hull. (All were over forty by the time the playoffs rolled around.) Name recognition certainly wasn't an issue, as the Whalers featured four future Hall of Famers in their lineup by the end of the regular season: Gordie and Mark Howe, along with Keon and Hull.

"For the rest of the season," Terry Price wrote in the *Courant* on March 1, 1980, "the Hartford Whalers can be called the Hockey Hall of Fame—East. With the signing of Bobby Hull, the Whalers have united the two most glamorous names in the history of professional hockey."

"They certainly didn't hurt the team," Mark Howe told the *Hartford Courant* when asked about the veterans in a 2020 interview. "They were still capable players who knew how to do their job. You think, you've got three guys that old on a team, how bad it's going to be. But they all contributed.

"Even when I got to the end of my career, and I was 40," Mark added, "I would ask, 'How the hell did Dad play at 52?' I still think it's the greatest thing I've ever seen in sports."

"The thing about playing at this age, it's like playing injured all the time," joked Gordie that season.

While Hull and Howe were the bigger names, Keon had a fine season by any measure. His 52 assists that season represented a career-best NHL total. His 52 helpers were tied for eighteenth in the league that season. In addition, he had 10 goals, fourth in team scoring for the season.

The good news? The Whalers finished thirteenth overall in the league that season. (If it weren't for a ten-game winless streak near the end of the regular season, they could have landed as high as tenth.) It's a proud moment for any young franchise when it lands in the postseason, but for a team like Hartford, in its first year in the NHL, it was cause for celebration. The Whalers were in the playoffs, while five of the NHL's established teams weren't.

"There have been some low points and some high points. But if you total it all up, it's been a very satisfying year for the entire organization and the players," Blackburn told reporters at the end of the regular season. "We've proved we're a legitimate team in the NHL."

The bad news? The Whalers were matched up with the third-seeded Canadiens in the first round—the winners of the last four Stanley Cups. And they were without Stoughton, Douglas, and Ley, three foundational players, because of injury. *Other than that? No worries!*

To their credit, the Whalers were aware of the massive challenge that lay ahead, and approached things with (mostly) good humor. "Talk about drawing the short straw," laughed Mark Howe.

When Kelley compared the Whalers' quest to the 1980 U.S. Olympic hockey team and their attempt to upset the Russians, coach Don

Blackburn said that was great, but the "Olympic team only had to beat the Russians once. We have to beat Montreal three times."

In advance of Game One, which was set for Montreal on Tuesday, April 8, Blackburn cracked, "The key to stopping Montreal is telling them the first game is on Wednesday."

"There's not a lot of pressure on us," Blackburn added. "We're lucky we've got guys like Gordie Howe, Dave Keon, and Bobby Hull who have been there before. We're going in relaxed. We're going to surprise some people.

"We won't disgrace Hartford by any means. We don't quit. We haven't quit all year, and we won't quit now."

But it was clear from the start that Hartford was in over its head. Montreal took an early 4–0 lead in Game One at the Forum and cruised to a 6–1 win. Game Two was more of the same, but it did provide hockey fans everywhere with one last Gordie Howe highlight, as Mark Howe set his father up with the last goal of the night to make it 8–4, Montreal.

"We were totally outclassed from start to finish," Blackburn said glumly after the game. "The only positive thing was that we didn't quit. This game showed a lot of our inadequacies. It shows we have a long way to go to be a good hockey club like the Canadiens."

To Blackburn's point, they didn't quit when it came to the next one. In Game Three–the first NHL playoff game in Civic Center history— the Whalers thrilled the crowd by taking their first lead of the series on a Pat Boutette shorthanded goal 7:03 into the game. After Montreal answered, Hartford went up 2–1 on a goal from Tom Rowe 1:27 into the second. A back-and-forth second half of the contest left it tied after regulation.

"Be ready," Blackburn told his team between the end of regulation and overtime. "They have a history of scoring fast in overtime."

Yeah. Twenty-nine seconds into OT, Yvon Lambert scored, and that was that.

For the Whalers, the end of the first season in the NHL was an unqualified success. Picked by most to finish dead last overall, they ended the regular season with 73 points. They were one of two former WHA teams to make the playoffs, along with Edmonton. While they were stomped in the first two playoff games against the defending champions, they pushed them to OT in Game Three before falling.

"That game was really close, and it looked like we could build on that," Debol said. "I remember when we got back to the room at the end of things, our coach Donnie Blackburn said, 'Get back out there.' We came back out, and we were getting a standing ovation." As fans filed out of the Civic Center, a banner hung from the balcony: "Thanks for the Great Moments. We Look Forward with Pride."

"Tonight, we showed why we had an excellent season," Blackburn told reporters. "We played well enough to win. We were a worthy opponent for the Canadiens."

"If the Whalers had a better than expected season, don't slight Don Blackburn when the dessert is passed," wrote columnist Owen Canfield in the *Courant*. "He had more to do with it than anybody. Give the man a raise and a [year's] supply of his favorite cigars. He's a genuine NHL coach."

"This was an excellent year for us," Kelley told reporters less than a week after Hartford's season ended. "Everybody from [Don Blackburn] on down did a great job. But that is behind us now. If we can find more consistency next year and avoid a long losing streak, we can finish 10th to 12th. We aren't looking for a huge improvement, but steady improvement."

To that point, the transition had already begun. Less than a week after the end of the season, Kelley professed to be unsure about the future of Keon, Hull, and Gordie Howe.

The first of the three who saw his situation resolved was Keon. The veteran, who had been contemplating retirement, decided to return on a one-year deal that May.

"Dave's experience and maturity adds much to the success of this team," Kelley said after the deal was done. "Considering Dave's performance this past season, I felt this wasn't the time for him to give up his hockey career."

Howe's future was decided in early June, when he announced his retirement—again. "It's not an easy task to retire. No one teaches you how to retire—I found that out the first time," Howe said. "I'd hate to go out after 32 years and find out in the middle of winter I'd run short. My goal was to provide a proper house and a proper heater for my parents when I started to play hockey. I just wanted to be lucky enough to have two suits. I still think I'm damned good enough to play.

"I made the decision about a week ago when I told the front office my feelings," he added. "I'd like to make it clear I'm not quitting. I'm not a quitter. I'm retiring. I feel very fortunate to have been able to play as long as I did."

As he hinted, Howe's retirement was anything but tidy. According to Mark Howe, Gordie had gone into Kelley's office at some point in that last season and presented a plan where he would serve as a player/assistant coach, an idea that Kelley summarily rejected. Kelley's plan was to go with a youth movement, according to Mark, which caused Gordie to tell Kelley to "shove it." Instead, Howe was named the Whalers' new director of player development, with him working with the younger players in training camp and in Binghamton, New York, as well as scouting the NHL and junior leagues.

"We will rely heavily on him on evaluating players we would like to accumulate," Kelley said when asked about Howe's new position. "We will also lean very heavily on him in appraising the juniors. He has new duties now and I can't think of a man more suited."

But retirement never really suited Gordie. He confessed as much in that gathering with the media, joking that when it came to his first retirement, it was a challenge. Within two years, Kelley was replaced, and Howe sounded dissatisfied with his role under new boss Larry

Pleau. He told the *Detroit Free Press* in June 1982 that despite having the title director of player development, he did not scout for the team that season, and he didn't travel to Montreal for the draft. "They left me out in the cold," he said. Instead, he was utilized more in a PR role, and also in community relations and ticket sales.

"You might call him 'Ticket Promoter of the Year,'" joked his wife, Colleen, when asked later about Gordie's role. "Gordie's not there to make decisions (about players). Pleau makes all the decisions. When *they* pay you, *they* decide what they think you're best at."

As for the third future Hall of Famer, Hull became a free agent on July 1, and while he expressed an interest in returning to the Whalers for at least one more season, the franchise didn't sound all that interested in having the Golden Jet back at his asking price.

"Bobby would like to play, and we would like him to play for us," Kelley told reporters that summer, while describing the conversations with Hull as "pleasant." "But it is a question of whether it is financially worth his while to play for us," he added.

Later that summer, Hull sounded like someone resigned to retirement. "I was ready to play when I talked to Hartford," he told the Associated Press. "But since then my desire has lessened. They only have so much money to spend."

"I appreciate what Bobby Hull has been to the game of hockey," Kelley said. "He has been great for the game. I just have to keep everything consistent with other players, period."

Three things likely complicated Hull's situation: First, he was going through a divorce, one that would eventually cost him $600,000 and would force him to move back home with his parents. Second, Hull's girlfriend had been critically injured in an auto accident shortly before the end of the season, throwing his personal life into chaos. And third, under the terms of his deal, if a team signed him, it would have to send compensation to Winnipeg. That season with the Whalers was his last in professional hockey.

DESPITE THE DEPARTURES OF THE FAVORED VETERANS HOWE and Hull, some sensed optimism around the team. The 1979–80 team had the highest point total of any of the WHA holdovers, and with some young talent, the hope was that they could continue to build on what would inevitably be recalled as a successful first year in the NHL.

But early on, it was clear the 1980–81 team wouldn't be able to sustain that momentum into a new season. Three days before the start of training camp, Stoughton—who had been playing under a four-year deal he signed as a member of the Cincinnati Stingers in the WHA—said he wouldn't report because of a contract dispute. He alleged the team failed to offer him a contract by July 1, which under the bylaws of the CBA, would make him a free agent entitled to $10,000 in damages. Meanwhile, the team argued that Stoughton was tied to them through an option clause.

It was all part of a bitter summer between the team and the high-scoring forward, who also said the Whalers sent out a letter to the rest of the teams warning them to not sign Stoughton, as he was not, as he claimed, a free agent.

The dispute landed him and the team in court before coming to rest on the desk of NHL commissioner John Ziegler. The two sides eventually agreed on a new four-year deal with Stoughton on October 29, but the damage had been done.

Stoughton's absence wasn't the only sideshow in training camp. The team's first-round pick, defenseman Fred Arthur, struggled out of the gate. A victim of unrealistic expectations, the teenager ended up playing only three games that year.

Despite the personnel losses—Hull, Gordie Howe, and goaltender Al Smith—and the missing Stoughton, the 1980–81 season started respectably enough, with the Whalers having a .500 record through the first fourteen games. Despite a nine-game winless skid, capped by a dismal 5–0 loss to the Islanders on November 20, they were still hanging around the upper reaches of the still-developing playoff picture.

The most eventful regular-season game of the year was a December 27 clash in Hartford against those same Islanders. Things started on a surreal note when, before the game, a water main broke in the building, forcing both teams to dress by handheld flashlight.

When things got underway, the Whalers rallied from a 3–0 deficit to take a 5–3 lead, a charge that electrified the Civic Center crowd. On the heels of two straight wins coming into the contest against New York, a win over the Islanders could provide a boost for a team looking to create some consistency.

But the third period saw a near-tragedy take place. Defending a breakaway, Mark Howe pivoted toward the net while facing a 3-on-2. After some incidental contact, he slid into the goal, where he was impaled on the sheet metal in the center of the net. Howe recalled the harrowing incident in his book.

"'The net went into my ass!' I yelled at trainer Joe Altott, the first to reach me. 'Cut off my pants. Cut off my pants!'

"I was certain I had punctured my intestines and was bleeding to death. When I looked up and saw that Fotiu's eyeballs were as big as bowling balls it scared the hell out of me—and my teammates too. Rogers, on whose arm [trainer] Altott had arrived, remembers seeing a pool of 'black blood' beneath me. They stuffed my wide-open wound with towels, put me on a stretcher and brought me to the training room."

Howe was rushed into surgery and eventually recovered. But it was a horrifying injury, one that nearly paralyzed him.

"Had the flange come in perfectly straight, it would have gone into my spinal cord, probably putting me in a wheelchair for the rest of my days," Howe wrote. "The sphincter muscle was only slightly torn, saving me a life sentence with a colostomy bag. My hamstring, which could've been severed, was missed completely, too, and my rectum only scraped."

The incident led to a lawsuit and increased the league's safety measures for the area in and around the goal. "In an era when players would drive the net with a little fear of being called for goaltender interference, the game became safer," Howe said.

Adding to the craziness of the night, a late noncall from referee Ron Harris caused the first sold-out crowd of the season to explode, littering the ice with debris—including a shoe, according to reports—and chanting, "Harris is a bum!" After the game, Kelley confronted Harris underneath the stands, and had to be restrained from going after him. Harris and linesmen Paul Flaherty and Kevin Collins had to be escorted out under police protection. "We were screwed by an official," Baldwin fumed after the game.

In the end, the Islanders rallied with a pair of late goals to tie the game. The deadlock left the Whalers with 34 points on the season and a respectable tenth place overall. But really, it was a tie that felt like a defeat for a few reasons: They lost one of their best players in Howe for an extended stretch, and they missed out on a statement win against the defending Stanley Cup champions. The fallout was tough to take, as they stumbled to a 2-11-4 stretch that eventually forced a change in coaching. Blackburn was out, and Larry Pleau was in.

"That year, the team was doing well until I got hurt and Mike Rogers got hurt," said Mark Howe. "I came back, but at that point, Larry Pleau and Rick (Ley) didn't like me and the way I was playing. I mean, *I* didn't like the way I was playing, so I could understand where they were coming from, at least then.

"Maybe they thought that would motivate me—get me going. But that wasn't the case. It just motivated me to do better so I could get the hell out of there."

In hindsight, Howe acknowledges the injury against the Islanders was the beginning of the end of his time with the Whalers. "I believe that to be so," he said. "I was really starting to improve, Mike Rogers and I. I could play thirty minutes a night, no problem. Things were going well—I was starting to become much more of a leader. For me, as far as I was concerned, things were really starting to come together. That's when things came crashing down.

"I tried to come back, but I was horrible. I had lost twenty-two pounds. I was weak in the noodle, but I was trying. But I really shouldn't have been out there. I was just nowhere near my capacity when it came to being ready to play, and it showed. . . . I felt bad."

By this point in his career, Mark had grown into being much more than the son of Gordie. He was an All-Star in his own right, and while he wasn't overly enthusiastic about the sudden move from left wing to defenseman, he made the switch and was in the process of becoming one of the best in the league at the position. He had carved out an impressive career of his own, earning the respect of fans and teammates as a dynamic sort who went hard all the time.

"There was just *something* about Mark," Rogers said. "You can go on and on about the skill level, the drive. He just had that will to be the best. And he just worked at it. A lot of times at practice, you're not feeling well, you don't want to be out there, so you go out and practice like that. Mark Howe never had a bad practice. He just went out and worked on things and just wanted to make himself one of the best players to play. I firmly believe he is right up there with the greatest defensemen to ever play the game."

The first move made in the hope of jump-starting the team after the stretch of dismal hockey following the injuries to Howe and Rogers came in January, when Ley's knee issues forced him to take a reduced role, one that saw him surrender the captaincy to Rogers. "Something has to be done," Ley, the last original Whaler, told reporters. "There's only one chance in 1,000 that I'll be back this year and it's only 50-50 that I'll ever be back. You can holler all you want in the dressing room, but you need someone on the ice to take charge."

"You've got to be realistic about coaching. You know it's a very short-lived job," said Blackburn about his firing. 'It's a lot easier to change a coach than twenty-two people. Anytime you're losing you've got to be concerned as a coach. It never comes as a surprise. I think the day you sign a contract as a coach you've got to realize it's going to end sometime.

"I don't think I have to make any apologies for the job I've done in Hartford. We came into the league last year and we did a fine job," he added.

Blackburn was popular with the players, but for some of the wrong reasons, at least according to a few of the players on the roster at the time. "Don Blackburn never made the transition from being a player to a coach and always wanted to be with the players on the road," wrote Lacroix in his autobiography. "There is an unwritten rule in hockey when you're on the road: The player and the coaches do not go in the same bar. If the players happen to be in a bar and the coach walks in, the coach will leave. Blackburn not only stayed; he had team meetings at the bar."

Eventually, Pleau completed a remarkably fast ascension, becoming GM and coach on April 1. It was shocking to many, given the fact that he had gone from assistant coach to GM and head coach in less than six months. But Baldwin sounded confident that Pleau could lead the Whalers into an exciting new era.

"Larry Pleau has come a long way in a short time, but having worked closely with him for the past two months, I see somebody that has all the qualities to move this franchise forward in a positive direction," Baldwin said. "This is the beginning of a new era for the Hartford Whalers. We have all learned from this year, and now is the time to take this knowledge and use it to our advantage."

At the time, Pleau was raring to go. But now, by his own admission, he was overmatched in that moment. "I went from being an assistant coach to head coach [quickly]. And ten games later, they asked me to be a GM *and* coach," he said. "I knew I always wanted to coach, but when I was coach and GM at the same time, I had no fucking clue—none. You know how you think, *Oh, when I'm coaching, I'll do it this way.* But everything I thought about coaching and player movement, it was all fucking wrong."

He had emerged from the rubble of the previous season, ascending from assistant coach to head coach/GM in the span of just thirty-nine days. If he had reached the surface any faster, he might have been checked for a case of the bends. But it was now his team.

Really, the team was never the same after that fateful December night against the Islanders. They were winless in eleven of twelve after his injury, with many of those losses coming in the final minutes. Maybe the most discouraging was a 6–6 tie with the Blues when St. Louis had a pair of power-play goals in the last eighty-eight seconds of regulation. When Howe did return, the horrific injury left him a shell of his old self. The Whalers won just eight regular-season games after January 1, an abysmal finish to a season that had started with real promise.

The team suffered at the box office as well; although the 1979–80 team could at least offer the chance to see future Hall of Famers in Hull, Keon, and Gordie and Mark Howe as part of an expansion team making a playoff push, there was no such pull in 1980–81. The novelty of the new building and the initial burst of excitement that came with that first season in the NHL had worn off. Now, the team appeared to be consumed by internal bickering—between the Howes and Ley, in addition to between others on the team—and an unstable situation in the front office and coaching staff.

The end of the 1980–81 season came on April 5, 1981, with a 5–4 loss to the Penguins. Hartford finished the season with a 21-41-18 mark, fourth place in the Norris Division, 4 points ahead of the Red Wings. It was the first time in franchise history—WHA or NHL—the Whalers had not made the playoffs.

"No players are untouchable," Pleau told the *Courant* shortly after the end of the season. "We are open to deals of every sort. We have to make changes. We didn't make the playoffs, and we finished 18th. When you do that, you have to make changes. I don't see why we can't even trade No. 1 draft picks if the deal will help us.

"We have to get good people and go with them."

That process would start with the draft and the franchise-defining decision that would shape the future of the team for the next decade.

6

Ronnie Franchise
1981-85

People were devoted to Ronnie because you could hook your wagon to him morally. You could have your kid idolize him. You could root for him and never be let down.
—Former Connecticut sportscaster Mike Adams, on Ron Francis

The kid is almost too good to be true. Losing Bobby Carpenter to the Washington Capitals may have been the best thing to happen to the Whalers in a long, long time.
—Terry Price, *Hartford Courant*, November 23, 1981

Every team needs *their guy*, whose mug is plastered on the front of the yearbook and the season-ticket brochure, who usually has the *C* on his sweater, and who stars in the commercials. He shows up on the posters, has the best-selling jersey in the pro shop, and lifts (God willing) everyone around him to another level come playoff time.

In the early days of the New England Whalers, that role fell to a variety of individuals. Ted Green and Ricky Ley were the closest to face-of-the-franchise status in the 1970s, and Larry Pleau had the benefit of being a local kid and playing professional hockey at a (relatively) high level in the NHL. They were all vital in the nascent days of the WHA for different reasons, but collectively, their presence was enough to help spark fan support at a time when the franchise desperately needed it.

When Gordie Howe first showed up, Mr. Hockey was knighted as the leader of the team, almost by default. You could make a serious argument that while Gordie didn't necessarily save hockey in Hartford, his mere presence gave the Whalers a certain legitimacy that didn't always exist across the WHA. Dave Keon was popular with knowledgeable fans and younger teammates. Later, Mike Rogers moved the needle—he was a consistent scorer and worthy of being named a team leader, cracking the 100-point barrier at a time when few of his teammates were able to consistently put the puck in the net.

But with Howe's retirement, the departure of Keon, and the eventual trade of Rogers to the Rangers, those sorts of familiar faces were few and far between. From 1980 through 1983, the Whalers had five different captains: Ley (who had the *C* on his sweater from 1975 to 1980), Rogers (1980–81), Keon (1981–82), Russ Anderson (1982–83), and Mark Johnson (1983–85).

All of them had their strong points: Ley was an original Whaler, a pugnacious, blue-collar defenseman who checked all the boxes: productive and willing to do the dirty work, he was a natural choice to be a leader. The high-scoring Rogers was the best player on the roster and one of the more well-liked guys in the dressing room, but when he was dealt, Keon seemed to be the best choice to replace him. A future Hall of Famer, the occasionally gruff veteran set the perfect example for the youngsters. As for Anderson, he was a tough defenseman who was nearing the tail end of his career but still engendered enough respect with his teammates to make him worthy of the *C*.

But Johnson may have filled the role best, at least from a recognizability perspective. Johnson, who was part of the 1980 U.S. Olympic Team, was a familiar face for even casual hockey fans. He was the lone Hartford representative at the NHL All-Star Game in 1984, a year when he finished with a career-high 35 goals and 52 assists. Overall, in three seasons with the Whalers, he had 85 goals and 118 assists. Although he wasn't an overly charismatic sort, his experience as a member of the "Miracle on Ice" team was enough, at least from a marketing standpoint, when the team needed household names.

Who could be considered the best captain changed with the arrival of Ron Francis. It's hard to overstate the role Francis played in the history of the Whalers. In short, he filled the team's desperate need for a brand ambassador who could also deliver on the ice as a scorer and in the dressing room as a leader.

"Ronnie was the ultimate first-class guy—he always said and did all the right things, helping teach you what it meant to be a professional," recalled Adam Burt, who was a teammate in the late 1980s. "One time, we were playing in Boston and staying at the Marriott Long Wharf. I was just a kid who hadn't been in the league too long. I went down to breakfast in a pair of crappy old sweatpants. He's down there first thing in the morning in a suit. He looked at me and said, 'Kid, get back up there and get changed.' It was all part of him teaching you how to do it right, both on and off the ice."

"I was *very* fortunate to be able to play with him," remembered Ray Neufeld, who played with Francis in Hartford for parts of five seasons. "He was truly a fantastic hockey player and even a better person. It would have been awesome to play my career with him, but hockey doesn't always work out that way. He was young when he first came to the Whalers but grew into being an excellent leader at a very young age and [could] really shoulder the leadership and responsibilities of the team.

"He led by example [and] was really one of the greats of the game—in my mind, he kept under the radar. I believe you needed to play with him to really appreciate how good he really was. I have nothing but fond memories of Ronnie—he earned and deserved everything he got out of the game. He was a great pro in all aspects of the game, on and off the ice."

Francis was all things for the franchise, a godsend for a team that needed to build an identity. A handsome, rugged, well-spoken centerman, he could meet with the Chamber of Commerce in the afternoon, score 3 goals to help beat the Islanders that evening, and be the first guy to talk to the media after the game. He was the *quintessential Whaler.* He would go on to hold every major record in franchise history, all while carving out a niche as a community leader who did hundreds of personal appearances in the ten years he was in Hartford.

The ironic thing? The team never wanted him in the first place.

IN THE DAYS BEFORE THE 1981 DRAFT, THE WHALERS WERE adrift. Gordie Howe was a year into retirement, the team was going into its third year in the NHL, and the young roster needed an identity. The Whalers were waiting on their next big star.

The way things had started to come together, it was clear that the Whalers, who had the fourth overall pick, would select Bobby Carpenter. The top American in the draft, he was on the cover of *Sports Illustrated,* heralded with the banner "The Can't Miss Kid." The three teams who were in front of the Whalers in the draft that year had their eyes elsewhere, so it seemed to be a natural fit. *A Massachusetts schoolboy star playing in New England?* It would be a dream, both on and off the ice. Drafting Carpenter would not only give Hartford its new centerpiece but also help boost Baldwin's chances to create a TV network focused solely on New England sports.

For his part, Francis was considered a highly touted prospect worth at least top-ten status. The son of a general foreman at a Sault Ste. Marie steel mill, he was no stranger to hard work. He was a high scorer with high character, a lot of the latter due to growing up with a brother, younger by two years, who was developmentally delayed and suffered from seizures—sometimes as many as twenty-five a day. Ron helped his parents care for his brother Ricky, occasionally accompanying them on late-night trips to the hospital.

All that being said, he wasn't Carpenter. And on the afternoon of the draft, the only thing worth mentioning was the fact that the Whalers had lost out on the Can't Miss Kid. A draft-day trade between Colorado and Washington allowed the Capitals to swoop in and take Carpenter third overall. Hartford's burgeoning fan base was crushed.

Pleau had a front-row seat for the circus. "So [Capitals GM Max McNab] comes up to me," recalled Pleau. "He says they're going to trade up. 'I know you guys want Carpenter,' he said. He showed me his list, and I basically told him, 'Look, you make your choice, and we'll take whoever is left.' So, he jumped ahead and took Carpenter.

"Carpenter's old man was sitting at our table, and all I heard when it went down was a huge *slam* down at his end of the table," Pleau added. "Turns out he got up and was all pissed off because he thought he was coming to New England.

"Turns out, we stayed put and got Ronnie Francis, one of the best fucking players *ever*. Carpenter's father got up from the able, stormed out of the Forum without talking with reporters, and was overheard saying, 'We won't be going to Washington.'"

McNab said he wasn't trying to undercut Hartford, only that the Caps had rated Carpenter and Dale Hawerchuk (the future Hall of Famer who went first overall to Winnipeg) "head-to-head," and they had been trying to find a way to land Carpenter for much of the last ten days. Washington was completely cognizant of Hartford's interest, and so the Caps kept their interest on the down low. They came to all his high school games but rarely tipped their hand by speaking with his coaches. Washington also followed him to the World Junior Championships in Munich, and the Caps were impressed after Carpenter was every bit as impressive as Hawerchuk.

"You do what you have to do," McNab shrugged. "There was no question we rated [Carpenter] the top player in the draft."

For what it's worth, even after Carpenter was drafted by Washington, there was no guarantee he'd end up in the NHL, as the Carpenter family weighed professional hockey against going to college. In the end, the Caps won out over Providence College, but the decision wasn't officially made until the end of that summer.

The disappointment in New England was palpable. Carpenter was supposed to be the guy to help usher in greatness in Hartford.

But the day after the draft, the *Courant*'s Terry Price penned a piece that gave some fans cause for optimism. Under the headline "2nd Choice Francis May Turn Out Best," Price wrote about a "relaxed and mature" eighteen-year-old who had all the tools necessary to succeed in the NHL. Former NHLer Terry Crisp—who coached Francis with the Greyhounds in Sault Ste. Marie—called Francis a "natural hockey player" who is "blessed with hockey sense."

"There are things you can't acquire through all the years of practice and play," Crisp told reporters who asked about the teenage Francis. "You have to be born with it. Francis is one of them. Another year and he'll be awesome."

"I was hoping the Whalers were going to pick me," said Francis, who was at the draft with his father. "I didn't plan on it, but when Carpenter went to Washington, I sort of thought I might go to Hartford. I'd heard they were interested, but I didn't count too heavily on it. I knew they wanted to take Carpenter.

"I'm just happy to be picked. I just met Gordie Howe at the Whalers' table. It's really a big day for me. I'm really enjoying it."

In the end, the top five in that year's draft went as follows: Hawerchuk (first to Winnipeg), Doug Smith (Los Angeles), Carpenter (Washington), Francis (Hartford), and Joe Cirella (Colorado). Hawerchuk went on to a Hall of Fame career as a high-scoring centerman, while Smith and Cirella also had long and successful NHL careers. Meanwhile, Carpenter went on to a steady and solid career in the NHL, playing eighteen years and finding glory with the Caps, Rangers, Kings, Bruins, and Devils. But Francis, the soft-spoken teenager from Ontario, served as the foundation for the best run in Whalers franchise history. "We think Ron Francis is going to be great," Whalers assistant GM John Cunniff said shortly after the pick was made.

The addition of Francis was just one of several moves Pleau made that offseason. He also drafted Paul MacDermid, who became an important complementary player. Pleau added highly regarded goaltender Greg Millen and dealt for veteran Rick MacLeish, who came by way of Philadelphia.

In the pre-internet era, draft weekend could be an adventure, both for the team and the prospect. The Whalers were no exception. MacDermid still recalls how he ended up with Hartford. "When I was drafted, I remember I went to school that day and was very excited to see if I was going to be even *drafted* or not," said MacDermid with a laugh. "Part of the way through the day, my landlady where I was staying to complete the school year called my school and left a message for me call her. By the time I called, she had gone back to school, as she was a primary school teacher.

"Then, I called my teammate Claude Loiselle's landlady, and *she* told me I had been drafted but couldn't remember who took me. I missed the call from Hartford but did finally get talking to Larry Pleau, the GM at the time. I wasn't familiar with the Whalers at all and had to look at an atlas to find out where Hartford was located. But it was all very exciting and something I'll never forget."

THE DRAFT WAS ONE WAY TO ACQUIRE TALENT, BUT TRADES were also part of the equation. And while the Whalers were able to add some intriguing pieces that offseason, those moves came at a price. They lost feisty Pat Boutette to the Penguins after an arbitrator ruled that they didn't give up enough initially for Millen. And just before the start of the season, Pleau dealt Rogers to the Rangers. Hartford's most prolific scorer since the team arrived in the NHL, he was coming off back-to-back 105-point seasons. In return, the Whalers got three prospects, including Doug Sulliman and Chris Kotsopoulos, a pair of talented youngsters who couldn't find a place in a New York system dominated by veterans.

Although one could argue that the previous deals were done with the goal of putting the best possible team on the ice as soon as possible, the Rogers deal was the clearest sign the franchise was operating with an eye toward the future. Pure and simple, the next couple of years would be rebuilding mode.

To his credit, Pleau took the slings and arrows that inevitably came with the decision to trade a high scorer and popular player for three prospects. "I know Mike Rogers is a popular player with the fans, but there is no other way to put it," Pleau told reporters after the deal was done. "My job is to develop a hockey team for three or four years from now. There are certain players on a team you can move. Rogers is one who had value. We may never replace the 105 points by him, but we can do other things to improve our club for the future. The trade is in keeping with our philosophy of putting a young, competitive team on the ice."

"Larry did get a bad rap. But at the time, you think you're ready," said Kaiton. "But Larry's draft in 1982 netted Dineen, Ray Ferraro, Ulf Samuelsson, and Paul Lawless. In 1981, there was Ron and MacDermid. All those guys were drafted before Emile Francis came in."

The 1981–82 team gathered for training camp that September at the Bolton Ice Palace. Sixty-eight players—rookies, veterans, and free agents—were all vying for a spot on the roster. Little was expected from the team that year, as the Whalers were coming off a 21-41-18 mark. (Only three teams in the league finished behind them.) It was their first nonplayoff year in franchise history. They were guided by the thirty-four-year-old Pleau, who had a grand total of twenty games of head-coaching experience at the NHL level. Although they had plenty of fresh faces, they had lost Ley to retirement and the popular Boutette in a trade. And they had relocated to the Adams Division, with the Bruins, Nordiques, and Canadiens. It was a grouping that would quickly distinguish itself as one of the most physical in hockey.

At least publicly, Pleau wasn't deterred when it came to his hopes for the season. "Our goal is to make the playoffs," Pleau said before the puck dropped to start the 1981–82 season. "We're in a tough division, but I believe it will make us better in the long run. We will be a better hockey club quicker."

Francis's future was a heated topic of debate—specifically, whether he should start the year in the NHL. Baldwin said yes; Pleau said no. "We had a lot of pressure on us to keep him with the big club, but we also wanted to do things right and give him the proper time to develop," Pleau recalled. "We brought him in for training camp and took it down to the end, and we just didn't think he was ready, so we sent him home to Sault Ste. Marie."

This did not go over well with ownership. Baldwin and Pleau spent hours arguing as to where Francis should be playing. "Larry, we finally get something to hang our hats on, and you're going to send him down?" exclaimed Baldwin. "That is ridiculous. We need to keep him here!"

"Well, I'm the GM," Pleau responded.

"Well, you're the GM, but *that can change* too," Baldwin retorted.

"We have tickets to sell and sponsorships to sell, and when we finally get a young player people can hang their hat on, you're going to send him back? That makes no sense."

"Larry's philosophy was like the old Montreal Canadiens in that he didn't want to give young players too much too soon," recalled Kaiton. "Bill Dineen, the chief scout, was always pleading with Larry: 'He's ready to go right now. Please.' Bill was saying, 'Just give him eight or nine games and then send him back if he can't play.' But Larry stuck to his guns."

A November trip to see Francis play was enough to change Pleau's mind. "We were playing in Buffalo and had a night off before the game, so I went across to visit him and watch him play," Pleau said. "He was great—he did one of those moves where he switched hands on his stick. He was just tremendous. I went down after the game and told him, 'Look, we had some injuries. I can take you back across and play.'

"We were just going to keep him for a few games, but he ended up [staying] around," Pleau said. "A little later, after we had him for a while, his mother called me up and said, 'Larry, I want to tell you something—when you sent Ronnie back, it was tough, but he wasn't ready. But he's ready now.'

"My biggest regret was that because I waited to call him up, I probably cost him the Rookie of the Year award."

Regardless of the ongoing feud between Pleau and Baldwin when it came to his future, Francis never complained when he was returned to his junior team in Sault Ste. Marie. After his call-up, he saw his first NHL action on November 14, 1981, at home against the Caps. Wearing number 4—the number most recently worn by former first-round pick Fred Arthur and franchise favorite Andre Lacroix—he centered the second line, with Don Nachbaur on the left wing and Don Gillen on the right. Later in the game, he was in the middle of a line combination that featured Garry Howatt and Sulliman. He didn't appear on the scoresheet his first night in the NHL, but in three of the next seven games, he had at least 3 points, with two of those contests coming against the Maple Leafs.

"Ronnie was Ronnie—he went back with a good attitude and then came back in November . . . and the rest is history," said Kaiton.

"It's hard to judge how I'm doing," Francis told the *Courant* in late November of his rookie year. "I'm just doing what got me here. I'm just trying to give it my best effort. I know I'm going to make a lot of mistakes. The coach told me just to play my style. Hopefully, when I make mistakes, I'll realize what I did and not make them again. It's going to be a game-by-game thing. I'll learn more every game I'm involved in."

But regardless of his lofty draft status, as a rookie, Francis was treated like any first-year player. He was tested on and off the ice—veterans wanted to see if the highly touted teenager could stand up to life in the NHL. That meant getting physical from time to time.

"Right from that first training camp when he showed up, you knew he was special," said Kaiton. "You knew something special was going to happen with him. He was so mature and so heady and so smart. But he also had to be tough. I remember Joe Reekie being rough with Ronnie at training camp at a scrimmage one day. It was probably the only fight that Ronnie ever had, but he was going to be tested by the veterans."

That November he was tied to the trainer's table, blindfolded, and given a full-body shave—*without shaving cream*. But once he arrived in mid-November, it was clear he was there to stay for several reasons, not the least of which was Baldwin's need for a recognizable, marketable face for the team. When you can't sell tickets based on the present, you shape a vision of the future. And Francis in a Hartford uniform was a sellable commodity.

In their attempts to bring Francis along slowly, Pleau and the Whalers were likely hoping their first-round pick wouldn't suffer the same fate as Ray Allison and Arthur, two of Hartford's most recent top picks who—despite sizable buildup—were underwhelming when they reached the NHL.

"If a No. 1 draft pick makes the club, it puts a lot of pressure on him right off the bat," Francis told reporters who asked about his preseason stretch in juniors. "When I went back, I started to work on the things I learned in camp. I had a lot more confidence when I got back.

"I was ready physically to play, but I wasn't mentally ready. There were so many things happening. I was a little in awe. Being sent down put everything into proper perspective. When I came back, I was ready physically and mentally."

The wins came here and there over the course of the 1981–82 season for Hartford—like four in six games late in November and into December, and a nine-game unbeaten string in late January and early February. But for the most part, it was the rebuilding year that many had anticipated. Three wins in their first twenty games put them in the basement of the Adams Division right out of the gate, where they remained all season long.

It was a long, cold, lonely winter for Pleau and his team, who were all learning together. Although there were some smart and heady veterans, including Keon, who would score 8 goals in his last season in professional hockey, for the most part, it was a younger team: Francis, MacDermid, Stoughton, Millen, Sulliman, Douglas, and Marty and Mark Howe were all twenty-eight or younger. (The 1981–82 Whalers had three future Hall of Famers on the roster in Francis, Keon, and Mark Howe.) Pleau added Pierre Larouche via a trade with Montreal for some offensive punch, and the twenty-six-year-old center added 25 goals that season.

The painful lessons they'd learn during the 1981–82 season would pay off down the road, but it was awfully tough to go out there every night, take a beating, and, later, remind reporters that they weren't necessarily playing to win the Cup that year but to be competitive a year or two down the road. In the end, the 1981–82 Whalers finished fifth with a 21-41-18 record for the second consecutive season and were at or near the bottom of the league in most major categories, including goals for (264, twentieth out of twenty-one teams) and goals against (351, sixteenth).

At the same time, the youngsters got a baptism by fire when it came to life in the National Hockey League. "This was a tremendous learning experience for us," Pleau told reporters shortly after the season wrapped up with a 7–2 loss to the Bruins on April 4, 1982. "That's the biggest thing about this year. We made a lot of changes. We got younger, and we found out a lot about the players we have."

It didn't escape notice that the Whalers' top minor-league club in Binghamton won the AHL's Southern Division title with a 46-28-6 record and advanced all the way to the Calder Cup final.

But with the big club, while there was a lot of young talent on the roster, Francis remained the best hope, the promise of a brighter future. In his first year in the league, he ended with 25 goals and 43 assists. He was tenth in Rookie of the Year voting, finishing behind . . . *Bobby Carpenter*, who was tied for eighth place. That summer, Francis threw himself into charity work and became one of the most popular players on the roster, all as a teenager.

"I brought him to school once for show and tell. I was like ten or eleven, and he was just a rookie. But it was amazing," recalled Howard Baldwin Jr. "He was like the big brother you loved to have. The other players, they'd stuff me in the dryer, and he'd pull me out. He always looked out for me."

Francis shunned the usual trappings that went along with being a star. There was no entourage, no special requests when he showed up at charity events. The roots of that approach went back to his youth.

"I think there were so many people that influence you over your career—it really started when my dad started working in steel plant," he said. "My younger brother had a learning disability and seizures. My mom was trying to raise two boys and make sure I get to the rink on time *and* take care of my brother. You just kind of see your family, and you grow up that way. The values they instilled in me, including the fact that you treat people with respect, that's stuff that stays with you."

That low-key approach was frequently on display. One afternoon, Francis and Mike Adams were at a golf event, and Adams thought it'd be a kick if he put the hockey star on the phone with his son, a huge fan. The two found a payphone, and Adams dialed up his young son.

"I have someone here who wants to talk to you," Adams told his young son before handing the phone to Francis.

"Hey there! Who's your favorite hockey player?" the game Francis asked Adams's son.

The young man waited a beat.

"Wayne Gretzky?" he replied.

"Uhh . . . no," replied Francis before quickly recovering. "How about your *second*-favorite hockey player?"

"Ron Francis!"

Francis and a handful of young players worth building around were in place, and that group took its collective lumps in 1981. The upshot? A subpar year yielded some excellent draft positioning, and they took advantage to add more foundational elements and create depth at key positions.

In the end, the 1982 NHL Draft didn't feature the above-the-marquee talent like Francis, but Pleau and the Whalers crushed it, coming away with four important parts of their future. With the fourteenth overall selection, they landed Paul Lawless, a winger with an eye for the net. They followed that with the best back-to-back-to-back draft selections in franchise history: first, in the third round, they landed Kevin Dineen, a gritty forward who was the son of Whalers chief scout (and former head coach) Bill Dineen, at number fifty-six—much to the younger Dineen's consternation.

"When it was my draft year and I was getting ready to play for the Canadian Olympic team, I went home for the summer," he recalled. "My brother Peter, he's pretty good at busting my balls. My dad was a scout for the Whalers. Pete comes in and says, 'Hey, guess what? Dad drafted you!'

"I was a little pissed; I mean, *holy jeez*, the one team I didn't want to go to because I knew everyone was going to think there was some nepotism involved. But my dad came in and talked to me and said I was the best choice in that spot.

"At that level, your play speaks for itself. I mean, if you were looking at the optics of it, I'd understand. But if you were looking to do something like that, it would usually happen in the later rounds. I mean, you wouldn't burn a third-round pick by just doing someone a favor. So I don't really think it was ever an issue."

In the fourth round (sixty-seventh overall), the Whalers drafted Swedish defenseman Ulf Samuelsson, an agitator who wasn't afraid to muck it up with anyone. And in the fifth round at number eighty-eight, they added undersized speed merchant Ray Ferraro.

"I hadn't considered Hartford a possibility and was surprised," said Ferraro, who would become one of the more popular players in the history of the franchise because of his quick smile and scrappy play. "Also, I was more concerned at the time that I went in the fifth round, which was a couple rounds lower than I hoped. But all in all, initially, I wasn't overwhelmed by the whole thing."

Of course, like the 1981 draft class, it would take time for the investment of the 1982 group to pay dividends. Those players were still far from making an impact. In the short term, the fan base saw the core being stripped away. That soon included Mark Howe, who had been at odds with Pleau for a long time and was ready for his time in Hartford to come to an end. When Howe sat down with the coach/GM, he presented Pleau with a list of four potential trade partners: Rangers, Islanders, Flyers, and Bruins. Howe knew the idea of trading him to Boston was pretty much a nonstarter—Howe said Sinden had told him Hartford wanted a pair of first-round picks in return—but he figured he'd give it a shot anyway.

"I remember when I talked to Harry when I was trying to get traded," Howe later recalled. "He would always say, 'Look, there's no way they're going to trade you to me.' I know that now. I've been working in the front office, where deals are made. In those sorts of situations, unless a team blows you out of the water, you're not going to make that sort of trade, especially in your own division."

That left the Rangers, Islanders, and Flyers, with Philadelphia ultimately yielding the best package. The deal, on its face, looked pretty good for Hartford: In Howe, they were giving up a player who had seen a significant drop-off in production following his scary injury in 1982. In return, they were landing Kenny Linseman, forward Greg Adams, and two draft picks. At twenty-three, Linseman—a legendary agitator—was coming off his best season with career highs of 24 goals, 68 assists, 92 points, and 275 penalty minutes.

Of course, the deal had been in the works for several weeks, but when it was announced on August 20, 1982, it still stirred emotions with the Hartford fan base—the Howes had become Connecticut's first family of hockey. With Gordie's retirement, and now the trade of Mark and departure of Marty (who would spend the 1982–83 season with the Bruins before returning to Hartford for two more years down the road), for the moment, it left Hartford bereft of Howes.

"I had a couple of talks at the end of the season with Larry [Pleau], and then, when Larry Kish got hired, I was really looking forward to playing for Larry Kish. I think it's a good change the Whalers have made [hiring Kish]," Mark told WFSB's Khambrel Marshal. "They called me in today, just like any other day, and they just kind of dropped one on me. They gave me the phone number to the Flyers and [told me] the deal had been made, and said if I did want to go, I could go, and if I didn't want to go, I could stay here. I told them that if they did trade me, I'd like to go to a winning team or a contending team, and if they did want to get rid of me, I'm not going to hold them to that no [trade clause]. I think it's a deal that's going to benefit hopefully both hockey teams. The Whalers have been very good to me, and the fans have been very good to me. I think it's a move where it's just time that something had to be done.

"I didn't have a great year on the ice, and I think I got in a lot of trouble here with management a little bit. Things got a little hot and heavy. But like I said, things had cleared up. But when I talked to Larry today, he said he thinks [the deal] is in the best interest of Mark Howe and in the best interest of the Philadelphia Flyers and the Hartford Whalers. . . . I'm just going to try and forget about everything here and look forward to, you know, my next five years in Philadelphia."

The Whalers then dealt Linseman to the Oilers with Don Nachbaur for Risto Siltanen and Brent Loney. While Siltanen had a fine NHL career, the double gut-punch of Howe finding his mojo in Philly and eventually becoming a Hall of Fame defenseman and Linseman going on to win a Stanley Cup in Edmonton was a tough twofer for Hartford fans to have to absorb.

On the ice, Hartford bottomed out during the 1982–83 season with a record of 19-54-7 (45 points), twentieth out of the twenty-one teams in the league. The misery was heightened by the team having to endure the year wearing Cooperalls—full-length pants that made hockey players the on-ice equivalent of baseball players in shorts. They were originally thought to be a nod to player safety and protection, but the pads under the Cooperalls were held snugly to the body and unable to shift out of place, leaving the player exposed to injuries, to his tailbone in particular. But the long pants, worn that year by the Whalers and Flyers, were later outlawed by the league, not because of crimes against sports fashion but because the players wearing them were basically sliding around on a windbreaker-type material that caused them to glide into the boards at a higher speed. *So long, Cooperalls.* The long pants were a fitting postscript to a less-than-memorable stretch for the franchise.

IF THE DECISION TO DRAFT RON FRANCIS WAS THE FIRST STEP in the right direction for the Whalers and the 1982 NHL Draft was second, the third came on May 2, 1983, when Baldwin pulled the trigger on the addition of the legendary Emile Francis as Hartford's new GM.

In his words, Baldwin had been seeking a "czar" to run the organization, and Francis was the only serious candidate throughout the process. Nicknamed "the Cat," he was old-time hockey, through and through. Raised in the game, he spent nearly twenty years as a goaltender for several teams, including the Blackhawks and Rangers. (His innovations led to equipment changes for netminders, including an expanded glove.) Always hailed for his leadership skills as a player, he quickly transitioned into a bench role, becoming an assistant GM with the Rangers in 1962 and eventually both general manager and head coach in 1965. Francis would remain behind the bench with the Rangers for most of the next ten years (except for brief moves to a solely front office position in 1968 and 1973), making the playoffs on a regular basis and leading his team to a loss in the 1972 Stanley Cup Finals. After he was let go by the Rangers in early 1976, he held several different jobs—coach, GM, executive VP—with the Blues until 1983, providing stability for a franchise that was going through a rocky stretch.

Although he never won a Stanley Cup while working in a coaching or executive role, he did take two wobbly franchises and set them on a path to success, making them perennial playoff teams. Could he do the same thing in Hartford? Baldwin certainly sounded optimistic. "Experience is something this organization has lacked, and it is something that Emile Francis brings us," the owner said after the announcement was made. "I can state with total conviction that we've added a man with the highest credentials."

"Our commitment to hiring the best possible candidate is fulfilled with this appointment," Conrad added when asked about Francis. "He has great insight into hockey and is as respected as anyone in the game. I now believe the Whalers have a management team which is among the best in the NHL."

"I live by the three D's: depth, desire and determination," Francis said when he was introduced at a press conference at the Parkview Hilton in Hartford. "I think there's a good nucleus here, and that if we add to our depth, we'll be competitive.

"The most important thing though, is to get things done *now*. Every one of us is going to be put on notice, and that's the way it should be."

Francis praised the hard work and effort put in by those who came before him, but at the same time, he heralded a new era for Hartford hockey. "What happened here last year can happen to anyone," Francis told reporters after the deal was made official, referencing the 54 losses the team suffered in 1982–83. "I've come here with an open mind. Loyalty and dedication are important. It's up to the people if they want to stay."

Just over two months later, on July 7, Francis hired Jack Evans to be the Whalers' new head coach. Francis and Evans had a longstanding relationship—they were teammates with the New Haven Ramblers in 1949—and although other younger, fresher faces were available, the two seemed to form a complementary pairing. A taciturn man not given to hyperbole, Evans was as low-key as they come. But that didn't stop him from getting off a memorable zinger in his introductory press conference. Evans recounted a joke he heard making the rounds among losing teams the previous season: "We were so bad Hartford could have beaten us." *Ouch.*

"We have to get some respect in the league," he added.

"I would like to be able to sit here and say I have a magic wand to turn things around in Hartford, but I don't," said Evans. "It will take a lot of hard work."

"I wanted a coach who had experience with younger players," Francis said, "a strong fundamentals coach and a good teacher, because we have young players, and we will have more.

"This is a new season," Francis added. "It's a whole new team and we're not going to be on the bottom. It's up to us to climb the ladder. We're not going out there to play any games just for fun."

Upon hearing Hartford had hired Francis, an old nemesis said what many across the league were thinking. "I had Montreal, Quebec, and Buffalo to worry about," said Sinden, acknowledging the rest of the Adams Division. "Now, I have to worry about Hartford too."

That June, Francis started with his reclamation project. He began by drafting Sylvain Turgeon and the following month made a deal with Calgary to acquire defenseman Joel Quenneville. There was the return of old friend Marty Howe, as well as the addition of Mike Zuke, Mike Crombeen, Bob Crawford, and tough guy Torrie Robertson. In addition, he fired Ley as head coach in Binghamton, while that summer, Bill Dineen—a longtime employee who served as the chief scout the previous two seasons—left to coach the AHL's Adirondack Red Wings, and assistant coach Jacques Caron left the organization.

It wasn't completely coincidental that Francis went after several of his former players in St. Louis, including Zuke, Crombeen, and Crawford. "I don't know if he specifically thought of bringing in a bunch of us from St. Louis, but he knew what we could do," recalled Zuke, who was known as a skilled penalty-killer in St. Louis for five seasons before moving to Hartford. "And the other thing is that he was very loyal to the guys he knew, those guys who were with him when he was with the Blues. He brought in something like ten guys over a couple of years who were with him in St. Louis, guys like me and Crombeen, Mark Reeds, Mike Liut, and Dave Babych and plenty of others. He knew quality players, and he respected us and knew what we did when we were together in St. Louis and thought we could help Hartford."

"When I first came to Hartford in 1983, the Whalers were 1 point from being the worst team in the league," said Crawford. "My first year, we brought a whole new team in there with Emile and Jack, and they brought in players from all over—a lot of new players. Things turned around pretty quickly."

The St. Louis influence was also felt in the front office. In a feature story before the start of the 1983 season, the *Courant* named the "St. Louis Six" as the leaders of a new power structure in town, with Francis and Evans joined by new Hartford assistant coach Claude LaRose, who played for the Blues at the end of his fifteen-year career before becoming a St. Louis scout; new director of player personnel Steve Brklacich, who held a similar spot in St. Louis; and scout Leo Boivin and trainer Tom Woodcock, both of whom moved from the Blues to the Whalers.

While there was some sense that things would *start* to turn around, there was also the understanding that Francis and his team were starting from a low point. If you were an optimist, the feeling was that things could only get better from here. *Right?* In its annual preview, the *Courant* picked Hartford to finish last in the Adams Division, with Jerry Trecker writing, "Some subtle changes have been made by the new Emile Francis regime, but this is a club that still falls far short in the raw talent department. If Mike Rogers, Mark Howe, Pierre Larouche . . . oh why bother? Suffice to say that Hartford can be 20 points better than a year ago and still miss the playoffs. Let's at least hope that they *are* 20 points better."

That didn't quell the optimism from the coaching staff. "Let's put the real bullets in the gun and see what happens," Evans told reporters at the end of the 1983 preseason, a stretch that included a 2-4-2 record.

Things started optimistically enough, with an 8-7-1 record over the first fifteen games—the first time in Hartford history the Whalers were over .500 so deep into the regular season. But the good times didn't last, as they slipped to 13-20-3 after a stretch that included an embarrassing 9–3 home loss to the Kings. After the loss—which dropped them 9 points out of a playoff spot—a weary Evans allowed his frustration to seep through. "I'm going home and pour me a scotch," he sighed.

A 2-8-4 January was the unquestioned low point—at that point, there might not have been enough scotch in the state of Connecticut to soothe Evans. But there was more roster maneuvering from Francis, and the younger players started to step to the fore and mix nicely with the veterans and other newcomers. It paid off with an impressive February, which saw them go 7-5-1—the first winning record over the course of a month for the team all season.

If there was any doubt that things were headed in the right direction, that was erased on February 12, 1984. That afternoon, the mighty Oilers came to the Civic Center—and were vaporized by Hartford, 11–0. The Whalers buried Edmonton with a second-period flurry, tallying 4 of their 6 power-play goals in a span of 4:06 when ex-Hartford tough guy Kevin McClelland was serving a five-minute major for knocking out Sylvain Turgeon with an elbow. In the process, they knocked all-world netminder Grant Fuhr from the game.

"Holy crap," remembered longtime fan Jeff Bamberger, who recalled the chant of "Double chili, Double chili" as the goal-count approached double digits. *Why?* "The Wendy's at the Civic Center gave you a free bowl of chili with your ticket stub from any game where they scored at least 5 goals," he said. "We didn't know if they would give two bowls. I never went to find out."

Chili aside, the game itself was one of the singular highlights of the Whalers' first five years in the NHL. "When people see that score, they're not going to believe it," Johnson told reporters after the game. "It wasn't 1–0 or 3–0 or 5–0, it was 11–0. That's scary."

"I think I'll go home and have a nice party," Millen said with a smile.

In the end, it was just one win, but it represented much more, and not just because Hartford had crushed the mighty Oilers. It was Hartford's fourth win in five games, and with more than a month left in the 1983–84 campaign, the victory equaled the win total of the previous year and 1 more point (46) than the team had in all of the 1982–83 season.

"I'm at a total loss to explain this, but I'm not surprised at the total reversal of form," Evans told the media after the game. "That often happens in sports after everything goes wrong. Today, everything went right."

The season ended with the Whalers going 5-5-1 over their final eleven games and included two more notable moves—the trade of Blaine

Stoughton to the Rangers for Scot Kleinendorst and the addition of free agent Dave Tippett.

Like the Mark Howe trade, the Stoughton move had been a long time coming—it was clear Francis wanted to move him and his sizable contract. Stoughton left town as the Whalers' all-time leading scorer.

"I really wasn't surprised at all—the stuff I'd been hearing for the last two or three weeks. It's no big shock to me. But when I found out it was the Rangers, I was pretty excited," he told WFSB's Dave Smith. "There were three or four places I didn't want to go and three or four places I'd like to, and this is one of the teams I'd like to go to. It's a lot better than going to Quebec or Winnipeg or someplace like that. Mr. Francis definitely did me a favor. I have no hard feelings—I'm leaving here with my head up high. I played here for five years and did everything that was expected of me. I have no bitter feelings at all. I just hate to leave all the people you've met over the five years out of hockey who you probably won't run into anymore."

Though it was tough to stomach the loss of Stoughton, the addition of a player like Kleinendorst represented a new direction for the franchise. He wasn't a high-wattage scorer like Stoughton but a cost-effective scrapper who would emerge as a glue guy in the locker room. Tippett was the same sort of player—signed immediately after the conclusion of the 1984 Olympics, he seemed to quickly find his form with the Whalers with 4 goals and 6 points in the last seventeen games of the 1983–84 season.

Tippett had carved out a reputation as a wildly underappreciated left winger who was one of the tougher players in the league. "Tippett was a Saskatchewan badass," said Adams, who covered the team in the mid-1980s. "One day at practice, Tiger Williams just unloads a slap shot, point-blank, from like fifteen feet. Tippett was skating through the zone at the time, and the puck just went ripping across his face and nose. I mean, you could just hear a *splat* from Tippett's face. He went down, and his face was just gushing blood."

"I guess he's not going to play tonight?" Adams asked Ron Francis.

"I bet my house he plays," Francis replied.

"Are you kidding? There's no way he plays."

"He'll play."

That night, Tippett was on the ice, with a bruised and battered face and gauze stuffed up his nose. "Like I said, a badass," recalled Adams with a smile.

"That's pretty accurate," said Dineen when informed of Adams' description of Tippett. "He didn't have the smoothest upbringing. I remember him telling me a story about how he hitchhiked his way across Canada when he was fifteen. He just went to the side of the road and stuck his thumb out. He wanted to see the country. He slept in hostels and by the side of the road. He's definitely a cool guy with a lot of great stories. When he lived in Connecticut, he would renovate and build houses and sell them. He had me over a few times swinging a sledgehammer."

"Oh, I did a few things like that in my younger days before I got to the NHL," Tippett said when asked about the hitchhiking story. "I mean, doesn't everybody have stories like that about their younger days?"

Playing through pain was a way of life for Tippett. He chuckles now at being called a Saskatchewan badass—for him, it was just about making sure he stayed on the ice. "I was an undrafted free agent, and you're coming in trying to land a spot, you're not going to tell anyone if you get hurt. I didn't want to tell anyone, ever," he said. "You had to compete for ice time. You had to compete for a job. But once I got into the league, it was a badge of honor. You had to make sure you showed up and played hard every day for your teammates. Back then, the game was different. It was a personal thing for me—I didn't want to leave the lineup.

"The other side of it? I always said that adrenaline was the best pain killer out there."

Tippett wasn't the only member of Canada's 1984 Olympic Team to find his way to Hartford that season.

ADAM BURT HAS A REALLY SIMPLE WAY OF DESCRIBING KEVIN
Dineen. "He was a *man's man*," Burt said of his Hartford teammate. "You
respected so much about him. He just carried himself differently—his
work ethic, his grind, his desire to win, it was intoxicating. It spread
amongst the team."

Though not the face of the franchise, he quite often personified the
heart and soul, the DNA, of the team. While the casual fan would pur-
chase the number 10 jersey to salute Francis, the hardcore fans would
point to Dineen—number 11—as their player of choice. Francis was the
gentleman, eventually a three-time Lady Byng Award winner who, for
his career, never had a season with 90-plus penalty minutes in a year.
He was on the front of the program, the one who would drive ticket
sales and wear the *C* with honor.

In contrast, Dineen was the grinder who was always willing to do
the dirty work, who never shied away from a scrap, and who served
as a reminder that size didn't matter when it came to hockey. In the
end, it was all about heart. He would become one of only six players
in NHL history to finish with more than 350 goals and 2,000 penalty
minutes. "He's got more guts than a slaughterhouse," the GM said of the
feisty forward who never got the acclaim of Francis but still managed
to propel the team through the biggest moments.

After an impressive career in junior hockey, it didn't take him long to
reach the NHL. Dineen was taken in the third round of the 1982 draft
by the Whalers after a freshman year at the University of Denver in
which he finished with 10 goals and 20 assists in twenty-seven games.
He spent one more year in Denver and then a season with the Canadian
National Team—which finished in fourth place and where he played
with Tippett—before joining the Whalers in 1984. After a brief stopover
in Binghamton, he was called up to the big club, making his NHL debut
against the Canadiens on December 3, 1984, at the age of twenty-one.

Even before he was signed by Hartford, he had New England roots—
his father, Bill, was the coach of the Whalers in their final WHA year,
1978–79, and would go on to scout for the team.

"I drank a lot of beer with him," Adams, a former sportscaster for WFSB in Hartford from 1985 to 1991, said of Dineen. "He came from a big family—four brothers and one sister. His brothers played hockey. I did a feature on him once—I asked him who the toughest member of his family was.

"'My mother,' he said.

"'What do you mean?'

"'She was the one who had to break up all the fights.'"

"That's pretty accurate," Dineen said with a laugh years later. "I think there are always fights and bickering between brothers, but you get into your teenage years, and guys get bigger and stronger. I think the last really good battle my brother Gord and I had—he was eleven months older than me—we were teenagers. We had a pretty good battle, and we both realized, with my mom trying to break it up, we were big and strong and probably shouldn't be rolling around like that. That was the last of our real battles."

Dineen joined a line that include Mike Zuke and Tippett. Evans said the trio was "like a bunch of mosquitos. They're all over you." They were dubbed "the Mosquito Line."

"Buzz, buzz," Dineen gleefully chortled when informed of Evans's quote.

Almost instantly, Dineen won over the fans. His first NHL goal came in a 4–3 win over the Canadiens, and a few days later, he celebrated in the locker room by handing out cigars. He added 2 more goals the following game, a 6–5 win over the Bruins, and then won over the hearts and minds of Hartford fans when he stuck up for the city. "Hartford is kind of like the little city down the road from Boston," he told reporters. "It's like the complex Canada has about the U.S. That's what makes it nice to kind of stick it to Boston.

"I just hope Sylvain Cote [who got his first NHL goal in the first period in the win over the Bruins] passes out as good cigars as I did," chortled Dineen.

This was the type of guy Whalers fans had been looking for: a shit-talking buzz saw who wasn't afraid to go toe-to-toe with the

Bruins. He finished his rookie year with 25 goals and 16 assists in fifty-seven games, and even though his games played were limited because of his delayed call-up, he *still* finished third on the team in penalty minutes.

"Kevin will do whatever it takes to make it in the National Hockey League. Fight, hit a guy, make a play, score a goal," Pleau said shortly after Dineen got the call to Hartford. "What more can you say about that kind of person?"

The arrival of Dineen was one of two seismic personnel events that season. The other came when Emile Francis pulled off one of the biggest heists of his time in Hartford, dealing Mark Johnson and Greg Millen to the Blues for goaltender Mike Liut and future considerations.

At the time, the trade was roundly criticized. Johnson was a popular player and former member of the 1980 U.S. Olympic team, and Millen was Hartford's starting netminder and one of the more notable members of the roster. The *Hartford Courant* ran a reader poll that posed the question "Do you agree or disagree with the trade?" The conclusion was that 17 percent agreed with the deal, while 83 percent gave it a thumbs-down. But Francis defended his decision.

"He is one of the premier goaltenders in the league," Francis told the media when the deal went down. "I know what he is capable of—Mike played for me in St. Louis for several years. He was there when we went through a rebuilding stage and was a big reason for our success. You don't often get a chance to trade for a goaltender of Liut's caliber. When you can, they don't come cheap. To trade Millen, it would have to be for someone like Liut."

The Whalers quickly recognized Liut's abilities as a leader. Hartford acquired him in February 1985, and less than a month later, after a bitter 7–6 overtime loss to Vancouver in which Hartford coughed up a 2-goal lead with less than two minutes in regulation and then lost in the extra session, Liut unloaded, scalding his younger teammates behind closed doors. According to Jeff Jacobs of the *Hartford Courant*, Liut overturned a tray of Gatorade, snapped the blackboard in half with two swings of Dineen's stick, and kept screaming, "You cannot survive in this cesspool!"

"I told them I was not content to play out my remaining years on a team that gave away points," Liut told reporters. "If we were, I was going to be one ugly SOB to be around. There were about eight guys with us then playing their first full season. I said, 'I'm only going to be here two, maybe three more years. You guys are going to be here six, seven, eight years. That's a long time to live in your own mess.'"

"He lost it *pretty good*," Dineen later recalled.

"He hadn't been there very long," Tippett said. "When we lost 7–6, he came in, and it was like an explosion. I remember him throwing a skate and it sticking in the wall.

"He had a great passion for winning. He was a friendly guy, but he wasn't necessarily there to make friends, but to win. Him coming to town, that was a big turning point for our group."

To Tippett's point, the acquisition of Liut, in many ways, represented a major culture change for the Whalers. No disrespect intended to Millen, but Liut was a well-established vet who had cachet around the league. A former WHA star (he spent two seasons with Cincinnati but signed with the Blues—who held his NHL rights—after the merger), he finished second to Wayne Gretzky in MVP voting for the 1980–81 season, when he went 33-14-13, and became the centerpiece of the Blues.

Of course, he was an admittedly *expensive* centerpiece, one of the reasons why he was likely available in trade. The Blues were known to be conscious of the bottom line, and the decision to move the former All-Star could be traced back to money. It was not lost on Liut—who was making a reported $900,000 at the time (tops on the team)—that he was dealt for two players who had a combined salary less than the his. But the Blues' financial prudence was the Whalers' gain.

"At the time of the trade, [the Blues were] back in first place in our division and rising, so the trade late in the season to a last-place team was disappointing because I was back where I was my first year in St. Louis. It would be the only year that I missed the playoffs," said Liut.

"On the other hand, I had played for Mr. Francis in St. Louis, so I knew what he expected from me. There was a job to do, and it was clear that Hartford had a dozen very good young players. We had a very good run to finish, and it carried over to the '85–'86 season."

In the end, a three-pronged approach would yield positive returns: The trades of marquee players like Stoughton and Rogers for young talent started the changes. The arrival of Francis in the 1981 draft, in addition to the Lawless-Dineen-Turgeon-Ferraro quartet of 1982, Turgeon and David Jensen in '83, and Dana Murzyn and Kay Whitmore in '85, set the stage for the rise of the franchise. And the pickup of veterans like Liut solidified the core of a team on the rise. The Whalers' combined win-loss record from 1981–1982 through the 1984–85 season was a gruesome 98-178-44. But in that same span, the newcomers all arrived in Hartford. The draft work, personnel maneuvering, and front-office additions that were made over the course of those four mostly forgettable seasons would lay the groundwork for the greatest run in franchise history.

7

Brass Bonanza
1985-88

The Hartford Whalers are the Green Bay of hockey.
—Howard Baldwin

I mean, yeah, it was like Green Bay. The only difference was that Green Bay plays in front of a sold-out crowd every game.
—Whaler Kelly Chase

During the 1984–85 season, the Whalers went unbeaten in eleven of their last fourteen games to finish with 69 points. The late push still wasn't enough for them to make the playoffs, but it still gave the franchise reason to think that things would improve when they'd drop the puck for the 1985–86 season. The *Courant*, sensing the optimism, went with a twelve-page season preview, plastering on the front cover a giant photo of a glaring Mike Liut and featuring a lengthy Q&A with Ron Francis, who had been assigned the *C* the previous season. He was asked if the team would make the playoffs that season. "I would think so. Honestly speaking, I think we can do it this year," Francis said. "We've got the potential to be better. And you saw that potential over the last 15 games. We've got to make sure we don't get into those lulls like last year. You look at the teams in our division and Boston had some key guys retire. A guy like Terry O'Reilly retires and they lose a lot because he meant so much to them. Yes, Barry Pederson and Gord Kluzak are coming back. So it's tough to tell. If we play the whole year like we did the last 15, we can play with anybody in the division. Last year, we played 15, nap for 15, play 20 and nap 20. We can't do that anymore."

As for the rest of the league, it wasn't so much *optimism*—more like a vague possibility the Whalers could achieve more that season than in previous years. "Hartford, 30-41-9, is the perennial division doormats," wrote the *Edmonton Journal* in its season preview, "but the Whalers believe they finally have the nucleus to earn their first-ever playoff berth."

The positivity stemmed from not only the on-ice product but also the very real stability at the top. Throughout it all, coach Jack "Tex" Evans and GM Emile Francis remained the centerpiece of the rebuilding effort. They didn't necessarily arrive in Hartford as partners, but they were fundamentally joined at the hip when it came to their philosophies on hockey and life. They were conservative, old-school guys when it seemed like NHL coaches and GMs were getting younger—Francis was fifty-six when he took the job in 1983, while Evans was fifty-five when he was hired by Francis. Basically, they had been around a few years—Francis occasionally reminded people he had grown up playing outdoor hockey during the Depression, when a puck cost five cents, "and even that was too much for me to afford," and they used that depth of wisdom to their advantage.

Of course, that conservatism came out other ways, occasionally around the players. "One night, we had a road game, and flew back to Hartford that same night—it must have been an East Coast game because we got home at twelve or so," recalled Zuke. "I was staying at the hotel downtown, and so Mr. Francis gave me a ride back to the hotel after we landed. Well, there was a [Grateful] Dead concert going on that night at the Civic Center, and we were trying to get through traffic, and people were smoking all sorts of stuff. All these Deadheads were in the street. The Cat was an old military guy—always did stuff on the straight and narrow. Needless to say, he was a little taken aback by what we ran into that night."

Regardless of his musical tastes, it was clear Francis had jump-started a turnaround, breathing life into a moribund franchise with a series of moves that got people excited again.

"We had a fairly young team, and a lot of us guys that got called up became very close, and we had a very tight team," recalled MacDermid. "As the next couple of years went by, we got better and better, and we won a lot of games. And when we got to the playoffs it was something that I won't forget—the fans in Hartford were right there with us through every game."

"It was kind of like Woodstock—you just had to be there. . . . It was a very special place to play hockey," remarked Bob Crawford, who played for the Whalers from 1983 to 1986.

"Sometimes you play with some assholes," added goaltender Peter Sidorkiewicz. "We really didn't have that."

Moreover, the understated Evans carved out a niche as a players' coach. "He had faith in us, and it was refreshing," veteran Stew Gavin said of Evans. "I liked it because I came from a rigid program. Nowadays, we're at a point in hockey where coaches try and overcoach and program the players to act every way in every circumstance. In my personal experience, that kind of restricts guys. The game is read and react and hope you're making the right decision. That's what Tex was all about. It was really refreshing. Other teams would get into micromanaging—where you were and how you should have played. It was just overkill. There was none of that with Jack."

"I loved Tex," said Neufeld. "He was fair to me treated me well, and I feel I played hard for him as well. I liked playing for him and the Cat."

"We pretty much had the same practice every day," said Gavin. "And he didn't tell us how to play—he would just say play hard and play defense. We really had very little actual coaching, which allowed us as a line to build communication and trust in each other. We were basically self-coached. I don't know—maybe that's why so many guys on the roster at that time went on to become coaches."

"Jack would say, 'Figure it out.' And those guys would figure it out and respond," Skip Cunningham said. "I mean, at the time, you didn't know they would all become coaches. It was really unusual. But Jack was good about just letting guys do their thing and listen to them. He never overcoached, that's for sure.

"I also don't think Jack liked to practice a whole lot—you just had to give him an excuse, and he'd call it off. One day, he and [trainer] Tommy Woodcock were talking, and Tommy said, 'Hey Jack, I think the guys should have a day off. It's the last day to see the peak foliage.' And Jack called off practice. Like I said, just give him an excuse."

"It was nothing compared to the workouts I'd been used to in Edmonton," wrote Dave Semenko in his autobiography, recalling his first practices in Hartford after his trade to the Whalers from the Oilers in 1986. "One of the Whalers told me in the locker room that if I sweated during practice in Hartford, it would be strictly my own fault. Jack Evans ran his practices almost exactly the same way every day, and they didn't amount to much more than public skating."

For what it's worth, the players certainly seemed to benefit from the occasional random day off. They also got an off-ice boost via a special mixture from Woodcock. Cunningham described it as a rub with "unidentifiable ingredients" that was created by Woodcock. Bud Gouveia, who worked as part of Woodcock's staff before taking over as trainer in 1990, said it was a combination of a few things.

"I believe it was some type of horse liniment that he would make and combine it with some type of applicable aspirin," Gouveia recalled. "I know Ulfie was a big fan."

That wasn't the only original concoction offered by the Hartford training staff. "I know he also made his own heat rub—[referee] Ron Asselstine would love it," Gouveia said. "He would come to Hartford and work games, and he would want a refill of the stuff."

But when it came to the mud, players say it worked wonders. "I never saw an ice bag," said Gavin. "Never. But there was magic mud. I had no idea, whatever type of concoction it was, but it kept us away from the ice bags. To this day, I don't know what it was."

"Tommy was my old trainer when I was in St. Louis, and he always had a concoction for what ailed you. I know he made a lot of that stuff in his basement, but it worked, so I wasn't going to say anything," said Crawford. "There were a lot of characters on those teams, and Tommy was one of them—such a good guy. Anyway, he was always talking about recovery drinks and different liniments for aches and pains. He was ahead of his time. Tommy was always a happy guy—some trainers were kind of ornery. But he was a fun guy who didn't take anything too seriously. Never knew what was in that mud, though."

"Woody always had *something*," said Kevin Dineen with a laugh. "That stuff ended up ruining a lot of suits, that's for sure. He'd put his magic potion on you, and it would squish out the sides. If it was on your knee . . . half your suit would be covered, and there'd be this strong odor on you the rest of the day. I never knew what was in the secret stuff, but it worked for sure. A lot of times, people would use ice, but we always got the mud."

THE PLAYERS WERE SET UP FOR SUCCESS BECAUSE THEY HAD a hand in game planning as well as execution. Of course, the flip side was that there could be breakdowns at the worst possible time, especially against the crafty Canadiens.

"The negative of Jack's system was that he didn't really coach when it came to facing Montreal," recalled Gavin. "They had a trap system, which we never really figured out. But from a coaching perspective, we weren't as advanced as what Montreal was using at the time. That was frustrating. If we had someone who was more of a technique coach, that could have put us over the top."

Evans's coaching style wasn't for everyone. Defenseman Dave Lumley was placed on waivers during the 1984–85 season after just forty-eight games in Hartford. He was quickly scooped up by Edmonton and shortly after he joined the Oilers reportedly said, "It's nice to be with a team where the coach takes a shower with the players." Soon after the statement surfaced, a handmade sign on Evans's door read "Any Player Wishing to Take a Shower with the Coach Need Only Ask."

But while Evans carved out a niche as a hands-off coach, he did have a knack for crafting successful pairings. That included the popular LEG line of Lawless, Dean Evason, and Gavin. "We all worked well together, but what made it *really* work was that Lawless and Gavin could absolutely fly," Evason would later recall. "It was just a perfect-storm type of thing, with the name combo—LEG line—and the fact that those two guys could skate as fast as anyone in the league. I was the hands of the LEG line. I just used to flip pucks into the neutral zone or bank pucks off the boards to those two, and it all worked.

"Man, Stew and Lawly could *skate*. I'm still not sure how the line was formed, but we definitely had some success—it was a fun line. It was a nice combination on the ice, and our personalities worked well off the ice. As a player, it was nice to have a line that stayed together for years—it was good to have that sort of stability."

The even-tempered and steady approach didn't mean there weren't missteps, particularly when it came to dealing with the media, with the most notable case coming in March 1986 when Evans clashed with veteran sportswriter Randy Smith. Smith had written that Evans had called a special practice in Winnipeg earlier in the year, a morning session after players had been out drinking all night. Evans denied that, saying that it had been a routine practice. After a game in Buffalo, according to Smith, Evans grabbed him and shoved him against a wall, all while shouting obscenities and threatening to hit him.

A couple of weeks after the incident happened, the franchise issued the following statement:

"An investigation of the alleged incident that occurred in Buffalo last Friday night has been conducted.

"Although the investigation revealed certain relevant facts and circumstances which have not been reported, we do not consider it appropriate to engage in a public dialogue concerning the facts and circumstances while legal action is pending or threatened.

"We do regret that the incident occurred and what happened was unfortunate and we are sorry for it.

"Our organization, including management, coaches, players and staff, has made every effort to establish a professional relationship with the media and we will continue to do so. We hope this unfortunate incident will not impair this relationship.

"The Hartford Whalers partnership is solidly behind the efforts of Emile Francis and Jack Evans to make the playoffs. This was our goal before the season started and continues to be our goal."

"I don't find it terribly satisfactory," Chris Powell, the managing editor of the *Journal Inquirer*, told reporters when asked about the statement. "If it's an apology, I don't see it. I suppose if it was an apology it would have been made to us.

"We're not looking for some big fight with the Whalers. This is something inflicted on us. I don't know why it should be such a technical or touchy issue for them to apologize to us. I don't see how this really changes anything."

Powell and the *JI* continued with legal action, but in the end, the incident was one in a series of jousting matches between the Whalers and the media throughout the mid-to-late 1980s. In their monthly luncheon with the media on March 19, 1985, Emile Francis characterized coverage of the team as being "the greatest sabotage job since Pearl Harbor." Afterward, *Courant* Sports Editor Jon Pessah reached out to try to smooth things over, but all he got was a curt "We have nothing to say" from Francis.

Several reporters who covered the team through that stretch could recall icy glares from Evans or Francis. Interviews with media members who covered the team at that time do not reveal why the mood was so tense, but an occasional inability to handle heightened expectations certainly played a role. As the team improved throughout 1985 and 1986, the slower stretches were met with critical press. That should be the norm in most big markets. But Hartford's ascent into the world of big-time hockey wasn't without its bumps, with a change in coverage being one of them.

"I think that it is probably fair to say that we're thin-skinned, but you have to look at where we're coming from. We've had six years where we've kind of struggled," Baldwin explained to the *Courant* in 1986. "When you go through a tough process you have your ups and downs and it gets frustrating at times.

"It's frustrating for fellas covering the team and it's frustrating for us. I'm not saying we're right, just why it may be so. We have to realize that you fellas have a job to do and we have a job to do. You aren't always going to like what we do and we aren't always going to like what you write. But that's life."

THE 1985–86 SEASON STARTED ON AN UNEVEN NOTE FOR THE Whalers, who won four of their first five but hung around the .500 mark a month into the season and needed a spark. That November, Francis swapped out Neufeld for Dave Babych. Neufeld was a grinder who was enjoying a good run in Hartford, a very nice complementary piece along the Ron Francis line, but the chance to get someone like Babych was too good to pass up. The rest of the league shook its collective head at Winnipeg's decision to deal the twenty-four-year-old defenseman, who already had a pair of All-Star berths under his belt. Babych immediately provided some punch—in his first three games in Hartford, he had 2 assists (including 1 in an 8–1 blowout of his old team) and the game-winning goal in a 5–4 victory against the Canucks.

Off the ice, the hirsute defenseman was memorable for other reasons. "He had hair where most people didn't have skin," one former teammate recalled of Babych. "He was like a bear—baldheaded, but *every square inch of his body* was covered with hair."

The trade was tough for Neufeld, who was struggling with addiction while with the Whalers. The deal marked the end of an odyssey for the first Black player in the history of the franchise.

"We all loved Ray," said teammate Jeff Brubaker. "Nobody ever looked at Ray like he was a Black guy or thought about him as a Black guy. The subject of Ray and race just never mixed, at least in my memory."

"I had my challenges with booze in Hartford," Neufeld confessed. "I didn't really pick my spots—as I've said, I just drank most of the time. I'm sorry about this as I look back on my career, as it wasn't fair to my teammates. It was really quite selfish of me. But I had a problem in a time [when] no one talked about having problems, especially with booze. I have to think it affected my play, but that's hard to know, as I had some great years in Hartford.

"Things changed for me my last year in Hartford just prior to the trade," he added. "I was on and off booze throughout that summer. I went to camp and had a good start to the season . . . and then they traded me to Winnipeg. It was during that winter I gave up the booze.

"I must say, it was tough, getting traded and trying to figure out my personal stuff with me and my wife and the struggles alcohol put on our lives. But my wife was a champ and supported me, and I found my faith through the steady support of my teammates Laurie Boschman and Doug Smail, and I managed to turn my life around."

The acquisition of Liut and Babych helped set the stage for an impressive stretch. In December, the Whalers put together a twelve-game string during which they were unbeaten in nine contests, and they followed that with a wild January—five straight wins, which got them to 26-21-1. In February, the city hosted the 1986 All-Star Game, a smashing success for the franchise and a financial windfall for those downtown—despite a skills competition planned for the morning of the game being called off because some All-Stars complained they hadn't been given proper notice. The game sold out three months in advance, and 15,142 watched as the Wales Conference (including Hartford's Sylvain "Sly" Turgeon, who took the place of an injured Francis) beat the Campbell Conference, 4–3, in overtime. Edmonton netminder Grant Fuhr was named MVP.

It was also a feather in the cap of the Hartford ownership group. The Whalers were the first former WHA team to host the NHL All-Star Game.

"People laugh when I tell them the last three years in the WHA [were] comparable to Russian roulette," Baldwin later recalled. "We'd deal out the cards and see who was in and who was out. In hindsight, if you compare 1979 to previous expansions, we got a heck of a deal. It would have cost us more to join the National Hockey League because we never would have had a chance to recoup our initial investment."

The highs of January and early February quickly faded, however. There would be a ten-game winless skid, and the Whalers slipped from second to fourth place. Liut recalled it as a particularly gruesome stretch, one that was caused at least in part because of injuries to several key players. But the booing got so bad, the team wouldn't introduce Evans on the PA before the game.

"The worst skid I had ever seen as a professional," Liut recalled in a 2015 interview. "I can't even begin to describe the frustration we all felt at that time. We were inventing new ways to lose games, and nobody had any answers. We were also missing important players like Ron Francis, who was injured, and we just couldn't seem to catch any breaks.

"It was easy to point fingers, and that's when the fans began booing Tex Evans. It was a brutal situation to be in because people were literally climbing on the glass behind the bench and screaming at him during games, but he never, ever turned on the players. That's something he refused to stoop to, and we didn't ever forget that loyalty and respect he showed us. Emile Francis, who was also under tremendous pressure because he had dealt two fan favorites in [Mark] Johnson and [Greg] Millen for me, gave the players a reason to fight for the team with his public outpouring of faith and support in us. [Francis and Evans] never cracked, never jumped on the team or made us the fall guys for our struggles at that time, which was so important because when you're in a slump of that magnitude, you never think you'll win another game."

But the Whalers would flip the script, and what followed was the greatest stretch of hockey in the history of the franchise. Buoyed by the fact that, despite their recent run, the five Adams Division teams were separated by a total of 16 points at the start of March, Hartford came alive. Francis acquired goal-scorer John Anderson and defenseman Mike McEwen, and that was followed by a rare win in Montreal, a 5–2 victory powered by a 3-point effort from Ferraro. Over the course of the month, the division started to stretch out, but the Whalers kept pace, putting together an eight-game unbeaten streak, which included an impressive 3–0 win over the Habs and an 11–4 thrashing of Chicago.

There was no denying that the Whalers had begun to gel. That unbeaten streak was a prime example of a carefully shaped team-building approach favored by Evans and Francis that mixed veterans and youngsters.

"When I was in St. Louis, we had a few younger players and a lot of veterans," said Liut. "As part of the group of younger players, we were learning as we went through the seasons. In Hartford, I was the older guy at twenty-nine, and we had eight or nine rookies, so the role was reversed."

Thanks in part to the leadership of vets like Liut, they came together in several other ways, including off-ice hijinks. In the late 1980s fans started bringing cookies and milk for players to enjoy after practice. During one stretch, Turgeon was "AWOL" (in the words of one player), and when he did show, he wasn't performing as well as he had in the past. As a result, it was no surprise his picture showed up on the side of one of the milk cartons. Then, there was the time when they were able to pull a fast one on Sylvain Cote—players were always getting offers for free stuff, and in early November one Whaler thought it would be a goof to post something on the locker room bulletin board about free turkeys.

"Coco took the bait," recalled one player with a laugh. "He went out there with his broken French accent and almost got into a fight with a guy over a turkey."

Cote was among the youngest players on the roster through the mid-1980s. That, as well as a generally guileless nature, made him vulnerable to an occasional slip-up. Tim Bothwell, one of the oldest players on the team through this stretch, remembers one night where Cote spent a little too much time gawking at what was going on off the ice.

"One night, we had the San Diego Chicken at the Civic Center," Bothwell said. "We were in the first period, and Sylvain Cote was next to me on one side, and Scott Kleinendorst was on the other side. The chicken is, like, five feet from our bench and trying to get our attention.

"Coco was sitting there, transfixed. He was just eighteen at the time—I don't think he knew anything about the San Diego Chicken. Joel Quenneville is coming off the ice and yelling 'lefty, lefty' for a replacement. I see Joel coming and elbow Coco: 'You're on.' Joel is getting closer to the bench, and Coco is still looking at the chicken. He finally wakes up and is all flustered.

"Meanwhile, Scotty sees what's happening, sees Joel, and figures Coco isn't going. Joel doesn't see anyone coming on the ice for him and turns back. But Scotty and Coco both jump over the boards and we have four defensemen out there, and we get a penalty. Tex comes sauntering down the bench and asks, 'What the hell is going on down here?'

"'Stupid fucking chicken.'"

That looseness also manifested itself in other ways. Howard Baldwin Jr., the son of the owner who worked with equipment manager Skip Cunningham, got some help from the players when he showed up at the rink after getting into a dustup at school.

"When I went to school, people would razz me about my dad and the team and all that, and I would have to fight," he said. "Well, one day I came into the locker room after school with a black eye, and the rest of the guys turned to Torrie Robertson and said, 'Look, you have to teach him how to fight.'

"But Ulf Samuelsson gave me the best advice—he was an unbelievable guy. He told me the best thing you could do is just laugh at them, because there's nothing more annoying to a person than when you laugh at them. And it worked."

Of course, Samuelsson was a different breed. One night, the Whalers were in the Forum, and Evans called for a Samuelsson-Quenneville pairing. Quenneville prepared to jump over the boards, but Samuelsson was still. "I can't go, Tex," he said.

"What the hell are you talking about?" Evans replied.

"I can't go, I can't go," he replied.

"What the hell is wrong with you?"

He paused for a second. "I got to take a shit," Samuelsson said.

"Next whistle, he's gone, off to the room," recalled one teammate with a laugh.

AS A YOUNGSTER, BALDWIN JR. HAD A TON OF JOBS, INCLUDING putting sandwiches on the opposing team's bus after the game. One night, an opponent took too many unnecessary shots at Francis and the Whalers. When they got on the bus that evening after the game, they found all their sandwiches had a bite taken out, courtesy of Baldwin.

"Skip knew the Canadiens would take the black tape with them back to Montreal," Baldwin recalled, "and so when they would ask for volumes of black tape, Skip said, 'Tell them *no fucking way.*'

"One day, (former Montreal trainer) Eddy Palchak asks me for more black tape, and I say, 'Skip says no fucking way.' The story gets back to Skip, and he calls me in. I thought I was in trouble, but all he did was smile quietly at me and says, 'I didn't think you'd actually use the *word.*'"

The hijinks weren't limited to the locker room and training table. The most notable team prank? *Hot news.* Players would be reading the newspaper, and someone would sneak up and light the newspaper on fire. "They'd arrest you today if you did something like that in an airport," laughed Bob Crawford.

Dineen was the master of another prank, according to former assistant equipment manager Greg Pacheco. "We're flying back from Los Angeles after a game—I think it's the red-eye because we end up stopping in Chicago to switch planes sometime between 3:00 and 4:30 a.m.," he said. "We're all half asleep because it's such a long flight. We're all hanging around the terminal, and suddenly, I hear the guys laughing. I walk over and see a dollar bill on the floor, and I'm, like, 'Wait, am I the only one who sees what's going on? There's a bill just sitting there on the ground.' Suddenly, I see the bill move. 'Wait, what just happened?' It turns out Kevin Dineen had fishing line, and he had poked a hole in a dollar bill and he had it strung off a ways so he could see what was happening. As soon as people tried to bend down to pick it up, he would pull the string and it would just flutter out of their reach."

Of course, not all plane flights were fun and games—traveling in the Northeast during the winter often meant bad weather. Zuke recalled one forgettable plane flight in the early 1980s. "One day, we were chartering up to Quebec City on the day of the game, and there was an awful storm. We had one small propeller plane, just big enough for the team," he remembered. "We get off the ground in Connecticut, and for almost two hours, it was the worst flight I was ever on. The plane was bumping up and down the whole time, guys were puking and soaked with sweat. We think we're coming in for a landing in Quebec . . . and the pilot says we have to turn back because things are closed up because of the storm. We have to go all the way back to Hartford in the same environment. It was just *absolute hell* for four hours."

HEADING INTO THE FINAL WEEKEND OF THE 1985–86 SEASON, Hartford and Buffalo found themselves battling for the fourth and final playoff spot. The Whalers took a colossal step toward closing out the Sabres with a 5–3 win on April 1 at the Civic Center, and they finished the job with a 7–1 blowout of Toronto. Hartford finished the regular season with a 12-3-1 stretch that was the envy of the rest of the league—thanks in part to the promise of free Gucci loafers.

What? During that run, John Anderson, in the locker room after a game, had remarked about Baldwin's new shoes. Baldwin replied that if the team made the playoffs, he'd buy everyone a new pair. The first postseason berth for the franchise since 1980 meant new shoes for everyone.

"We used to give Howard grief about his shoes all the time," Bothwell said with a laugh. "He had these—I think they were suede—shoes that were really in style at the time. One night, he comes into the locker room and says, 'If you guys make the playoffs, I'll give every one of you guys a pair of Guccis.' These shoes were like, between $300 and $400 a pop. So we made the playoffs, and we all got Guccis.

"Stew Gavin and I, that year at the banquet, we gave Howard the Imelda Marcos Award for Footwear. We got this really nice shoe, and we nailed it to a piece of wood—he wasn't there for the banquet, but the next time he came down to the locker room, we gave it to him."

"Suffice [it] to say I was out several grand," Baldwin said later, "but the guys had new shoes for the playoffs."

Regardless of the free shoes, the Whalers entered the playoffs as one of the hottest teams in the league, which wasn't lost on the coaching staff. "We did suffer through February, but March and how we started April has been great," Evans told reporters when the regular season wrapped up. "It's important that you are on a roll going into the playoffs. I like the feeling on the team and the way we are playing.

"Maybe we'll surprise a few people," he added. "I had talented players before, but never the depth or great goaltending like this team. The playoffs are unpredictable, but one thing you do need is good goaltending. [Not having] it can limit what you can do."

Hartford would face first-place Quebec in the opening round, which—on paper—appeared to be a good match for the Whalers. The two teams had split the season series with four wins apiece (2-2 at home and 2-2 on the road), and both teams had scored 33 goals in the eight games. To Evans's point on goaltending, Quebec had the talented Clint Malarchuk, but Liut was in the midst of one of the best stretches of his career, and he was one of the key factors in the Game One win over the Nords in Quebec. He made 37 saves in the overtime victory, which ended when Sylvain Turgeon scored at the 2:36 mark of the extra session to give the Whalers the first playoff win in their NHL history.

"I really think that the biggest difference for us was the first ten or so minutes in Game One," remembered Bothwell of that series. "It was like the ice was tilted, and Liut stood on his head. We scored, and the series just flipped at that point. We won three straight. Without that goaltending to get us through the first ten minutes, maybe they bounce us out of the building, and everything is different. The importance of quality goaltending at the right time is always huge, and thanks to Mike in that situation, we just got better and better and more and more confident as a group."

Game Two wasn't nearly as close. Hartford took an early 2–0 lead and maintained control for most of the evening, eventually coming away with a 4–1 win. Up 2-0, the Whalers returned home to a sold-out Civic Center crowd that spent much of the night chanting, "Sweep! Sweep!" Hartford crushed the deflated Nordiques by a 9–4 score in Game Three to win the series.

The usually laconic Evans enjoyed the moment. As he walked up to a handful of reporters after the game, Evans said, "Well, you all wanted to see this. I'm going to give it to you. Once." Then, he smiled—*briefly.*

The hockey world was on notice: Hartford was for real. "I think Hartford can beat Montreal if they don't get psyched out," Malarchuk told reporters after Game Three. "The Whalers have won only once in the Forum, but the way they are playing now, they can win anywhere."

THE WHALERS-CANADIENS SERIES THAT SPRING WAS THE MOST compelling of the second round of the playoffs for several reasons, including the first-round upsets of Quebec and Philadelphia, two regular-season division winners. Whichever team came out of the Adams Division that postseason would have an excellent chance at winning the Cup.

For the Whalers, it would not be easy. Like most other NHL teams, they had always struggled in the Forum—they had recently endured a twenty-three-game winless streak there before a late-season victory the month before—and with Montreal holding home-ice advantage, the Whalers would have to win at least one away from home if they wanted to advance to the next round.

But Hartford liked its chances. The Whalers had been competitive with the Habs all year long. Montreal had taken the regular-season series, 4-3-1, but just about every game was a tight one. And sparked by their late-season run and playoff sweep of Quebec, Hartford had every reason to feel optimistic heading into Game One. That feeling was well-founded, as Hartford shocked the hockey world with a 4–1 win in Montreal to open the series. Gavin had a pair of goals, and Liut turned back just about everything to give the Whalers the advantage.

But that euphoria was short-lived, as the Canadiens won the next two, regaining home-ice advantage with a Game Three win in Hartford (4–1) that left the Whalers reeling. Compounding Hartford's troubles was the news that Liut suffered a knee injury prior to Game Three. But backup Steve Weeks held the fort, and a 2–1 overtime victory in Game Four—the first of two OT games in the series—knotted the series at 2–2.

In that dramatic contest, between the end of regulation and the start of overtime—with the score tied at one—there was a conversation in the Hartford locker room. "We looked around the room and started asking for volunteers to be the hero tonight," Francis told reporters after the game.

Dineen ended up as the hero. Early in the extra session, he scooped up the puck along the left boards, spun past Montreal defenseman Larry Robinson and headed for the net. He beat Patrick Roy high to the glove side, just over a minute into OT. It set off a wild celebration.

"I caught him flatfooted, so I took off at full speed, held off until I was right on top of Roy, and then sent it upstairs," Dineen said afterward. "Thank God, we're tied at 2–2. I know we can't get too excited, we're only back to being even with them, but believe me, this feels like a really big win."

"He was able to get around Larry Robinson and cut in alone," TV play-by-play man Rick Peckham said of Dineen's play. "You're just not expecting him to do that, but that's how bold and daring Kevin Dineen was. He would just grab the moment and make something happen."

For Peckham, it provided the signature broadcasting moment of his career. "I remember that play—it was one of my favorite calls for a few reasons, including the fact that it happened at the Civic Center," he said. "I don't think the fans got the credit they deserved for the noise they made, especially in that series. It could get loud in that building, and in that series—in that moment—it really felt like the roof would come off. But yeah, it was one of my all-time favorite calls."

"It just brought the house down," said Chuck Kaiton.

"Single greatest night in Whaler history," recalled longtime fan Dan Tapper. "I was there with my dad in our front-row seats. I thought the roof would collapse again."

The goal was a postseason culmination not only for the Whalers but also for Dineen in general. "Kevin, he just sort of exploded in those playoffs, with that relentless pit-bull kind of mentality," Ron Francis later recalled. "He had a very underrated wrist shot and that high compete level. For him to score that goal . . . you never stop believing in that situation, but when it came to that series, that just kept our beliefs alive, all the way up to Game Seven."

"I think things were going well for me in that series—I was having some success offensively," Dineen later said. "I had still played a bit of a game that had different style to it than I was able to play in the past when I more physical—when a confrontation happened, I always tended to be in the middle of it. But I was also scoring more goals than I had before. In that series, I realized I was more valuable on the ice than in the penalty box. That was a telltale sign.

"Brian Burke was my agent at the time—we were buddies—and he said after that one, 'You weren't very good, right up until you scored that goal.'"

It was never going to get better than that moment. Indeed, if you wanted to carve out a statue of the most iconic moments in Hartford hockey history, you'd choose an image of Dineen, celebrating off-balance while stumbling toward the boards in a postgoal celebration.

At that point, maybe for the first time since the merger, it felt like the Whalers *really belonged* in the NHL. Everything had been building to that: the collapse of the old arena, the 91 Club, the fight to make it to the NHL, Cooperalls, just missing out on Bobby Carpenter, and the jokes about the "Forever .500s"—a tongue-in-cheek term for the team coined by Boston sportswriter Kevin Paul Dupont. All that was in the past. In that moment, Hartford was standing toe-to-toe with the legendary Canadiens, holding its own in the postseason. The Whalers had a terrific young core, a boisterous fan base, robust local ownership, and a front office willing to do whatever it took to improve the team. That series, and that moment, represented the best professional sports moment in the history of the state.

They split the next two games, setting the stage for a dramatic Game Seven in the Forum. Montreal jumped to an early lead in a game marked by near-misses and crisp play. But the Whalers responded late in regulation. Taking a drop pass from Evason, Babych ripped a slap shot from the blue line that beat Roy high to his glove hand at 17:12 of the third period to make it 1–1. The legendary Forum was silent, and a Montreal team that thought it was capable of waltzing into the next round started to really sweat.

"I remember the feeling when Dave Babych tied it with less than three minutes left," recalled former Montreal forward Chris Nilan. "I remember thinking 'I can't believe we're at this point. We were supposed to win this series.'"

The extra session was similarly dramatic. With the Forum crowd on its feet urging its heroes, Montreal was denied on multiple occasions by Liut. On the other end, Hartford had its chances, but Roy was up to the task.

"They wanted to come out of that room and finish us off," Nilan said of the extra session. "They had us back on our heels."

In the end, it would be Montreal; 5:55 into overtime, Claude Lemieux picked up a loose puck behind the Whalers' net, whipped around in front, and beat Liut for the game winner—*season over.*

"I was never so happy—and relieved—in my life," said Nilan.

"The letdown is hard to take," Evans said. "The team played so well. I can't say enough about Mike Liut."

"Losing the last game is the worst feeling in the world," Tippett said afterward.

"After a magnificent March stretch drive and ten tumultuous playoff games, the Whalers improbable dream is dead," wrote Alan Greenberg in the *Courant*. "If not for Liut, it would have been buried by the end of the first period, crushed by the convincing superiority of the Canadiens' skating and checking.

"But it wasn't, of course. It wasn't because the Whalers, so meek for so many years, no longer go gentle into that good night. But for an errant bounce of the puck, they might not have gone at all. The team that two months ago figured to be watching the playoffs at home took the Montreal Canadiens into overtime of the seventh game of the Adams Divisional final. And that, sports fans, is about as gallant as it gets."

To Greenberg's point, there was a genuine sense of accomplishment. A team ticketed for another last-place finish pushed the powerful Canadiens to the brink. They were a young and hungry bunch, a mix of eager youth and salty veterans. Their time would come sooner rather than later.

"It was really a tough loss, but you know what I had in my head? This is a freaking good team, and this is not the end of something, but a beginning," recalled Victor Masi, a longtime team employee. "We all felt this was a team that was going to be around for a long time."

"To say at the beginning of the year that we would be one goal away from winning the division, nobody would have thought it was possible. We have to be proud of what we accomplished. This team made believers of a lot of people," Ferraro told reporters after the game. "To be honest, the Stanley Cup is up for grabs. If we had won this one, we might have walked into the finals. Who knows?"

Ferraro was right. The Canadiens blew through the next round and the finals with ease. Montreal needed only five games each to finish the Rangers and the Flames for the title. From a league-wide perspective, it was a wide-open year for a few reasons, not the least of which was that Calgary upset Edmonton—in the seventh game of the Smythe Division final, the Oilers knocked the puck into their own net, beating themselves and handing the Flames their ticket to the final series against Montreal.

Without Gretzky and Edmonton in the picture, who knows what might have happened? The Canadiens had Roy, sure, but they also had thirteen rookies on their roster and benefited from the fact that the Oilers—which had won back-to-back titles the previous two years and finished the regular season 56-17-7—were out because of a fluke Game Seven loss. This would have been the year for Hartford to steal a Cup, especially considering that the Whalers had dominated Calgary and New York.

"We beat the Flames two of the three times we played them," recalled Bothwell. "We went to Calgary in January, and they were struggling. They were a great team, but they were struggling. They were really good for the first eight minutes of the game against us that night, but we scored first, and I've never experienced anything like it in my career—you could just feel the air go out of the balloon that night in the Saddledome. We beat them 9–1, the worst home loss in franchise history. And they were the ones who got to the finals that year? That would have been a real interesting matchup.

"I mean, if we had beaten Montreal, we would have played the Rangers, and we beat them in two of the three games we played too. Honestly, beating a team in the regular season doesn't mean you'll beat them in the playoffs, but we wouldn't have been big underdogs."

Regardless of what might have been, in the immediate wake of the loss to the Canadiens, any bitterness was quickly put aside. The City of Hartford threw them a parade, and thousands of people showed up to cheer on a team that had just won a single playoff series, an admittedly strange sight. But for Hartford, a city that had been starved for a winner, it was a welcome party. In Connecticut there was no modern-day equivalent for the success the Whalers had just achieved. UConn basketball had won some big games in the nascent days of the Big East, and the men's soccer team had captured two national championships. A professional sports team winning postseason series? *Sure, it's probably a bit much. So what if we went a little overboard? It's been a long time coming.*

The governor proclaimed Hartford Whalers Day across the state. Businesses gave employees the day off and encouraged them to attend the parade. Police estimated that between ten thousand and fifteen thousand people showed up to brave the surprisingly blustery conditions. Players rode in the back of pickup trucks and sat in convertibles. Liut's young daughter Jenna sat on her father's lap and smiled at the *lee-oot* chants that echoed off the buildings downtown.

Baldwin said that next year fans wouldn't have to put up with the winds. "Next year, it's going to be a lot warmer when we have the parade, because we're going to have it in June, after we win the Stanley Cup," he said.

"The parade after we lost to Montreal was *unreal*," remembered MacDermid. "We couldn't believe all the people that came out to show their support and appreciation for the team. It meant a lot to us players—we joked if we had won the Cup they would have to shut the city down for that parade."

"I was a Boston guy—grew up in Framingham. So the most embarrassing thing I can remember when it came to covering the team in that stretch was that parade," said Gerry Brooks, longtime New England TV and radio news reporter. "We were talking about how we were going to cover it and what it was going to look like, and I just kept saying, 'They're a fourth-place team! We're throwing a parade for a fourth-place team!' I remember doing a live shot near the Civic Center on a street corner, and on the air, I'm going, 'Isn't this great?' Inside, I'm thinking, *This is so embarrassing.*

"But I can see why they had that parade. There was a great feeling downtown—places were opening, clubs and restaurants were hopping on game night," Brooks added. "Navigating downtown Hartford around the Civic Center wasn't like the area around Boston Garden or any other major city. Hartford is a small city, and the whole place was like a party on game night in those years. They made the city feel good."

Although the Canadiens captured the Stanley Cup, let the record show that the Whalers were the only team that ended up pushing them that postseason. Montreal's only seven-game series in that playoff run came against Hartford.

Small wonder that there was a terrific sense of optimism around the team heading into the offseason. It had a solid nucleus, steady veterans mixed with smart young talent on all three levels. The coaching staff, front office, and ownership were all committed to taking things to the next level. Hartford was a team on the rise.

"We started to feel it as a team—we could and would win games," Gavin said of the Whalers heading into the 1986–87 season. "We started to believe in ourselves, and we knew we had a lot of good character guys. We knew that if we worked hard, we would be successful.

"We were gaining confidence and believing we had something special as a team. There were some really good, young players who grew into the core of that team, guys like Francis and Dineen," he added. "They were leaders and students of the game. I came from Toronto, and by Christmas, we were out of the playoffs. That was very frustrating as a player. For me, it was a positive to be on a team like that and contribute and to feel a part of it."

The 1986–87 team had stars, to be sure. Francis was established as one of the premier players in the league at that point, while Dineen and Liut had also become leading lights in their own right, and players like Turgeon delivered plenty of flash. The fan base was energized.

"My dad got season tickets that season," recalled fan Stephen Popper. "It was one of the greatest years of my life. Between having my driver's license, total access to tickets to the Whale, being a junior in high school, and seeing U2 play the Civic Center instead of going to my junior prom, there was nothing sweeter for a teenager in central Connecticut."

The roster was greater than the sum of its parts, a deep and talented group that was full of steady and sturdy contributors who came to play every night. Although there were a ton of those type of players up and down the lineup, the two who best personified the overall approach were Tippett and Jarvis. Tippett was the "Saskatchewan badass" who never asked out. And whereas Jarvis was a little more mild-mannered, he and Tippett were kindred spirits when it came to their hockey philosophy. Tippett never wanted to tap out for fear of losing his spot in the lineup. The same was true for Jarvis, a thirty-one-year-old centerman who had built a reputation as one of the sturdiest players in the game. Acquired from the Caps on December 6, 1985, he had already had a lengthy consecutive-games-played streak by the time he got to Hartford. His approach was forged in the cauldron of Montreal, where asking out of the lineup could leave you on the outs with coaches and teammates.

"The depth on that team, especially when I was in the minors, they had guys on the roster who could have been in the NHL," Jarvis recalled. "You didn't want to come out a game because you knew there was someone else there who could take your spot, and you wouldn't be able to get back in. You didn't want to give up that opportunity. That built over time, and that just became my mindset all those years. You didn't want to give anyone a chance to take your job."

When he arrived in Hartford, he was paired on the same line with Tippett. The two ended up rooming together for a stretch. "Dave and I looked at the game very much the same way; as players, you have a role on a team, and you fill that role to the best of your ability," continued Jarvis. "We were defensive-minded guys who had mostly checking assignments. Jack was big on matching lines, and we handled a lot of that. But it was a lot of face-offs in the defensive zone and killing penalties for a couple of years.

"What I appreciated about Dave was that there was no question he was a competitor. He was a gamer who wanted to be in there, he wanted to compete, and he competed hard . . . no matter what it took. It was joy to be honest, to be alongside a guy like that. There was no question that when you came to the rink or went to a game you wanted your linemates to be self-motivated guys who wanted to be their best, and that was the case with Dave."

Jarvis's consecutive-games streak continued when he joined the Whalers, and it soon became clear he wasn't just in the lineup because he was a sideshow aiming for a record. A perennial Selke Trophy candidate who was also one of the oldest guys on the roster, Jarvis had a professional approach and positive attitude that added another layer of leadership for a relatively young team.

"I just tried to play the games one at a time," he said later. "It's not one of those records you set out to break—basically, by the grace of God, you stayed injury-free and kept playing. I just enjoyed playing so much and tried to go about it the right way, a game at a time, and it added up.

"I didn't really think about the streak at the start—you'd pass someone on the ladder, or hit four hundred or five hundred or seven hundred games, and then, it would be forgotten again," he added. "It seemed like going into the 1986–87 season, though, in Hartford, that's when it started to catch on. The media started talking more about it, and I would get asked about it by the media when we would go into visiting cities. That's when it really started to gain some note that the streak was in play."

One of the highlights of the 1986–87 season came in Hartford on the night of December 26, 1986, when Jarvis broke the record, which had belonged to Garry Unger, of 914 consecutive games played. Jarvis's record would eventually stretch to 964 consecutive games, a mark that stood until 2022. The team presented him with a trip to Hawaii in a ceremony prior to the game against the Canadiens.

"That night, my family was all there," said Jarvis. "I can remember the graciousness of our team, the players and ownership, as they presented a trip to Hawaii to me and my family, and the players and management picked up the tab.

"To be able to set the record against Montreal, a team I had started with and against a number of players I played with when I was with the Canadiens, that was special."

Perhaps influenced by Jarvis's record-breaking performance; by the continued elite level of play from stars like Francis, Dineen, and Liut; or by the Whalers being in the midst of a stretch in which they would go unbeaten in seven of nine games over late December 1986, legendary sportswriter Frank Deford was asked on the January 1, 1987, episode of *Nightline* for a prediction for the coming year. "The Whalers will win the Stanley Cup," he replied.

As March gave way to April, the Whalers appeared hell-bent on making Deford's prediction come true. They inched closer to a division title, thanks in large part to a dominant stretch of nine wins in thirteen games that included a thunderous 10–2 victory over the Bruins in Hartford on March 5, which had eighteen penalties, including eight for fighting. They lost out on a golden opportunity to clinch on April 1 when the Canadiens surprised them with a 3–2 win, courtesy of a late goal from Bob Gainey. After that, they had to wait an extra ninety minutes—a delay from the closed-circuit broadcast in Pittsburgh for *WrestleMania III* pushed back the start of the Penguins-Canadiens game—before they saw Montreal stay alive in the division race with a 4–1 win over Pittsburgh.

But Saturday night was the Whalers' time. After dominating the Adams Division for the better part of the 1986–87 season, on April 4, 1987, Hartford beat the Rangers, 5–3 to claim the division title. Though falling behind in the early going, the Whalers scored 3 goals in less than four minutes in the third period to put the game away. "Going into the third period, I was thinking the table was kind of set for someone to take charge," Ron Francis said.

It was the first division title for Hartford in its eight-year history in the NHL and the first time the franchise had finished on top of *any* division since the WHA days.

"There was a time when we'd get standing ovations for just coming close," Francis said after the division clincher. "I remember when we won 19 games here."

"Our goal was to win the division outright," Liut said flatly after it was all done. "You have to take things a step at a time. Once we made it our goal to finish first, and the closer we had it in reach, we took command of the situation. To fulfill that, a goal set and a goal achieved, is great."

That night was a validation, even more than the late-season and playoff push the team had made at the end of the previous year. Critics could dismiss that run as a lightning-in-a-bottle burst of success, which resulted from the combination of a little luck and a hot goaltender. No, this was very different. The 1986–87 Whalers won one of the toughest divisions in hockey that year. They stood toe-to-toe with the rest of the league from the start of the year to the finish and were equal to the task. Hartford lost four in a row just once over the course of the regular season, a stretch that was punctuated by their team bus being stolen in New Jersey. They were among the best in the NHL. The postseason would bring even greater glory, and another bigger, grander parade. Right?

OVER THE TWO PREVIOUS SEASONS, THE WHALERS HAD CARVED out a niche as a smart and steady hockey team. Though physical, they didn't take stupid penalties and were usually tough to goad into fights. And after wins in the first two games of the opening series against the Quebec Nordiques, it looked like that was going to be the case that postseason.

But in Game Three, the Nordiques started gleefully getting under their skin, poking at Hartford time and again and getting the Whalers to take a series of foolish penalties that quickly changed the complexion of the series. It started when Dave Semenko went after Robert Picard after a clean hit, delivering a high stick to the back of his head. With Samuelsson also in the box for a previous misdeed, the Nordiques connected for a power-play goal. Quebec took a 5–1 win.

After receiving a game misconduct in the first contest for being the third man in, Samuelsson received a second game misconduct in Game Four—a 4–1 win for the Nordiques that evened the series at two games apiece—and was suspended from Game Five for an obscene hand gesture.

"This is a tough, tough series," Ferraro told reporters after Quebec had evened the series at two in another slugfest at Le Colisée. "The fans get on you here. They're borderline disgusting. That shouldn't affect anything, but it makes you want to beat them all the more."

Making it harder was Nordiques coach Michel Bergeron, who gleefully poked at the Whalers who landed in the penalty box in the games in Quebec. The penalty box was adjacent to the Nords bench, and Hartford wasn't pleased that Bergeron chirped throughout the series.

"Every time there have been any penalties assessed, your players are over there and he's got his darned nose stuck out and 'Yap, yap, yap,'" said Emile Francis. "There is one darned, unwritten law in this business that you can yell all you want at your players. But as a coach you don't yell at the opposition. You stand behind 20 guys and it doesn't take much courage to yell.

"That's what led to Ulf Samuelsson being thrown out the other night here," he added. "Sure, you can blame Ulfie all you want, and he shouldn't have paid attention to Bergeron. But it's a son of a gun, because he's playing on that side two of the three periods, and that guy Bergeron keeps yapping at him."

In Game Five, Dineen cross-checked Peter Stastny, and Ferraro slashed Goulet. That led to a pair of power-play goals for Quebec, and the third straight win of the series for the Nords, a 7–5 victory that had a total of twenty-one combined penalties and left Ron Francis with a broken cheekbone and the Whalers on the brink. Game Six went to overtime at Le Colisée, but Stastny beat Liut at 6:08 of the extra session to give Quebec the victory and the series win.

"The loss tonight is part of growing up," Ron Francis told reporters after the game. "But it was a hell of a price to pay for a learning experience. We've just got to store it away and use what we learned down the road."

In the end, the Nordiques extracted a dose of revenge for what had happened the year before when they finished the regular season in first place but were shocked in the first round by the fourth-place Whalers. This time, Quebec was the one that pulled the upset, knocking off the division champions and teaching them a lesson about keeping their collective cool. The two teams combined for a whopping 199 penalties and 611 penalty minutes (317 of which were assessed to Hartford) in the seven-game set, both NHL records at the time.

"I know I learned something from this series," Samuelsson said after things wrapped up. "They tried to intimidate me and Kevin, and I got the real bad end of that. I've never played games where a few players intentionally tried to hurt you every time they see you. I only wish I would have known the way they were going to play. I feel like we got robbed."

It was a bitter defeat, though not as gutting as the year before when they nearly shocked the eventual Stanley Cup champions. The 1986–87 team was better than the previous season—deeper and stronger on all three levels and poised to play deep into the playoffs. But players allowed themselves to be pushed into mistakes at the worst possible time, and they paid dearly for it.

Others in the organization noticed a false sense of security that crept in late in the regular season and served as at least *part* of its downfall against Quebec. "I think one of the things that hurt was a sense of complacency that set in," said team employee Mark Willand. "We as an organization didn't have that same edge had we had previously in 1987. That playoff series, we were flat all the way through."

But outwardly, the general sentiment was the playoff loss was just a blip, a bump in the road on the way to bigger and better things. Once the season ended, the team released an impressive full-length highlight video. And because it was the 1980s and any successful team had to make its own version of the "Super Bowl Shuffle," the Whalers included one of the most forgettably unforgettable music videos of all time, "Whalermania," which included several members of the team in sunglasses, trying to play guitars (or other instruments) and lip-syncing to lyrics like this:

> Be a part, of Whalermania
> Be a part, a part of the fun
> Come see the Hartford Whalers
> Become hockey's number one!

Ron Francis can be seen in front of the group, pretending to play guitar as teammates "sing" around him.

The "Whalermania" music video aside, the feeling was that the season was the start of something. It was the dawn of a new era for sports in the state, and for the Whalers in particular. The franchise had grown slowly and steadily since the WHA days, taking incremental steps forward throughout the 1970s and early '80s, and had reached a point where that careful planning was going to pay off. The Whalers had lost to the Nordiques that postseason, of course, but all good teams go through growing pains. Right?

Wrong. The division clincher against the Rangers and the first two playoff wins over Quebec did not herald the start of a new era. No one knew it at the time, but instead, it marked the beginning of the end of the Whalers as we knew them. A franchise that had worked so hard to succeed would soon experience a ten-year stretch that led to their departure.

It began immediately at the start of the 1987–88 season, when the team lost five straight. Though an off-season interrupted the four straight losses in the playoffs and the five losses to start the new year, those working in the organization saw the losses as a troubling sign.

"We won the first two games of the 1987 playoffs when we beat Quebec at home, but from a larger standpoint, we didn't play particularly well, and you didn't feel a whole lot of confidence going up to Quebec. But we won Game Two, and that was that end of it. *Nine in a row,*" Willand said of the streak spanning two seasons, "and you could sort of feel things slipping away at that point.

"I remember thinking in 1986–87 it'll never end, and then, the next year, it all just unraveled against Quebec."

There were other changes—red flags began to pop up with employees. The franchise lost some of the family feeling. The sense of community that had always permeated the organization was starting to slip away. Part of that was because the NHL was changing; revenues were increasing, as well as cost, and financially sound but small-market organizations like Hartford faced a new set of challenges. Professional sports had always been big business, but now, the deals were in the tens of millions of dollars as opposed to the tens of thousands. The NHL landscape was changing, and the Whalers felt the impact.

Another change was that Baldwin started spending more time on the West Coast. "One other thing that changed around that time behind the scenes was that Howard started spending more time in Hollywood, and his lieutenants were left to run the organization," said one staffer. "The people who remained behind did as well as they could, but it just didn't have the same feel to it because he was never around."

On the ice, the franchise had ascended to become a playoff team, building a steady roster of talent that could compete with the rest of the NHL's elite on any given night. They made the playoffs in back-to-back years in hockey's toughest division. Forty-plus regular-season wins and a playoff spot was now the baseline for success. Stars like Francis, Dineen, and Liut were among the best in the game at their position, and the Whalers did have good depth. But how do you make that leap from being a playoff team to a serious Cup contender?

That season, the Whalers tried to build back after the five-game losing skid started the year, seemingly always chasing respectability, but despite the roster, it was a maddeningly inconsistent team. In February, that could very well have been one of the reasons why Evans, in an offhanded comment with the media, said he wasn't planning on coaching beyond his latest contract, which ran through the 1988–89 season. (Another reason could have been the "Jack Must Go!" chants at the Civic Center in the wake of the multiple losing skids.) And even though Emile Francis had been Evans's most rabid booster over the years, the losing was enough to cause him to pull the plug on his friend. Later that month, he fired Evans—the winningest coach in franchise history to that point—and replaced him with Larry Pleau.

But the change did little. The Whalers did reach .500 a few times and peeked over the break-even mark in late January when a 4–2 win over the Canucks in Vancouver made them 22-21-7. But things were never quite right; their defense and penalty-killing unit were among the best in the league, but an inconsistent attack left them struggling at times to put the puck in the net. They were twentieth out of twenty-one teams in scoring. Facing an ignominious fate—they were in danger of becoming the first team in NHL history since the 1943 Rangers to go from division champions to cellar-dwellers in one season—they rallied to win five of their last six and barely sneak into the postseason. Could that late-season momentum provide the boost needed to fuel an upset of the mighty Canadiens?

In a word, no. Hartford fell into a quick 3-0 hole in the series, and while the team rallied to win a pair of games to cut the deficit to 3–2, despite injuries to Liut and Samuelsson, the Habs ended things with a 2–1 win in Game Six in Montreal. The finish was a pleasant surprise for a team that was up and down for much of the season, and the Whalers could take some solace in that three of the four playoff losses were by 1 goal. But there was no getting around the frustrating fact that the season came to an end at the hands of the Canadiens—again. It felt like *Groundhog Day* on ice. (Unlike previous postseason losses to Montreal, however, the Whalers couldn't even comfort themselves with knowing the mighty Canadiens would end up playing deep into the spring. Montreal was steamrolled in the second round by Boston.)

"You guys played well in adversity," a reporter told Pleau after the narrow Game Six loss.

"You've got to *win* in adversity too," he replied glumly.

In stark contrast to the end of the previous regular season, where it was all possibilities and tomorrows, now, things were considerably gloomier. The Whalers finished the regular season with 77 points, 16 fewer than the previous year when they won the division title. They needed to hire a new coach. Key personnel and front-office questions were on the horizon. Suddenly, a franchise that appeared poised to take the next step on the road to greatness instead found itself at a crossroads.

"In the mid-1980s we had gotten to a point where we felt we could compete," said PA announcer Greg Gilmartin. "But at the same time, it's not over until it's over, you know? The whole concept of getting to the playoffs is okay, but I mean, at some point if you don't win the whole thing, what are we doing here?"

8

The Trade(s)
1988-92

Eddie Johnston always said he was going to build a Stanley Cup winner. He didn't tell us it was going to be in Pittsburgh.
—Ex-Whaler Ray Ferraro, on the deal that sent Ron Francis from Hartford to Pittsburgh

Ronnie should have been a career Whaler. That's all there is to it.
—Hartford goaltender Peter Sidorkiewicz

At the dawn of the 1988–89 season, the Whalers were in a transitional period. They had established themselves as a playoff team, one with a capable roster that appeared to be poised to make the leap to consistent contender. In the previous eighteen months, they had posted playoff wins and won a division championship. But they changed ownership and the coaching staff.

Despite the inconsistency that marked the 1987–88 team, they still had many elements needed to be a success. There was the easy-to-measure on-ice success when it came to wins and losses, but they also found success away from the rink, in the community. The players and their families were active in charity organizations throughout the state—the team prioritized appearances at fundraising events.

Those appearances had two primary benefits: they would help needy organizations and would help win the hearts and minds of the fan base. "Once they meet you, they'll never boo you," play-by-play man Rick Peckham recalled telling the players who first arrived in Hartford.

"One of the greatest things about being a small-market team was the fact that we were all very active in the community," Tippett said. "The one that really stands out to me was the Whalers' Waltz, where we helped raise money to fight childhood cancer. [Mike Liut's] wife, Mary Ann, ran it one year; my wife ran it one year; [Ron Francis's] wife ran it one year. Those sorts of things really brought the players and the community together.

"Our family and the Liut family lived side by side—we were two of the three houses on a cul-de-sac at the end of a nice little street in Simsbury," he added. "Mike drove this big, black Mercedes; I drove a half-ton pickup. They called us the odd couple. We'd ride together to practice all the time."

"As it turned out, the Tippett and Liut families were next-door neighbors—Dave and I drove to the rink together almost daily . . . so I was closest to him," said Liut. "But we had a good group—we did a lot of things as a team, and the smaller groups were never the same . . . just whatever circumstances dictated.

"The other thing—and I know it's different in sports now, where guys have one house where they play and one house in their own community. When we were in Hartford, I mean, that's where we lived. We'd go away on vacation, but we were home. All the guys who played in Hartford, pretty much all of us, lived there year-round. It was that sort of community."

But that sense of community, one of the genuine strengths of the team throughout the mid-1980s, was starting to show some cracks. Baldwin eventually departed just before the start of the 1988 season. In

September of that year, the sale of the team was approved by the NHL Board of Governors, with the final price tag at $31 million. Real-estate developer Richard Gordon and Donald Conrad, the Aetna executive, ended up owning 74.5 percent, worth $23 million. Aetna owned 13 percent, while Cigna and Travelers owed 2 percent each.

As for Baldwin, his place in Whalers history is immense. Simply put, the franchise—initially in WHA form, or later, as part of the NHL— wouldn't have existed without him.

"I feel great pride when I look back on the Whaler experience," Baldwin wrote in his autobiography. "I would be the first to acknowledge that there were certain decisions I had made that were impulsive, yet overall I was pleased with the job I had done. When the sale was officially approved by the NHL in the summer of 1988 and the power was transferred from my hands and the hands of the corporate partners to the Gordon/Conrad interests, I felt they were taking over a team that was poised for great success in the 1990s."

Things were changing on the ice as well. In October, Stew Gavin was taken by the North Stars in the waiver draft. Gavin wasn't a superstar but was a respected member of a team that surged to prominence in the mid-1980s, so much so that a fan-generated petition protesting the move garnered thousands of signatures.

He ripped management's decision to leave him unprotected. "I was floored Friday when I found out I wasn't protected," he told the *Courant*. "A lot of people we met in our three years here have been really supportive. When you hear you might get picked up pretty high, it gives you a sense of pride again. You get dropped and aren't good enough to be in the top 18 skaters, a lot of emotions run through your mind . . . humiliation. I was mad. My wife's expecting a baby. I was really ready to contribute this year. My life was going great, then it's 180 degrees the other way."

Even with Gavin gone, 1988–89 really marked the last gasp for the old guard. They got a full season out of stalwarts Francis and Dineen, but it was an inconsistent regular season. That year, the Whalers were never over .500—they reached the break-even plateau just once after October. There were acknowledged high points, including January 19, 1989, at the Civic Center, when they scored 6 straight goals in twenty-two minutes to erase a 4–0 Montreal lead on the way to a 6–4 win, the biggest comeback victory in franchise history.

The season ended in an uneven 37-38-5 record, fourth place in the Adams Division, and a first-round date with the Canadiens—*again*. But the difference between the regular-season and postseason performances for the Whalers was nothing short of stunning. After dropping Game One, 6–2, Hartford and Montreal played three 1-goal games, with two of them going to overtime. The Whalers hung with the Canadiens throughout, playing tough, smart, fast, and physical hockey. Hartford was ultimately swept out of the postseason by Montreal, but the competitive nature of the series gave fans hope that the performance could be replicated moving forward.

"The last three games could have gone either way. It's kind of amazing we didn't get one of them," Joel Quenneville said after the Game Four loss, the fourth time in five years the Whalers had been eliminated from the postseason by an overtime goal.

"If we can remember the work ethic we showed in this series and play like that in the regular season—because we were inconsistent in the regular season—if we can remember that we'll be much better off."

"We're at the hump," added Ray Ferraro. "We have to make a move and go over or go back."

To Ferraro's point, changes were in the offing. On the ice, many youngsters were pushing for playing time, with the most notable case coming between the pipes, where youngster Kay Whitmore had supplanted Liut, at least in the eyes of the coaching staff. Whitmore was the starter the last few weeks of the regular season and into the playoffs. While Liut said he had no plans to retire, the writing was on the wall, at least at that point.

Off the ice, there were changes as well, as Gordon moved into the primary ownership role, while Emile Francis was relieved of the

GM's job. Although Francis would remain with the franchise—he was reassigned as team president—it marked the end of an era for Hartford hockey. Francis had helped shape the roster into a playoff-ready group, shaking the franchise out of its doldrums and producing a consistent winner in the process. Simply put, you couldn't tell the story of the rise of the Whalers without putting Emile Francis in the first paragraph.

But a very real backslide followed that rapid ascent. The two previous years, the team had struggled to make the playoffs and was eliminated by Montreal. (The *Courant* noted smartly that the same arc had occurred in Francis's two previous stops as GM—with the Rangers and Blues—where a quick rise from mediocrity to the playoffs was inevitably followed by a slide back to .500.) For his part, Francis didn't seem thrilled at the idea of being replaced and blamed the *Courant*'s negative coverage for the playoff finale drawing just 12,245, a season low.

"If the fans are disappointed then a lot of it is because of what you people have written," Francis told reporters at his year-end press conference. "I've never seen so much negative press, and I'm talking particularly about the *Hartford Courant*. The past few months, I'm talking about the ownership squabble, as to who's going to do what when they take over, is probably the most negative press I've ever seen as long as I've been in this game."

Several names were offered as possible replacements for Francis, with the biggest name likely being Bob Johnson, a hockey legend with a lengthy resume that included college titles at Wisconsin and a berth in the Cup finals with the Flames. But in the end, Gordon settled on Eddie Johnston, a former Bruins goaltender who had also served as the GM of the Penguins. On May 12, 1989, the team announced that it had hired Johnston as its new vice president and GM. He was given a three-year contract.

"The easy decision was obviously to hire Bob Johnson," Gordon said. "Bob's articulate, has an impeccable résumé and he's exciting.

"But the *right* decision was Ed Johnston. Our goal in Hartford isn't just to make the playoffs and make money. It's to be the best team in the NHL and win the Stanley Cup. I think E.J. can do it."

"There is no question that there are going to be changes. I'm going to evaluate everybody," Johnston said after being introduced. "We have a good nucleus here, what we have to do is make a few trades. I want to change attitudes. That's a No. 1 priority."

The voice who put Johnston over the top? Bobby Orr—the Bruins' legend and an associate of Bob Caporale, who worked for the Whalers and was on Gordon's selection committee. Caporale introduced Orr to Gordon, and Orr soon became a committee member and recommended his old Boston teammate.

"He's a friend," Orr told the *Courant*. "But I wouldn't recommend anyone if I didn't think he could do the job. In time, you'll find it's the right selection. Eddie's a great guy, straight shooter, knows the game, no bull."

A stable of ex-Bruins suddenly had their fingerprints all over the franchise: Orr had the ear of the owner, Gerry Cheevers was in the broadcast booth, and Johnston was in the front office.

Almost a month later—and after dalliances with Bob Johnson and Bob Berry—Johnston installed Ley as the new head coach. Ley followed Pleau as the second former player to step behind the bench in Hartford.

It was clear that Ley was going to be as intense a coach as he was a player. "I'm excited. I'm ready to start work yesterday," Ley said at his introductory press conference. "I'll promise you this: we will get 100 percent 100 percent of the time. We want to create an atmosphere where it hurts you deeply to lose."

The hiring of Ley was met with two reactions: One, there was a question that, with the possibility of hiring someone else like Johnson, why would the Whalers go for someone like Ley? He was an original Whaler, sure, but his coaching background was painfully thin, having worked only in the minors before landing the head-coaching gig in

Hartford. *This was the guy who was going to reinvigorate the locker room?* Two, there was a flip side. A super-intense and fiery leader, he would be the sort of coach who could provide the necessary spark to get a talented roster deep into the playoffs. *This is just the sort of guy who will reinvigorate the locker room!*

The Johnston-Ley pairing got to work immediately. Even the most cynical fan realized that the duo had its good points—namely, Johnston had zero allegiances to anyone within the organization, while the no-nonsense Ley wasn't afraid of pissing anyone off. Together, they were clearly willing to do whatever they felt was necessary to shake things up and get the Whalers to the next level.

The first move was a firecracker—on June 17, 1989, Johnston heisted the gritty Pat Verbeek from New Jersey for underachieving forward Sylvain Turgeon. "Verbeek can score and will provide toughness," Johnston said after the deal went down. "Sylvain was having a tough time in our organization, and we just felt it was best to do something. We're very happy to get Verbeek."

Turgeon had played six seasons with the Whalers and had great success in the early days, including an impressive 40-goal season as a nineteen-year-old with the 1983–84 team—he finished third in Rookie of the Year voting—and a 45-goal campaign in 1985–86 at twenty-one, which caused some to tab the left winger as one of the league's next great snipers. But those numbers tumbled as he was plagued by abdominal issues and a shoulder injury. He was set to become a free agent that summer, and with that in mind—and with the Devils dangling Verbeek—Johnston pulled the trigger on the trade, the same day as the 1989 NHL Draft.

Whereas Turgeon tailed off (he would break the 30-goal barrier just once in his career after leaving Hartford and end up leaving the game after the 1994–95 season), Verbeek was seemingly built for endurance. He would play until the age of thirty-seven, racking up all sorts of awards along the way. In Hartford, his presence fit squarely with the likes of Dineen, Francis, Tippett, and Quenneville.

The Whalers never had a *truly great* team, but they had a few good ones. The 1989–90 team was one of the best of that vintage, probably the best one since the Adams Division champion from a few years before. They finished fourth in a stacked division race with 85 points, but their final point total would have been good enough to finish tied for first in the Patrick Division with the Rangers, or second in the Norris Division behind the Blackhawks, which ended up with 88 points. They were the second-best road team in the league, and a stout defense yielded just 268 goals, sixth-best in the NHL, while an evenly distributed scoring attack saw five different players finish with 20 goals or more.

But Johnston kept dealing. On March 5, 1990, Liut was sent to Washington for Yvon "Ike" Corriveau. Liut, who would be recalled as the greatest goaltender in franchise history, won 115 games in his five-plus seasons with the Whalers. It was a shocking move for the fans, as well as those on the roster.

"If you're not disappointed, what does that say about where you were?" Liut asked shortly after the deal went down. "I liked Hartford and liked the organization, and in that situation you give yourself to the team. It's tough when you wake up the next day and you're not teammates anymore."

A few things were at play in the Liut trade: One, at the time, he was probably one of their most tradeable chips. A former All-Star who had a suffered some bumps and bruises along the way, he was seen as a known commodity who, when healthy, could provide stability in goal for a veteran team in need of a final piece. Two, with that in mind, the thirty-four-year-old Liut could probably bring a decent return of young talent from a team in need of some help. The deal was not unlike the Stoughton or Rogers trades Pleau had made a decade before. Three, despite Liut's legacy of success in Hartford, the Whalers felt like they had a pair of young goalies in Peter Sidorkiewicz and Kay Whitmore who could grow into the role at a much cheaper rate than Liut's annual $455,000 salary.

All that said, Liut had grown into a foundational figure in Hartford. In his six years with the Whalers, he might not have been the all-out star that Francis became or the gritty, working-class hero that Dineen evolved into. But in terms of changing the culture, raising expectations, and shaping a new era of hockey, Liut did more than just about anyone. Dismissed by fans when he first arrived, he gave the franchise a sense of legitimacy. That was why this deal was such a bummer in the eyes of many Hartford hockey fans. His critics could accuse him of being a locker-room lawyer and someone too canny for his own good. ("Mike Liut is the smartest man in hockey. *Just ask him*," said one media member who covered the team in the late 1980s.) But he legitimately cared about the Whalers.

At a time when some players teared up when they learned they were going to Hartford, Liut teared up when he was told he was *traded away* from Hartford—in a postswap Q&A with Channel 3, Liut got emotional when talking about leaving the Whalers.

But he and Johnston had clashed on a number of topics, and although the deal couldn't be classified as being personal, it was easy to see how personalities may have factored into the move, at least on some level. At one point late in his Hartford career, Liut believed himself to be an All-Star goaltender if he had not gotten hurt. Johnston responded with, "With all respect, I don't see any Stanley Cup ring on his finger." So when Johnston was asked for an assessment of the deal, it wasn't a surprise to hear his response.

"In all honesty, Mike was not in our plans for next year," Johnston told reporters. "We would have been forced to give him a termination deal. If he stayed next season we'd be looking at a situation that would hinder the development of a young goalie. And then at the end of the season, to boot, Mike would be a free agent with no compensation."

Now, the starter's role would be passed to Sidorkiewicz, a youngster who had made his bones as a minor leaguer and a backup to Liut. He may have felt some butterflies in the moment, but with the benefit of hindsight, he said there was no added pressure in succeeding someone like Liut. "I didn't even look at it that way," Sidorkiewicz said. "One thing I tried to learn early in my career—there are only so many things you can control when you are a player. When you start to think about other things, like what management thinks, you can drive yourself crazy. The only thing I focused on was the fact I had an opportunity to be a starting goaltender in the NHL, and that's what I was going with."

Corriveau, who came back in the deal, was a first-rounder who hoped to regain some mojo after a couple of lost years with the Capitals. The veteran left-winger was well liked across the league, thanks in part to an ability to keep everyone loose.

"Yvon Corriveau . . . he would be the kind of guy you would look forward to talking to in the locker room," said Adam Burt with a laugh. "That's where he would hold court and tell his road-trip stories. You'd hear him and think, *If he did half the stuff he said he did, I'm not sure how he's still alive.*"

"He seemed like he was always bouncing off the walls," Sidorkiewicz said of Corriveau. "He was a fun guy, but sometimes, you just wanted to say, 'Oh my God, just stop.'"

"Legend," recalled defenseman Al Pedersen. "Led the league in dance shoes on the road. Everybody loved Ike."

"Ike was a great guy—a lot of fun, and fun to be around," said goaltender Frank Pietrangelo. "He loved life—when he came to the rink, he put a smile on everyone's face.

"But man, he was a hairy bastard. He looked like a monkey. He was covered in hair. We used to *give it to him*—I remember some guys saying they couldn't wait to get to the beach. Someone asked Ike about that—he said, 'Are you kidding? You add water to me, I'm like a Chia Pet.' He had a full-grown afro on his back."

Corriveau had 4 goals in the last three regular-season games and was part of a team that went unbeaten in eight of its last ten games to head into the playoffs on an up note.

Against this backdrop, the Whalers-Bruins first-round playoff matchup was one of the most anticipated in the league. Boston was the winner of that year's President's Trophy, awarded to the team with the most points, but Hartford won the regular-season series between the two teams, 4-3-1—six of the eight games were decided by 1 goal or fewer.

"I laugh about this now because I'm in the media, but it always feels like any matchup in the playoffs is the worst possible matchup. But the first round that year, in part because of geography and everything else, we had our work cut out for us," said Dave Poulin, who was a part of the 1990 Bruins. "We knew it would be a tough matchup. That was almost a 100-point team, filled with guys who weren't just good players, but hard players: Francis, Verbeek—the original little ball of rage—and the rest. There was Kevin Dineen, as good a leader and as tough a kid as they come. They were hard to play against.

"That was a really, really rough matchup for us. They played hard every night—Hartford was a really, really good team, an underrated team. The number of those guys who have gone into coaching and working in different aspects of the hockey world should tell you that."

As players, Ley and Mike Milbury, Boston's coach, had been pugnacious, and for the most part, the stars of each team were more than willing to follow their lead. So it wasn't a surprise the teams engaged in some memorable brawls in the late 1980s and early 1990s, including a November 1990 contest with a series of memorable skirmishes, including when Boston's Cam Neely cracked Hartford's Randy Ladouceur over the head. Afterward, the Bruins alleged the Whalers started the whole thing by taking a series of runs at goalie Andy Moog.

"I was told [Milbury] said we ran the goalkeeper. You've got him quoted on that? Well I'll go down there myself and punch him right in the mouth," Johnston told the *Courant*. "If I was coaching, I would have been on my bench, over the glass, and in his bench right after him. Did he say that Todd Krygier got pushed into the net and into Andy Moog [by Ray Bourque] too? I didn't think so."

Although individual grudges were on both sides, the one most people remember is between Neely and Samuelsson. The gleefully annoying Samuelsson took great delight in provoking stars throughout the league and never missed a chance to poke at Neely when Samuelsson was with Hartford. (That personal rivalry would ultimately extend for the rest of their playing days. After Samuelsson was dealt to Pittsburgh in March 1991, a knee-to-knee hit from Samuelsson resulted in a devastating knee injury to Neely that would limit his effectiveness for the next two seasons.)

"I remember playing against him one night—we were fucking slashing and cross-checking the shit out of each other, but I could never get him to drop the gloves, that fucking puke," recalled Chris Nilan, who mixed it up with Samuelsson for more than a decade as a member of the Canadiens and Bruins. "He would irritate the shit out of you and not fight. We would have fights every so often, and it was crazy—just two gladiators in a ring, just trying to beat the other one to death.

"Every chance they had, guys wanted to finish their checks on him and give him a shot. Fuck, *I* wanted to run him. He wasn't small—a good-sized kid. He played hard, and he played with an edge. But when I was with the Bruins, guys freaking hated him. They all thought that was a cheap shot on Cam. The Bruins certainly never forgot that.

"I mean, you don't go into every game saying, 'Let's go kill this guy.' But you had to be aware where he was any time you played him. You had to pay attention when he was on the ice at all times."

Harford won two of the first three games of the series, which included a split in the first two contests at Boston Garden. All three contests were the usual rock 'em, sock 'em Adams Division playoff contests, with plenty of stoppages in play and a long list of penalty minutes. The Whalers jumped to a 3–0 lead on the way to a 4–3 win in Game One, and added 3 third-period goals in Game Three to capture a 5–3 decision.

The series was billed as the Battle of New England, and for some, that was not much of an exaggeration. "That spring, my college roommate—who is from Lynn—and I got into a fistfight during one of the Bruins-Whalers playoff games," said Hartford fan Stephen Popper. "I don't recall what started it, but both of us ended up at the hospital later that week with broken bones. Drinking may have been involved."

Except for a brief Game Two letdown in the Boston Garden, the Whalers were in control for most of the first three games. Now, with a 5–2 lead going into the third period in Game Four and twenty minutes from a commanding 3-1 series lead, they were poised to seize control.

At that point, two things broke right for the Bruins: Milbury decided to pull goaltender Reggie Lemelin, and they had Dave Poulin. Poulin, who was acquired by the Bruins in a midseason trade, had a knack for coming up big in big moments. "We're going to steal this one," Poulin said in the Boston locker room, over and over between the second and third period. Meanwhile, in the upper reaches of the Civic Center, Bruins fans were keeping the faith.

"The civilized Hartford fans didn't know what hit them," said hockey writer Mick Colageo. "They were just enjoying the hockey, and they were behind their team. They had no idea how deep the passion ran for the Bruins. In the balcony in back of them, a group—which included myself—was completely crazy. We completely lost it when the Bruins made that comeback. I brought one of my friends, a fantastic street hockey player named Mikey Dowd, and he was all bummed out. 'It's not like this is even fun,' he said with his head in his hands. I told him, 'Mikey, wait until they come back and win this game.' I mean, I felt like an idiot at the time.

"But then it happened, and the back end of that balcony all filled with Bruins fans, there were guys who didn't know each other who were standing face-to-face, four inches apart from other guys and they were screaming at each other. The Hartford fans were looking back at us like, 'What is wrong with those people?' Those were the same people who were on the concourse during intermission who were talking about the next series and could they win it in six or would it go seven. I just thought these people don't get it. This'll be a fight."

Poulin started the comeback with a goal at 1:28 of the third and added an assist on Dave Christian's game-tying score. Meanwhile, Mike Tomlak and Scott Young missed out on prime scoring opportunities for the Whalers. With no answer for Poulin or Moog and the game slipping from its grasp, Hartford was unable to clear the zone with just under two minutes left. Boston's Randy Burridge collected the puck at the top of the slot and sent a slow backhander dribbling toward Poulin, who was on his way to the Hartford goal. Poulin and Samuelsson were jockeying for position, and the two of them—and the puck—were nearing Hartford goalie Peter Sidorkiewicz. The puck ricocheted off a skate and skittered past Sidorkiewicz: *6–5, Bruins.*

"The puck moved pretty good laterally, and it basically came down to me taking Ulfie to the net, and eventually I was just down on my knees, banging away at the puck," recalled Poulin. "Kerry Fraser was the ref, and he had great position down below the goal line. The puck just slid inside the post, and he motioned goal. In this day and age with instant replay, it might have been waved off."

"I don't even know who had the puck," Sidorkiewicz told reporters after the game. "He just seemed to slide it in their feet. I was looking at feet, and the puck . . . and I just couldn't pick it up in time."

"We had a lot of situations where our third man gambled and lost in the third period," Ley said afterward. "We didn't really use our heads. Plus, our old team reared its ugly head. We had players working as individuals instead of as a team. There's nothing we can do about this game now. I just wish we could have thrown a blanket on the ice and stopped the game at a certain point."

It was a gutting defeat. Afterward, the Whalers knew they had missed out on a colossal opportunity.

"We blew it in the third period," Samuelsson told the media after the game.

"We're going to find out a lot about our team," Ferraro said to the *Courant.* "We'll see how much inner strength we have. We can't sit and sulk about this. We can't have an official day of mourning. But it sure does stink. You have a three-goal lead in the third. And it should be in the books."

"The Whalers trail this best-of-seven playoff series, 2–2," wrote Alan Greenberg in the *Courant.* "No, that's not a misprint. They were on the verge of writing a bright new chapter in Whalers history, only to have Gang Green turn the third period into Nostalgia Night at the Civic Center. And when you're talking Whalers nostalgia, it ain't exactly *Happy Days*. It's *The Twilight Zone*."

To their credit, the Whalers kept battling. The two teams split the next two games, with Hartford rebounding after a Game Five loss to take the sixth game at the Civic Center on the strength of a 3–2 overtime win, with Dineen connecting for the game-winner at 12:30 of the extra session.

But in Game Seven in Boston, the Bruins jumped to an early 2–0 lead with a pair of first-period goals (including on a 5-on-4 power play) and added to their edge with a second-period tally. They also got an emotional boost with the return of Ray Bourque, who had been sidelined with a hip injury sustained in Game Two of the series.

"I thought we were going to be fine for Game Seven, especially after I saw Ray step on the ice," Poulin said. "A Willis Reed moment. And Cam Neely was tremendous in that game as well."

Meanwhile, the Whalers couldn't convert on multiple scoring chances against Moog, as Francis and Verbeek were off the mark with their first-period opportunities. In the end, Moog made 27 saves—18 of them in the first period—the Bruins advanced, and the Whalers went home for the summer, losing by a 3–1 score.

The Whalers had played well over the course of the year, and while they finished fourth in the Adams Division, they had managed to be a pain in the ass for the rest of the league from start to finish. Ley had instilled a feistiness that made them tough to play against every night, with elite talent such as Francis, Dineen, Verbeek, and others.

But in hindsight, the Liut trade took an awful lot of wind out of their sails. While Sidorkiewicz would grow into an excellent goaltender, the loss of a veteran of Liut's stature so late in the season would be difficult to overcome, especially when stacked against a team like Boston in the postseason.

"I loved Eddie Johnston as a Bruin, but I really felt like he blew it as a GM. Trading Francis and Samuelsson, he not only set up the Bruins in that division, he created a great team with the Penguins," Colageo said. "And if Liut was still Hartford's goaltender, they win that 1990 series against the Bruins. I firmly believe that. I mean, the Whalers might have won the *Cup* if they had kept it together. And Pittsburgh would not have won because they wouldn't have gotten that great second-line center in Francis they needed so badly. If Hartford doesn't make that trade, who knows what happens to the Penguins?"

That 1990 series was another chapter in the fierce Adams Division feud between Boston and Hartford. Although the Bruins didn't always focus on the Whalers as their primary foe—that ire was usually reserved for the Canadiens—Hartford almost always viewed Boston as its number-one rival. And because tickets at the Civic Center were easier to get than seats in Boston Garden, it seemed like there was just as much black and gold as green and white when the Whalers and Bruins met in Hartford.

"That was *always* a problem," said PA announcer Gilmartin. "I mean, the season tickets sold well, but there was always room for Bruins fans when they played in Hartford. There was fighting going on a lot of times. Put it this way: everything was either cheered or jeered, one way or another. There was a sense of real animosity at those games, to a point where there was some real intensity."

"When the Bruins and Rangers were in town and you were on the concourse, if someone scored, the cheers were such that you had to wait a couple of seconds for 'Brass Bonanza,'" said longtime Hartford sportscaster Rich Coppola. "If you heard it, you knew the Whalers had scored. If you didn't, you knew it was New York or Boston. That's what the cheering was like." Fifteen years later, Baltimore's Camden Yards would provide Red Sox fans with the same experience—cheap seats, easy location, and a division rival their team could beat up on—that Bruins fans had at the Civic Center.

"I loved going there through the 1990s," Colageo said. "I loved driving into town and seeing this parade of black and gold walking down Asylum Street an hour before the start of the game. It was like Camden Yards for Boston hockey fans—just a pure takeover. And let's face it, it was easier to get a ticket."

You could argue that the rivalry peaked during the 1990–91 season, which included a bitter brawl at the Boston Garden on the back end of a home-and-home series. There were 100 penalty minutes handed out in that one, many of which came after a third-period hit Hartford's Ed Kastelic put on Boston's Craig Janney that set off a memorable melee.

"I was coming back into my zone as a winger, back-checking in the slot, and I was on the ice with Janney and Neely. It wasn't my normal matchup—thinking about it now, I'm not sure why I was out there," Kastelic recalled. "But I was just coming back, and I had settled into the slot, and Craig [Janney] was coming into that area, maybe five to ten feet away, and he was looking in the other direction. I hit him. I didn't mean to clock him, but he was coming my direction, and he didn't see me. I didn't hit him hard, but he looked like he was hit and he went down. I just didn't move out of the way."

The hit produced plenty of fireworks. Dean Evason started tangling with Neely, and Nilan and Kastelic went at it for a bit. "Then, there were a couple of guys trying to get at me. . . . I think Nilan was one of them. Nothing really happened at first, but they were escorting me off the ice," he added.

"The benches at the old Boston Garden were side by side, and you basically had to walk through the Bruins' bench to get to the locker room," Kastelic said. "I saw [Lyndon] Byers there, ready to meet me. I anticipated the door opening up, I gave him a quick jab, and that's when he tried to punch me, and that's when the benches erupted. You had Verbeek, who is good with the stick, working there as well. He was a stand-up guy who would score goals and was feisty. The glass between the benches started shaking. *Oh my God. What's going on?*

"So yeah, every time we played them, there was a lot of intensity. You could feel it all the time."

"It was a *great* rivalry," recalled Bobby Carpenter. "The place was always packed—it was very exciting. Hartford always rose to the occasion against the Bruins, so we never went in there and played soft or we'd get beat pretty good. But you always knew you were going in there to play a game. It was always a tough one. It was a great place to play."

One night, after Neely gave Geoff Sanderson a cheap shot, Adam Burt went after him. "The thing about Cam was that he was a lot tougher than me, but I knew I had to get into it with him after that, especially because Sandy was our best scorer at the time," recalled Burt.

"So, we're going at it pretty good, and I get the idea to switch up hands and clock him with my left. I gave him a black eye and knocked him down. Well, our bench wouldn't shut up. They're egging him on. 'Burt kicked your butt, Cam.' You could see Cam getting more and more mad as it went in. I was like, 'Shut up, guys. I don't want to fight him all night.' Sure enough, when we got out of the penalty box, he came after me again. He wasn't going to stop, and he eventually got some payback."

Things were equally as spicy off the ice. One retired Hartford policeman—who chose to remain anonymous—recalled one night in the late 1980s where the Bruins' bus was boxed in after an overtime win for the Whalers at the Civic Center, and Boston coach Terry O'Reilly wasn't happy about it.

"When the Bruins arrived at their bus to travel home, a car had blocked the bus in. Terry became so upset, he was screaming every swear in the book. 'Fuck Hartford. This city sucks.' Well, the Bruins bus waited five minutes when Terry lost it. He grabbed a hockey stick, whacking the parked car. He destroyed it. He then had some players pick up the destroyed car to allow an exit for the bus.

"Hartford Police were required to make an arrest. We called a commander to the scene to make the call. Terry was foaming at the mouth. I was just thinking that if we arrested this guy, the bus full of Bruins were going to fight back. Well, the district chief issued a summons to O'Reilly for criminal mischief, with a court appearance. The ticket was issued, and four police motor units escorted the bus out of the city. By the way, the chief was disciplined for his actions, [for] not making a custodial [physical] arrest."

IF YOU'RE LOOKING FOR A POINT WHEN THINGS REALLY started to turn for the Whalers, you can trace it back to the spring of 1990. And it had absolutely nothing to do with losing to the Bruins in the playoffs.

Basketball had been coming on in Connecticut for the last several years. Jim Calhoun had replaced Dom Perno as the University of Connecticut head coach in the spring of 1986, and by 1988, he had the Huskies competing on the national stage, winning an NIT championship. In January 1990 UConn opened Gampel Pavilion, a state-of-the-art on-campus facility. And later that spring the Huskies made a memorable tournament run that captured the hearts of college basketball fans everywhere and was sparked by a last-second jumper from Tate George, lifting Connecticut over Clemson and into the Elite Eight. It started a legendary run that decade that saw the Huskies turn into a full-fledged college basketball hotbed.

While the Whalers were coming off an impressive first-round series against the Bruins, which would make it all the way to the Cup finals that year, the season was still a loss. Meanwhile, UConn basketball had suddenly become one of the darlings of the sports world—the women's team would break through in 1995 with its first of many national championships—and the charismatic Calhoun and the affable Geno Auriemma, the women's basketball coach, were able to charm Connecticut sports fans.

The rise of UConn basketball—presented the first substantial in-state challenge to the Whalers in terms of sporting dollars. They had never faced this sort of threat within the borders of Connecticut—a big-time athletic program that was winning consistently and picking up momentum. To their credit, the Whalers' recent run of success appeared to have them on good footing, but the surging UConn basketball program would leave them no margin for error anymore. From that point on, mediocrity was no longer an option. The state wanted a winner, and they had one building in Storrs, Connecticut.

"UConn basketball became larger than life," said Whalers broadcaster John Forslund of the seismic shift that was taking place, "and Jim Calhoun became the most important guy in the state."

Adding a new layer to their troubles was the deteriorating relationship between Ron Francis and the front office. The first signs of trouble came as early as April 1989 when Francis started speculating about his future with the team, saying after the playoff loss to the Canadiens, "If I get traded, I get traded. Maybe that would be for the best. Maybe it's time I move on." During the 1989–90 season, contract negotiations with new ownership and management stalled, and in December 1990 coach Rick Ley inexplicably stripped Francis of the captaincy, giving the *C* to Pat Verbeek. "I was not happy with the direction the team was going or the leadership, and I felt a change was necessary," Ley told reporters.

"Maybe it will take some of the pressure of me," Francis said. "I said, 'If you think that's better for the club, I'm all for it.'"

The move had an immediate ripple effect throughout the franchise and the fan base. You were either a Francis guy or a Johnston and Ley guy. As for the owner, he immediately let people know where he was aligned.

"Ron Francis is a good player," Gordon told the *Courant* shortly after the decision was announced. "Ron Francis is the kind of person every family would want to have as a son. He's been a great asset to the Hartford Whalers. But I think management felt that for our team to improve and to get to the next step we need a little different direction. I think that's really what made the decision.

"This didn't just happen overnight. I've known about this a long time. There's been a lot of discussion about this for months and months. There's no easy way to do this. There is no nice way to do this. There is no consenting way to do it. It's probably the hardest decision Ricky ever had to make, but I think he felt it was the right thing to do at the time."

One of the things that was certainly part of the conversation was that Francis was coming to the end of his contract. That season, he was making $380,000 and, according to the *Courant,* was angling for a raise that would make him between $700,000 and $750,000 in the first year of a new four-year contract.

The discussion around the sort of financial commitment the Whalers might have ended up making to Francis has to be put in the context of NHL salary structure at that time. Even though the salaries were a few years away from truly heading for the stratosphere, it was evident that the Whalers were a small-market team rapidly getting left behind most of the rest of the league. A National Hockey League Players' Association (NHLPA) survey for the 1990–91 season showed the Whalers had an average salary of $186,000. Only Quebec, at $169,000, was lower. (Hartford's total payroll of $5.2 million rated nineteenth.) With those sorts of parameters, the idea of doubling the salary of a player, even a beloved franchise cornerstone like Francis, was a less-than-palatable option.

But the ownership roundly rejected the idea that Francis's contract status had anything to do with the decision. "The issue really is not a question of free agency and contracts. It has nothing to do with that. That was never even thought about," Gordon told the *Courant.* "The real issue was, here's where we are, here's where we want to go, how are we going to get there?"

In hindsight, the gamesmanship between the two sides was the clearest symbol that the franchise and the franchise player were headed for a divorce. When this sort of passive-aggressive bickering takes place, it's usually a sign that there is a much deeper divide present between the two camps, and that was fairly evident here.

When it came to the stretch between Ley's decision to switch captains and the trade of Francis to Pittsburgh, the one thing that many people around the team seemed to agree on was that, while Francis was no longer the captain in name, he was still just as much of a leader as he had been before. That was no disrespect intended to Verbeek; Francis's stature in the room was so great, nothing was going to change it. "They still looked to Ronnie," said one staffer. "I think the guys in the room knew who the leader was."

TAKEN INDIVIDUALLY, NONE OF THOSE EVENTS—THE DRAMATIC ascension of basketball as a big-time competitor, the playoff loss to the Bruins, the unrest simmering between the superstar and the team—would necessarily be enough to submarine a franchise. But the combination of those things happening within months of each other was enough to shake the foundation.

Against that backdrop, the Whalers still turned the calendar from 1990 to 1991 with a sense of hope about the new year. Despite the recent drama, they went unbeaten in seven of their first ten games of 1991 and started to make a move on the rest of the Adams Division. *Did the decision to switch captains actually work?* For his part, Francis continued to put points on the board—in four of the Whalers' first eight games in 1991, he had at least 2 points, including 1 goal and 2 assists in a January 10 win over the Canucks in Vancouver.

But the good times didn't last for Hartford, and another losing skid left the fans sour and the team looking for answers. On March 3 Hartford blew a late lead at home and the fans booed the team as the game ended in a tie with Toronto, putting the capper on a six-game winless streak. Afterward, Verbeek said angrily, "This town doesn't deserve an NHL team."

"It was so positive at that time for our team, and the group was so together, that when things got broken up like that, it was tough," Evason later said of the stretch that led to Verbeek's outburst. "All of a sudden, if you don't have success, you have to move the pieces around to see if you can tweak it and have things end up different.

"The room wasn't the same. We weren't winning. It was a difficult situation—my penalty minutes went way up. Things were changing, and people were trying to make a difference. It was just frustrating to lose what we had because we were so close to that breakthrough."

221

To that point on the calendar, a collection of events conspired to hinder the Whalers franchise as it looked to build on the achievements of the late 1980s: the ultracompetitive Adams Division, the rise of basketball, injury.

But on March 4, 1991—well, like Chuck Kaiton said, it was the day the music died. That was when Johnston shipped Francis, Samuelsson, and Grant Jennings to the Penguins for John Cullen, Zarley Zalapski, and Jeff Parker. Even though Johnston defended the deal until the day he was fired, it turned out to be an unmitigated disaster for several reasons, not the least of which was that it sent Francis—the most popular player in franchise history—packing.

"I think it's a great deal for the Hartford Whalers," owner Richard Gordon said. "It gives us tremendous scoring down the middle. It gives us the offensive defenseman we so badly need. You look at the age, and there's an advantage there for us, too.

"But it is a difficult thing. Ron Francis and Ulf Samuelsson are great people and great players. They've helped this franchise a great deal. But I am convinced this is the best thing for us."

Years later, Gordon would sing a different tune. "Probably was the worst trade in the history of hockey," he said in a 2021 interview with the *Religion of Sports* podcast.

Now, more than thirty years later, Francis can see it was all connected: the decision to strip him of his captaincy, his contractual situation, and Ley's feelings about what a leader should look like. "There were a lot of things that led up to it," he said. "It was the last year of my contract. . . . They took the *C* off my shirt. They wanted me to say I wanted out and make it easy for them to make a trade. I wouldn't do that. I loved that community and loved that team. I had a lot of ties in the area.

"They had called me a little before the trade deadline and said they wanted to sign me, and we said we'd talk after the trade deadline. We just had our first child—Caitlin, my parents' first grandchild—and they were itching to come see her. So they got into town a few days [later], and one night at dinner, the phone rang, and I got the news from Eddie I was traded."

Ley did not respond to requests to be interviewed for this book.

"Ricky never really saw Ronnie as his type of captain," Kaiton said. "I don't know the ins and outs, but I have to believe that when they took the captaincy away from him, that was it. I remember when it was announced—he didn't really say a word. He always kept quiet. Shortly after that, they traded him. It's still hard to believe now."

"We're all fools," said Viv Bernstein, a *Hartford Courant* reporter. "We should have seen it coming after they stripped the captaincy from him."

Though he was just twenty-seven, Francis had seen a lot of hockey in his life. He was a teenage hockey star, a first-round draft pick who quickly ascended to the role of leader, and the centerpiece of a division winner. But he could not shake one nagging feeling. "The first time when you're traded, it's obviously a shock. You're not expecting it. You almost feel like you failed—they didn't want you.

"But there wasn't a lot of time to reflect. I got the call at 9:00 or 9:30 that night, and then, the next morning, I was on a plane to Pittsburgh, and I was playing the next night. When I got to the Penguins, I started looking around the room, and I started to get excited about the situation I was coming into. Fortunately for us, three months later, we were lifting the Cup."

Whether it was the flap over Francis's contract and his potential free agency, the desire to hit the reset button on a roster that never seemed to be able to get over the top, or something else, a lot of it seemed to come back to one thing: an inability on the part of the coach to mesh with his star player and captain. "All season, Ley had complained publicly about a lack of leadership on the Whalers," wrote columnist Alan Greenberg in the *Hartford Courant* after the deal went down. "You don't need a roster to know at whom his stubby index finger was pointing.

"Ley is a simple man, and he likes his players, and his captains, loud and feisty, the way he is," he added. "He might have been willing to make an exception for Wayne Gretzky. He wasn't willing to make one for Ron Francis."

"We were doing okay as a team there, but I know that we had problems with Ronnie," Jennings later discussed in a 2011 interview with the *Pittsburgh Post-Gazette*. "They took the *C* from Ronnie. Then, the coach was Rick Ley, and he just wasn't getting along with anybody except Pat Verbeek, basically, and we just had some turmoil there."

Viewed as a consolation prize a decade before, he was leaving Hartford as the most decorated player in franchise history. "Well, it's done," Francis said glumly after the deal was announced. "I'm gone. I'm looking forward to Pittsburgh, but I'm going to miss this place. I came here as a kid. I've met a lot of great people here. A lot of great friends. It's tough from that standpoint. The fans have been super. I'm disappointed, really."

Francis told the *Courant* that even with everything that had gone down between him and the team over the last year, the news still came as a shock. "There was a lot of talk and stuff all year. My guard was up," he said. "But two weeks ago, when they said they were interested in re-opening talks, they said they were very happy and had no intention of moving me. They said they'd wait until after the deadline. From that standpoint, it's very surprising.

"People here aren't stupid. They read the situations. I'm not bitter, but I'm disappointed that they publicly demeaned me. Every second day, there [were] stories about the contract, the captaincy, the trades. If they wanted to trade me, it's their prerogative. But after 10 years of giving everything I had when I stepped on the ice, I feel they could have done it differently."

The reaction across the state was seismic. To this point, this was the biggest story in franchise history. Former Channel 3 sportscaster Mike Adams recalled what happened. Adams got the initial call something was happening late in the day.

"Everyone at Channel 3 was trying to figure out how we'd get him before the plane left for Pittsburgh. We caught him the next morning—it was an early-morning flight out of Bradley [International

Airport]. We got there, and he was just standing there, and I walked up to him. He got all choked up—he said he didn't want to cry on camera, so he walked four or five steps away. I got choked up—it was sad, because you loved the guy. Everyone who was a Whalers fan felt the same way."

On the surface, taking out the emotional connection to Francis and looking solely at the numbers (financial and otherwise), the trade looked like it was a winner for the Whalers. Consider that the twenty-seven-year-old Francis had been leading the Whalers with 21 goals and 76 points in sixty-seven games that year, the last year of a contract that paid him $370,000. Meanwhile Cullen, twenty-six, was making $130,000 in his option year and was fifth in the NHL in scoring with 31 goals, 63 assists, and 94 points in sixty-five games.

For his part, Cullen handled things as diplomatically as possible, saying all the right things about Hartford and Francis after he arrived. "I can't replace Ronnie Francis, that's all I can say," he told the media. "He has all the records here. I am just a new face. I hope I can do well. When Mario Lemieux came back from his back injury, let's face it, I had to take a backseat. He's the best in the game."

As for Jennings, he had an inkling he was going to be dealt as well. "I knew that they were trying to move me," recalled Jennings. "I found out at ten o'clock on the trading deadline [day] that I was going to Pittsburgh. I had to be on the plane at six o'clock in the morning. They said there were some other players involved, and I'm like, 'Whoa—who?' And they were like, 'We don't know yet.'

"I think I was the first guy in the trade. I found out later that night that it was Ulfie and Ronnie Francis. So I was like, 'Yeah, right on.' I get to meet those guys at the airport."

When Jennings got to Pittsburgh, he had an immediate sense of what was missing in Hartford. "[With the Whalers] we always made the playoffs. We came close with Boston the year they went to the finals—we took them to seven games. We had a good team. We were missing that one ingredient," Jennings explained in 2011. "We had

Ronnie, and we didn't have Mario, basically. We didn't have two all-star centers, and that's basically what it took.

"Our team was basically defensive-minded in Hartford, and we had systems for killing penalties and all that. When we got to Pittsburgh, it was like they were more than welcome to take us and use us in that aspect. We were all big guys and size and defense, and that's what they were needing at that time. They had all the scoring power that they needed.

"They were leading in goals for, and once we got there, we started winning some games, and we started peaking at the right time. That was pretty obvious. Everybody was pretty excited about that. We didn't really know what was going on. I didn't really realize what we brought to the team at the time. Looking back now, it's a pretty good mix, that's for sure."

Frank Pietrangelo, who was the backup goaltender with the Pens when the deal was made, said the deal was a massive move for an already stacked Pittsburgh team. "That was huge," said Pietrangelo. "Ron was a captain and a superstar who was known around the NHL. We didn't know much about Grant; Ulfie was a stay-at-home defenseman. But we already had a lot of great players on that team—we had Mario and [Jaromír] Jágr and [Paul] Coffey and a Hall of Famer like [Bryan] Trottier and a bunch of other great players, but Ronnie added a whole different dimension for us as a strong, two-way forward who was a great guy in the room. When they got to Pittsburgh, to see him and Ulfie and Grant, they were great teammates and really physical, physical specimens. They helped make us a great team. All three of them just added so much."

The Whalers were reportedly awfully close to a second blockbuster deal at the deadline, as the *Courant* reported that they had been in talks for a three-way deal involving the Oilers and Flyers that would have included high-profile talent like Dineen, Scott Mellanby, and Joe Murphy. But that was scuttled at the last minute. "I was talking to Edmonton at the end, but it fell through," Johnston told the *Courant*.

Predictably, the Whalers went into a bit of a tailspin following the Francis trade. The game after the deal was consummated, they were listless in a 4–1 loss at home to the Blues. Hartford had just 19 shots on goal all night—including 8 in the second and third period combined. The game was stopped when fans threw debris on the ice after protesting a call from referee Don Koharski and chanted "Thank God for Quebec" and "Let's Trade Johnston" throughout the third period. "We weren't ourselves," Verbeek told reporters after the game, which stretched their winless streak to seven.

And in a weird twist of fate, less than a week later, the Penguins came to Hartford—with Francis and Samuelsson—to face the Whalers. That night had one of the biggest crowds of the season at the Civic Center, with many folks back in the building to see Francis. There were a ton of old number 10 jerseys, as well as a few with Francis' new number 9 with the Penguins. After the game, Francis confessed to having some serious anxiety about the contest, but the fans stood and cheered when he was introduced. All four ex-Whalers (Francis, Samuelsson, Jennings, and Scott Young) got the start against their old team, and the crowd chanted Francis's name throughout the evening. It reached a crescendo when he assisted on a goal from new teammate Mark Recchi. In the end, the contest was a relatively easy 5–2 win for Pittsburgh.

"This is probably the toughest game I've had to play," Francis told reporters in the locker room. "I kind of wish I had a few games under my belt. But hey, it might be just as good to play it and get it over with."

"I've got to cut the cord," added Samuelsson.

The trade caused some of the fan base to do the same. Predictably, the average attendance took a serious dip. The team averaged 12,404 for the 1990–91 season. The following year, it was 10,896.

"From the time they made the Francis trade through that summer, the attrition of season-ticket sakes was unbelievable," said Forslund of the summer of 1991. "We were doing damage control with the fan base, and no one wanted to hear it. We were marketing John Cullen and Bobby Holík and Zarley Zalapski, and that was not going over well at all."

Cullen was a well-respected veteran, but he wasn't capable of replacing Francis, either on the ice when it came to scoring or off the ice when it came to leadership. In two-plus seasons in Hartford, he managed 39 goals and 63 assists—respectable numbers, to be sure, but far short of the impact Francis would have in the same span. In addition, there were leadership questions—Cullen was a talent, but fairly or unfairly, players looked to him to be Francis 2.0. And that just wasn't who he was.

"I felt like John had a lot of pressure on his shoulders after Ronnie was traded," said center Andrew Cassels. "He was the main guy. Replacing someone like him was tough to do."

"Let's look at it this way—when he was in Pittsburgh, Mario had the back problems, and so the younger guys like Cullen and Mark Recchi and Kevin Stevens, those guys were really helping carry us when Mario was recovering," recalled Pietrangelo, who played with Cullen in Pittsburgh and Hartford. "We had player on top of player on top of player in Pittsburgh. No disrespect to Hartford, but when Ronnie left Hartford, they just didn't have that kind of depth. The two of them were just different players in different stages of their careers. Ronnie was older and more established as a star at that point. It was just unfair to compare John to Ronnie."

"John Cullen is a great guy—a tremendous guy. He really had some special skills as a centerman," said Peckham, who built a long friendship with Cullen later when the two were with the Tampa Bay Lightning. "But it was a tough place for him to come into. He was behind Mario in Pittsburgh and got some favorable matchups. All of a sudden, he's expected to be the guy replacing the icon of the franchise. It was a very, very different spot for him to be in. It was hard for him to step into that role, and honestly, he didn't have the talent around him for most of the time like Ronnie did for six or seven years."

"Here's the other problem that Hartford had to deal with when it dealt Ronnie, and [it] really ended up sinking them," said Bernstein.

"Their best players after that, most of them didn't want to be there—[Chris] Pronger, [Brendan] Shanahan, those guys. . . . Hartford was dull. It wasn't sexy. It was not a premier market.

"Ronnie? He wanted to play there. *He liked it.* The fans loved him. He was never whining when things were going bad. And guys wanted to play with him," she added. "When they traded him, they lost that."

The Whalers finished 3-11-5 in the final nineteen games of the 1990–91 season. Despite the late-season struggles, there were plenty of fireworks, including one March contest between Boston and Hartford that featured 210 penalty minutes, including 42 for the Bruins' enforcer, Chris Nilan. When the regular-season finale for the two clubs that weren't particularly fond of each other rolled around, playoff seeding was already set. It was a recipe for disaster, according to Nilan. "It was one of those 'fuck you' games. It didn't mean anything—everything had been pretty much decided, and we knew we were playing them in the playoffs. That's the worst recipe for something bad to happen. Back then, Rob Brown had that face you just wanted to punch. He was such a good little player and goal scorer for them, but honestly, I could not stand that kid.

"Later on, I met him in Edmonton after I retired, and the kid was a sweetheart. I remember thinking, *What the hell did I not like this kid for?* But that night was a different story."

Nilan took 10 penalties, including two for fighting (where he mixed it up with Hartford tough guy Jimmy McKenzie), as well as a game misconduct. "I mean, we were just going to bruise them up a little bit before the playoffs. But I remember Bobby Holík, he was running around and coming up the wall, and I was heading off for a change. He had his head down, and I just elbowed him right in the nose. Got two minutes for that one. Today, I'd be in jail for what I did.

"That game just got chippy and stupid. You could see it coming back then, and the referees had a tough time controlling the situation. But in that type of situation, I mean, are you shitting me? When guys are like that, you can't control shit, unless you're the good Lord himself. I remember Brown, he was losing his hair, and I didn't know this at the time, but I found out later he was getting plugs. He said something fresh to me, and I remember grabbing him. He turtled, and I got his hair and pulled some of the plugs out of his head. I got back to the [dressing] room and I still had some of his hair in my hand."

The start of the postseason afforded the new-look Whalers an opportunity to hit the reset button. And despite the uproar, they were almost able to salvage their season in the first round of the playoffs—Hartford took Boston to six games before falling. It was another year, another playoff elimination at the hands of the Bruins.

"Those were both epic series—*fantastic*. Everyone was so invested—that one game, one bounce, was the difference between moving forward and packing your bags," Kastelic said of the 1990 and 1991 postseason series between Boston and Hartford. "If we had ever gotten past them either of those years, that might have changed things in Hartford. It was a tough pill to swallow. But that was a great rivalry, a fantastic rivalry, with good character people on both sides."

While the Whalers' season was ending, Pittsburgh reaped the benefits of the Francis-Samuelsson pairing. Buoyed by the deal with Hartford, the Pens won the Norris Division and, after surviving a seven-game series with the Devils, rolled into the Stanley Cup finals against Minnesota. Hartford fans watched from a distance as the former franchise icon finally got a chance to taste the sort of success he had craved for long. Francis finished with 17 playoff points—7 goals and 10 assists, including 3 goals in the Cup finals—as the Penguins won in six games.

"I have had this dream since I was two years old growing up in Sault Ste. Marie. God, to see that big silver Cup—and it's a heavy sucker—and dream about that ring, it's a thrill beyond belief," Francis said after the Penguins closed out the North Stars.

"Unbelievable! Tell the boys in Hartford I just wish they could feel like I do," Samuelsson told Jeff Jacobs.

The gut punch to end all gut punches was delivered—without malice, mind you—by Mario Lemieux. He was asked when he felt like the Penguins, who had made the playoffs only once in the previous eight seasons, had a chance to not only do well in the playoffs but also win the Cup.

"When we made the trade with Hartford to get Ron Francis and Ulf Samuelsson," he told reporters. *Ouch.*

"The Francis trade was a turning point, no question about it," Peckham later recalled. "In terms of corporate ownership and sponsorships, it started to melt away. The commercial real estate downturn, the recession of the late 1980s, that really had a devastating effect on the city, and it impacted the Whalers too. The corporate support that had really helped boost the team was moving away. And Richard had a different philosophy than Howard, and he started getting advice from a lot of different areas. Things got *very* disjointed from that point on."

"When you lose that touch—when Baldwin left and Gordon bought them out, that initial feeling was gone. . . . When the guy with the original vision, when he leaves, whether you like it or not, things are going to change. And that's what happened," said Upton Bell. "When people who were either founders or part of a family give it up, usually it all goes south. And in the early-to-mid-1990s, that vision that Baldwin had, that was gone. It really doesn't have a lot to do with who has the most money in those types of situations. It has to do with a vision, and that's where the Whalers sort of lost their way."

"That foundation cracked," said Gerry Brooks. "That was all there was to it. The nature of the business changed, and they no longer found it prudent to own a piece of the Civic Center and be involved with the Whalers. In many ways, that process was the beginning of the end."

"The team offices moved across the street into this antiseptic atmosphere, and it was really a symbol for the organization at that point," recalled Mark Willand. "We started losing core guys and bringing in guys who didn't want to be there. We went from green carpeting and paneling to hardwood floors and glass. It all felt colder and less familial. I felt the on-ice product was the same way. We were becoming just another organization—treading water."

WITH FRANCIS GONE, THE ONE GUY WHO WAS CAPABLE OF
carrying the load was Dineen, but he was suffering through a unique
set of challenges. The feisty veteran had missed a series of games in
December 1990 and January 1991 with a recurrence of Crohn's disease.
The ailment, which was first diagnosed in 1987, had returned to plague
the forward. He was hospitalized on January 2, 1991, and lost ten pounds
in eight days. Later that month, he returned to the lineup, but he wasn't
the same player the rest of the way and finished the 1990–91 season
with 17 goals, 47 points, and 104 penalty minutes in sixty-two games.

Initially, after the Francis deal, the hope was the offseason would
bring rest for Dineen and a return to his old form. But privately, there
was concern that he would not be able to regain his scoring touch. He
was coming off a rare down year, and after a slow start (4 goals in the
first sixteen games), it was clear the team would entertain trade offers.
On November 13, 1991, the Whalers sent Dineen to Philadelphia for
veteran Murray Craven and a 1992 fourth-round draft choice.

"Dineen is not a superior hockey talent. Anybody who has seen him
practically beat the puck to death while attempting to carry it down
his wing can attest to that. Dineen does not have great speed or a great
scoring touch," wrote Greenberg in the *Hartford Courant* the day the
deal went down. "What he has is heart. Through sheer relentlessness,
he would bust out of the crowd in the corner or in front of the net,
and make the big play.

"Some players are less than their stats. Dineen was more. When
others laid back, Dineen led the charge. He wasn't pretty or graceful
out there, but he was beautiful to have on your side.

"Now he's on the other side."

Francis and Dineen were shipped out of town within ten months
of each other. *Ugh.* While the players Hartford received in return were
solid vets, they weren't foundational elements you could build a team
around, like Francis and Dineen. The Francis trade was a seismic event
that robbed the team of its centerpiece. While the Dineen trade got
significantly less play—and moving the undersized forward wasn't as

impactful as dealing Francis—the ramifications echoed throughout the locker room.

"Kevin was always for the boys—the social coordinator," said Kastelic, his former roommate. "I remember a lot of concerts with Kevin, like going to see Midnight Oil. He'd always take the guys out. And not just the stars, but a lot of the younger guys. I remember once when we were in Calgary, and we must have had a day or two off, a little layoff, and we went to Banff [in Alberta]. He would be the guy who would get the van. He would be the guy who made sure the reservations were made—music, food, whatever. Kevin was the guy."

"Kevin was professionalism personified," said Cassels. "You wouldn't say he was the most skilled player, but his work ethic was just . . . you watched him and what he would do in practice, as well as off the ice, and that was just the way you should do it.

"He would lead by example and wasn't afraid to call guys out," he added. "Not in a bad way, but he wanted to get the best out of you. He wanted the best. He was a leader and a captain. He talked about doing the right thing, and he went out and did them on a consistent basis."

ULTIMATELY, WITHOUT FRANCIS, DINEEN, AND LIUT, THE 1991–92 season was a strange and surreal year, led by new coach Jimmy Roberts, the former bench boss of their AHL affiliate in Springfield. A five-game win streak early in the season sparked some hope, but a .500 mark the next couple of months relegated the Whalers to the lower levels of the Adams Division much of the rest of the way. They went an abysmal 3-10-6 in January, but landed a playoff berth in large part because the Nordiques were one of the worst teams in the league—the Whalers' final mark of 26-41-13 was the worst of all sixteen playoff teams.

They saved the drama for the postseason. Facing the first-place Canadiens—*again*—Hartford didn't seem to have a shot. And after the Canadiens won the first two at home—so easily that the Montreal fans chanted, "Na na na na, hey hey hey, goodbye" at the end of Game Two—it was clear the Hartford fans felt the same way. For Game Three, only 6,728 fans showed up at the Civic Center, one of the smallest crowds in franchise history, regular season or postseason.

"There were less than 7,000 of them, but they sure were loud," Cullen told reporters after the game. "Those are real hockey fans. I won't forget them."

Despite the small crowds, the Whalers scrapped their way to wins in Game Three and Game Four, with the latter drawing more than ten thousand fans and featuring 24 saves from Pietrangelo and power-play goals from Corriveau and Randy Cunneyworth. It was as shocking a two-game turnaround as anyone could remember. After the Canadiens took a 3–2 Game Five victory in Montreal, the two teams returned to Hartford.

That's when an unlikely hero—Corriveau—took center stage. To that point in his time with Hartford, Corriveau had distinguished himself as an off-ice joker known for keeping the locker room loose. But now, he followed up his Game Three heroics with an overtime goal in Game Six, setting the stage for a dramatic Game Seven in Montreal.

The Canadiens jumped to a 2–0 lead after one period, but Cassels and Sanderson knotted things at two in the second period. It stayed that way throughout the third period and into overtime.

"We were down 2–0 but battled back," recalled Pietrangelo, who made 53 saves that night in Montreal. "I still remember Yvon Corriveau with a couple of breakaway chances—as he was coming down the ice, I was thinking, 'Boy, this is going to happen.'"

Corriveau's best chance came at the three-minute mark in the second overtime, when he went high and wide on a clean breakaway.

"I was going top corner all the way from the red line in," Corriveau said after the game. "[Patrick] Roy gave it to me. The bottom line is I missed it."

In the end, it was Russ Courtnall who killed the Whalers. He put one between Pietrangelo's pads at 5 minutes, 26 seconds of the second overtime to lift the Canadiens to a 3–2 victory. It may not have been as painful as Claude Lemieux's goal six years before, but it was a heart-breaker nonetheless.

"We've showed a lot of character," Corriveau said, "but that [OT] breakaway was the difference between winning and going golfing." The Canadiens moved on. The Whalers went home—again.

"For some reason, it wasn't meant to be," Pietrangelo said after the game, his voice cracking with emotion. "But we can hold our heads up high. It wasn't a lack of effort. We had a lot of heart and desire."

In hindsight, May 1, 1992, may have been the beginning of the end for the Whalers in Hartford. That gutting Game Seven loss—the longest game in franchise history and (at that time) the fourth-longest game in the history of the NHL—was their last playoff game before the franchise moved to Carolina in the spring of 1997.

The writing was on the wall—they were still struggling to draw fans. The Whalers drew an average of 8,354 in three playoff games.

"I always wonder . . . who knows what would have happened if we had won that series?" asked Pietrangelo. "Little things make a difference in the history of a franchise. Who knows? If we had won and then moved on, we could have helped save hockey in Hartford. It was a good group of guys, and we all really cared."

Ten days after the double-overtime loss—and three years to the day after he took the job—Johnston was fired by the Whalers. "This is a very small town in many ways," Gordon told reporters in announcing Johnston's firing. "This town needs to know you, all about you. It's a Yankee mentality. That means you've got to reach out and be involved in the community. That's something we negated the last three years. We lost track of our roots.

"This is a hard feeling, a difficult thing to do. But I'm kind of relieved in a sense. We've got to fill the void. Our next move has got to be much more positive, more experienced. Ed did a good job in the draft and rebuilding the farm team. But we didn't win enough and it showed up in the box office."

"Ed Johnston didn't reshape the Whalers, he bulldozed them beyond recognition," wrote Greenberg the day after Johnston was fired. "Where many saw a leaky roof and some sagging timbers in need of replacement, Johnston decided to dynamite the foundation and start from scratch.

"He was a foreman without a conscience, certain that you tear apart and rebuild one NHL team as you would 21 others, and never mind whether the franchise is operating on solid ground or quicksand."

And shortly after that—with Gordon in Paris for the French Open—Ley was fired. "I think the people who've been around our club all year have a pretty good idea what was going on. I mean, I don't think it was a hidden fact. Everything was very uneasy around here," Johnston explained to reporters. "It's obvious there's been a conflict, a difference between Mr. Ley and Mr. Gordon."

"I'm shocked," Verbeek said after the announcement was made official. "I thought he was good for next season and how we played would dictate what would happen with Rick."

For his part, Ley made it clear to Jeff Jacobs that his firing was because of his disagreements with Gordon. "This was Richard Gordon's decision. I know it isn't Ed Johnston's. I feel bad for him," Ley told the *Courant* in a wide-ranging interview a few days after he was fired with a year left on his contract. "He's a good man. He is a terrific general manager. There are a terrific bunch of people in this organization. There's only one man who doesn't think I'm part of that."

Johnston eventually landed on his feet back in Pittsburgh, setting off a bit of a legal skirmish. *Oh sure*, thought many Whalers fans. *It's a natural move to eventually lead the team you helped shape while you were running the show in Hartford.*

"The wicked wise guys among us would insist the Pittsburgh Penguins pick up the lion's share of Ed Johnston's $875,000 contract over the next three seasons. After all, EJ—as general manager of the Whalers—did one heck of a job leading the Penguins to back-to-back Stanley Cups," wrote Jacobs that September.

While the dissembling of the old-school Whalers may have started in 1988 with the loss of Gavin and departure of Baldwin and been hastened by the trades by Johnston, the 1992 playoff defeat to the Canadiens was really the end of a transitional era for the franchise. The good times that had marked the rise of Whalers through the late 1980s and into the 1990s were over. Now, the franchise would try to balance between a rebuild and an effort at trying to be competitive in a rapidly changing landscape.

The final tally? From December 1989 through March 1991, the Whalers traded away the following players: Paul MacDermid, Mike Liut, Dave Tippett, Joel Quenneville, Ray Ferraro, Ron Francis, Ulf Samuelsson, and Grant Jennings. The very heart of the team, the core of a roster that was playoff-ready and battle-tested night in and night out in the feisty Adams Division, was carved out and shipped elsewhere.

None of this is designed to malign the players they received in return, like Cullen, Zalapski, Cunneyworth, and Corriveau. But with the benefit of hindsight, that period was arguably one of the worst personnel stretches suffered in recent hockey memory. There were other reasons, to be sure, but in the end, the breakup of a once-great nucleus spearheaded by Francis, Dineen, and Liut would mark the beginning of the end of hockey in Hartford.

"We had so many great, great players," lamented Gavin. "In the end, they took a dollar and made it into 75 cents."

9

End of Days
1992-97

This is a human moment, a moment in sports you don't hear and
talk about very much. You talk about salaries. You talk about work
stoppages. You talk about owners relocating teams. You talk about
politicians not getting the job done. You talk about players who
maybe don't care about the city or town that they play in. But these
guys do. And the fans care. And that's why this moment is so special.
—TV play-by play man John Forslund, in the final moments of the
final Whalers TV broadcast

The Whalers, those perennial misfit losers, played their last game
before bleary-eyed, red-nosed fans at the Civic Center. The makeup
ran like Pete Karmanos.
—Michael Arace, *Hartford Courant*, April 14, 1997

In the spring of 1992, after the franchise jettisoned Eddie Johnston,
the GM role—and future of the franchise—came down to two guys:
Brian Burke and Mike Liut.

Liut has just recently decided to hang up his skates. The former Hartford goaltender, who had played the final two seasons of his career with

the Caps after being dealt away by the Whalers, had long expressed an interest in getting into management when he was done as a player. As early as the 1980s when he was playing for Hartford, he seemed ticketed for a front-office job. And Liut, who teared up when he was told he was traded by the Whalers, seemed to be a really nice fit for Hartford. He cared about the Whalers' future and was a recognizable face from the glory days. On the surface, if there was anyone who might be capable of restoring a little shine to the logo, it would be Liut.

"Am I ready to be a GM? I don't know. Can I do the job? Sure. I'm a fast learner," Liut told the *Courant* when he was asked. "It would be a terrific challenge and a great opportunity, but it's a little presumptuous at this point. If [Richard Gordon] calls, we'll get together."

"I think Mike is a quality person, bright and articulate," Gordon said. "He knows Hartford as well as anyone. He's a very positive guy, so we'll be talking to him."

The other finalist was Burke, the vice president and director of hockey operations for the Canucks. Burke was a serious sort—on the surface, the exact type of guy the franchise could build around. He had a relentless work ethic; the Canucks said they'd have to hire two guys to replace him. Armed with a bachelor's degree from Providence College and a degree from Harvard Law, he was seemingly a mixture of old and new school, a big believer in physical hockey but also aware that teams would have to adjust to the NHL of the 1990s.

Burke had been in the mix for the GM job in 1989, but the Whalers blanched at the idea of yielding a first-round pick to the Canucks, so they went with Johnston instead. This time around, they were determined to get their man; they offered him an annual deal of $275,000—a sizable contract for a first-time GM and, as Burke later recalled, three times what he had been making in Vancouver.

Of course, sealing the deal didn't come without a few odd wrinkles. Burke would later tell the story of one of his interviews with Gordon, during which he walked into the room expecting to speak with the owner one-on-one, only to find him joined by one of the season-ticket holders, a gentleman named Jerry. "I want him to be comfortable with this hiring too," Gordon explained when Burke asked what Jerry was doing there with them.

Burke later said his friend and former Whalers winger Tommy Rowe initially advised him against taking the job—in the strongest terms possible. "You're going to kill Richard before this is over," Rowe told Burke. "He interferes. He changes his mind constantly. *You're going to physically kill him before you get out of here.*"

Rowe wasn't the only one who felt that way. Burke later claimed that several people tried to talk him out of taking the Hartford job, including Rick Ley and Bobby Orr. "Maybe I should have listened to them," Burke later wrote. "Though in hindsight, I still wouldn't trade that experience for the world."

THROUGH THE YEARS, THE WHALERS' ROSTER ALMOST ALWAYS had a nice balance of finesse and physical players. There were the high scorers, sure, but there were also plenty of muckers and grinders, guys who weren't afraid to mix it up and drop the gloves if necessary.

Under Burke, Hartford would leave no doubt. In his introductory press conference, he made no bones about not being a fan of the 1992 team for a few reasons. "There is room for small, skilled players, but only if you surround them with enough size that your team doesn't get pushed around," he said. "I'm determined this team will get bigger and more physical. I like high-paced high-pitched offensive hockey.

"Thirteen wins at home is not acceptable. To have a team pushed around at home is not acceptable. That will change."

On the heels of his blunt assessment of the roster at his introductory press conference, and with no Ron (or Emile) Francis or Dineen to market the team around, Burke became the very public face of the franchise. He was part of a "No More Mr. Nice Guy" ad campaign. He did numerous public appearances, all designed to jump-start the fan base. The occasionally pugnacious exec was part of a weekly radio show.

And he certainly wasn't afraid to shake things up a bit: He hired former Flyers tough guy Paul Holmgren as coach on June 15, 1992. Holmgren hit on many of the same points that Burke did when he was introduced, so it was clear that the Whalers were aiming for a new approach: they were no longer to be considered a soft, finesse team. Their emphasis would be on physical hockey. If you were coming to play the Whalers, you better be prepared for hurt.

"My philosophy is simple: If you play hard-nosed and you outwork the other team every night, you come out on top, most times," said Holmgren, who had 1,684 career penalty minutes in ten seasons as a player. "I'm going to rely on players like John Cullen and Pat Verbeek, players who are proven point-getters in the NHL, and they're premier players for a couple of reasons. No. 1, they're highly skilled players. No. 2, and I think most important, they play with grit and determination and that's something I demand from every player, whether you're skilled, or whether you're not so skilled. It's a demand. I will not tolerate anything less than that."

When it came to the rebuild, Burke traded 1989 first-round pick Bobby Holík and draft picks to New Jersey for goalie Sean Burke (no relation) and defenseman Eric Weinrich on August 28, 1992. Burke had been an electric presence as a rookie, going 10-1 in his first season in the NHL (1987–88), but he had ridden a roller coaster since then, eventually reaching the end of his rope with the Devils, choosing to sit out the entire 1991–92 NHL season out of sheer frustration over the way things were being run in Jersey. (He played for the San Diego Gulls of the IHL and the Canadian National Team at the 1992 Olympics, winning a silver medal.)

Now, he had a fresh start in Hartford. "It's not the way I had planned things to go," Sean Burke told reporters after the deal was done. "I felt that after the last year in New Jersey I would get traded, I'd get another chance to get a fresh start with another NHL club. But it was a year coming. I'm glad that it's finally over. I have an idea where I'm going to be and I'm excited to get started."

The trade upset incumbent Pietrangelo, one of the centerpieces of the 1991–92 team that took the Canadiens to a double-overtime in Game Seven. Pietrangelo, who was acquired at the end of the previous season, sparkled in the playoffs, outplaying Patrick Roy and causing many to believe he was the no-doubt number-one netminder for Hartford for 1992–93.

"I think I earned the opportunity to come into camp and get a shot at playing No. 1 goaltender for the Hartford Whalers from what I accomplished last year," Pietrangelo told the *Courant*. "Sean Burke hasn't even played in the NHL for how long now? He had a great playoff his first year. After that, check his stats and put mine up against his. I think I did more than what was asked of me when I came to Hartford.

"But for some reason, Brian Burke was not happy with how I performed."

Burke *also* wasn't happy with "Brass Bonanza." One of the most sacred traditions in Hartford hockey was eliminated when the team announced in late September it wouldn't be using it as their goal song anymore. (For the record, this was the second time the team tried to ditch the now-familiar fight song. The team tried to swap it out in 1990, but fan outrage brought it back.) Now, Burke said it was all part of an attempt to change the narrative around a team that had started to skid. That meant new uniforms and a change in the music—a loud foghorn blast would accompany Whalers' goals from now on. "I don't like the song," he told the *Courant* in September. "I don't think it has a place in a National Hockey League rink."

John Forslund, who was working in the PR office, recalled one of his first conversations with Burke.

"The song is done," Burke told Forslund.

"Seriously?" replied Forslund.

"Yes. I hate it, and the players hate it," Burke replied.

"So we took it away," recalled Forslund. "That season was the only season when the Whalers came out to 'Thunderstruck' by AC/DC. That was not appreciated by most of the fans. They put a petition together, and I showed him. The Rutherford group eventually brought it back."

"Everything they had done in Hartford to that point had less than desirable results," Burke told NHL.com a few years later. "We changed uniforms, we eliminated the fight song, we made some major moves that would have led to long-term success but it just didn't work out between me and the owner and I went back to the [league office]."

In a 2019 interview with *The Athletic*, Burke was asked about the decision to end "Brass Bonanza." "My players came to me," he said. "This is one where I have been maligned and castigated for eliminating it as a goal song. The players came to me and said, 'It's like a college fight song, it's embarrassing, can you get rid of it?' That's why I got rid of it. It was so unpopular, I couldn't believe the strength of the reaction. And to this day, people bring it up, 'Brian Burke got rid of "Brass Bonanza."' I'm like, 'Well, I'm not going to hang out the players who came to me—but it was my players who came to me.'"

LED BY SEAN BURKE, THE NEW-LOOK WHALERS DROPPED THE puck on the 1992–93 season on October 6 in Montreal—and it was not good. They lost 5–1 to the Canadiens in the opener and were outscored 19–7 in their first four games, losing them all and marking the second-worst start in team history, trailing only the 0-5 opening in 1987–88. Brian Burke, Holmgren, and the players were all preaching patience, but a winless start didn't augur well.

They did, however, live up to Burke's black-and-blue vow. While they didn't win many games in the early going, they won a lot of fights—in the fourth contest, they set a franchise mark for penalty minutes in a game with 125 in a 6–2 loss to the Rangers. That season, the Whalers were second in the league in penalty minutes per game. Forslund estimated that was one of the toughest teams in franchise history.

"That was a *really* tough team," recalled the play-by-play man. "Their whole plan that year was to get a goalie and build a tough team and then try and find some skill guys. But that team, *whoo*, that was a tough group, with the Jimmy McKenzies and Mark Janssens.

"That was also a fun team. They loved that old song 'Brandy.' They'd be at an airline gate, and someone would grab the PA system and start singing."

But they would lose five of their first six and won just five of their first twenty games. Winning fights was fun. Losing games was not.

"I think I was ready to trade or shoot half the team that night," Brian Burke told the *Courant* after an 8–2 loss to Quebec left them at 5-14-1.

Though not the only reason for their early-season woes, their physical approach was costing them games. Opponents were scoring power-play goals on them at a rapid rate to start the year—teams had thirty power-play opportunities against Hartford in the first three games of the season, including ten in the previously mentioned loss to New York. The Whalers were still trying to find the line between physical, hard-nosed hockey and steering clear of the penalty box. At the end of the season, they had given up the fourth-most power-play goals with 107, accumulated the second-most power-play opportunities against with 493, and finished second in penalty minutes per game with 27.7.

The best thing to come out of the 1992–93 season might have been the creation of the CVS line: Cassels, Verbeek, and Sanderson teamed up to form one of the most potent scoring combinations in the league that season. Cassels was a soft-handed playmaker who could set up the speedy Sanderson or physical Verbeek. The group peaked during a March win over the Nordiques—with Quebec making a playoff push, the Whalers dealt the Nords a 4–2 defeat, with Verbeek finishing with 2 goals and an assist, Cassels contributing a goal and 2 assists, and Sanderson adding a pair of assists. The victory marked the first three-game win streak of the season for Hartford.

"What was so great about that line was that we had three really different types of players who did such a good job working together," Cassels said of the group. "Pat was a grinder, a get-in-your-face guy who wasn't afraid to be a shit-stirrer. Guys hated to play against him.

Geoff was all speed. I was more of a playmaker, a guy who was about giving up the puck and seeing other guys score.

"All three of us weren't exactly defensive specialists, but we were all willing to play and work in our own end to create chances on the other end of the ice. It was an absolute blast being able to play with those guys, and the results really came through."

Although a certain level of uncertainty was around the 1992–93 team, the expectations were certainly higher than a fifth-place finish in the Adams Division. Was it the most disappointing finish in franchise history? That's debatable. But at the very least, given some of the splashy additions, it was at least in the top five. Maybe the biggest takeaway for the glass-is-half-full crowd came in the development of the younger players, including Cassels, Sanderson, Michael Nylander, and Robert Petrovicky.

The other bit of good news Hartford fans clung to was that a high draft pick was in the offing—number six overall, to be specific. Having a pick that high had the potential to bring an impact player to add to the young nucleus, but Burke was eyeing something bigger. He decided to deal up for the number-two overall choice, sending the Whalers' number-six overall choice, in addition to their second- and third-round picks and winger Sergei Markov, to the Sharks. Could they find the next Ron Francis, a franchise player for a new generation who could turn around their failing fortunes and lead them to the postseason?

Their choice? After Alexandre Daigle went number one to the Senators, they selected eighteen-year-old defenseman Chris Pronger. Even though the team mortgaged most of that year's draft to land Pronger—and handed over its second-round pick in 1994 to Florida to ensure the Panthers would not select Russian sniper Viktor Kozlov, allowing him to drop to sixth, where the Sharks drafted him—the Hartford front office was ebullient. Pronger, a six-foot-six, 190-pound defenseman, had 15 goals and 62 assists in sixty-one games for Peterborough the year before.

Brian Burke loved Pronger. No, *loved* is probably too casual a term. In his book, *Burke's Law: A Life in Hockey*, he recounts the first time he saw Pronger play as a junior and was clearly smitten with the teenage defenseman who was on the ice at even strength, while shorthanded, *and* on the power play. "Pronger never left the ice. I think he played 50 minutes that game," wrote Burke. "And what a player. He was the best first passer who ever played for me—better than Scott Niedermayer. Even in junior, his first pass was a thing of beauty. He could put it right on someone's tape full speed.

"And he was mean. I just fell in love with the guy, and I thought, *We have to draft him.* There's no doubt in my mind that he was going to be a star."

With steady Sean Burke in net and good depth up front, Pronger was viewed as the missing piece that could make Hartford a contender again. "We had a unanimous vote by our scouts," Burke gleefully told reporters. "Pronger was rated No. 1 in the draft."

"I was kind of expecting to go to Tampa," Pronger said of the Lightning, who had the third overall choice. "It was a little bit of a surprise. I didn't really know Hartford was in the running.

"They are an up-and-coming team with a lot of young players," Pronger added of the Whalers. "I think Hartford needs some help. If I'm ready, I think I can go there and step in and make a contribution."

He arrived with a four-year, $7 million contract and an enormous set of expectations, because the team needed a boost.

"Pronger was so young and so skinny. He had this massive frame and these little skinny legs—it looked like he wasn't wearing shin guards," ESPN's Steve Levy said of his early impressions of Pronger. "I don't think you could tell at the time he would be a Hall of Famer and an unbelievable defenseman and mean and nasty and play with such an edge.

"The other thing? Absolutely everyone will tell you that it takes so much longer for a defenseman to mature. A forward could jump right in, but every mistake a defenseman makes ends up in the back of the net. There was that pressure on him early."

"I remember Chris just being *so young*," remembered Jimmy Carson. "I mean, I played in the league when I was nineteen, and it forces you to mature. The thing I remember the most was the fact that when he gets more experience, he's going to have a very solid, very long career. It's tough, coming into the league like that and people saying he's going to be the best defenseman in the league and be the next Bourque or Paul Coffey. That's a tough thing to put on a teenager."

Compounding the issues was a constant state of turmoil in the front office. After roughly a year as the Whalers' GM, Brian Burke left in late summer of 1993 to take a job as the senior vice president and director of hockey operations with the NHL. There were reports that Burke and Gordon had been at odds for several months, and Burke had threatened to quit on a number of occasions but had to be talked into staying. Now, roughly five weeks before the start of the season, Hartford was left without a GM.

"I love the guy and he's done a magnificent job," Gordon told Bernstein when asked about Burke's decision to leave. "But I don't think it's devastating to us. The big consideration is that with the new state deal, a lot of the things that Brian oversaw—and remember, he probably had more power than any general manager—are gone. He would be mostly a hockey GM now."

"Continuing disagreements with Richard on the business side were part of it, but not the major part," said Burke when asked by the *Courant* why he left. "The major part was the [NHL] job itself. I think it is a very important job for the league. I was concerned they wouldn't get the right person for the job."

Regardless of why Burke left, all would probably agree that a GM jumping ship weeks before the start of the regular season is indicative of a dysfunctional front office. Maybe that was why no one seemed genuinely interested in the job. (Several names were floated for the job, including Liut—the runner-up to Burke when he was hired.) In the end, Holmgren ended up taking on the dual role of coach and acting GM.

All that being said, there was *some* optimism before the start of the 1993–94 season—most of that was because of Pronger's arrival, as well as the relatively strong playoff outing the year before—but that was tempered by the Whalers' absolutely brutal schedule out of the gate and the relative inexperience of the coaching staff and front office.

"I told our players I expect us to make the playoffs," Holmgren told the *Courant* before the regular season began. "We should expect to make it. But I know how tough it's going to be. Hey, it's one tough subject to approach. I don't want to put too much pressure on our guys. I keep saying we need a fast start. But we got Montreal, Philly, Buffalo, Pittsburgh, Quebec right off the bat."

Holmgren's worst fears were soon realized, as the Whalers lost fourteen of their first twenty, a stretch that included a ten-game winless streak. That prompted a change; Holmgren moved from his head-coach/acting-GM role to full-time GM, and Pierre McGuire, who had been assistant GM, was named head coach.

"I wasn't entirely happy coaching," Holmgren said. "I was frustrated not only by the team's performance, but by individuals."

The thirty-two-year-old McGuire became the ninth coach in the history of the franchise, and the fifth in the previous six years. He was a former scout and assistant coach with the Penguins when they won back-to-back Cups at the start of the decade; this was his first shot at being a head coach in the NHL. Known as a relentless optimist, he was ready to put a positive spin on just about anything.

"If somebody in the media says, 'Your power play went 0-for-8,' I'll answer, 'Yeah, but our penalty-killing went 8-and-0,'" McGuire told reporters when he took the job.

"My goal right now is to get the team playing enthusiastic," he added. "My goal is to get the team to cut its penalty minutes. My goal right now is to get the team to be more productive on the power play. My goal right now is to get the team more productive when it comes to penalty-killing."

Despite the positivity, McGuire came to his new position with some baggage. "He was with me in Pittsburgh—he just rode on Scotty Bowman's name," Pietrangelo said of McGuire. "He was very destructive in

Hartford—he caused nothing but problems. He came into Hartford, and people said he was one of Scotty's assistant coaches, but he was a scout. Scotty brought him in as a spy, basically, and after the Penguins said, 'We have to get rid of this guy,' he jumped to Hartford."

"What a *terrible* mistake it was hiring Pierre as the head coach," said Bernstein. "The players did not like him. I remember him coming out after a loss and saying the players had messed their pants. I mean, he just ripped them to shreds. The end of that season, I can recall several players going to management and saying they wanted them to get rid of this guy. It was an insurrection. I mean, he was so ill-prepared to be a head coach. He thought he was Scotty Bowman, but he wasn't.

"Scotty was brilliant. Pierre just couldn't pull it off. Covering him as a reporter, [I saw that] Scotty was a tough man to deal with, but you couldn't argue with his results. Pierre had all of the bluster that Scotty had and none of the skill as a coach."

Brian Burke also alleged that McGuire tried to undermine his authority while he had served as GM. In his book, Burke said McGuire and Gordon spent time together at the practice rink, watching playoff games while McGuire would critique players and coaches. When Burke found out, he wasn't happy. "He was trying to work his way into Richard's good graces, while at the, same time, undermining me," Burke said, who added that he had since made peace with McGuire about what happened. "But Pierre had poisoned the well," he added. "The damage was done."

All the optimism in the world couldn't save a rapidly slumping situation. The team went 23-37-7 that season under McGuire and Holmgren. It was an up-and-down year, but McGuire was willing to use a variety of approaches to get the team out of a rough patch. Some of them worked, and some of them didn't. Cassels recalled one afternoon when the coach thought of an outside-the-box approach to fix their scoring woes. "We're in the room and hear all this commotion in the hallway. The door opens. Pierre is dragging in a net from the ice," Cassels said. "Now, it's tough to get that thing off the ice, down the hall, and into the room. He's huffing and puffing. Anyway, he has a string hanging from the crossbar with a puck tied to it. He calls us over and starts his spiel. 'I know we're struggling to score. Now, take a look at this puck. Look at how small this is and how big the net is.'

"[McGuire] looks around the room, and he sees Robert Kron—he hadn't scored in what seemed like months. 'Bobby Kron, step on up here and shoot the puck in the net and see how it easy it is.' He goes to shoot and hits the crossbar. 'Just focus,' Pierre says. His next shot, he hits a post, it bounces off the post and hits Sean Burke—who had a locker right next to the net there—in the head. Burkie was pissed, and I think he had to go get stitched up. Pierre looked away and said, 'Well, maybe we need to try something else.'"

While McGuire was muddling through his first stint as a head coach with a team struggling to put the puck in the net, far more troubling issues loomed for the franchise. Whereas he was an obvious talent who would go on to accomplish great things in the NHL, Pronger, that spring, clearly wasn't ready to take on the role of franchise savior. On March 24, 1994, at 3:55 a.m., Pronger, Verbeek, Geoff Sanderson, Mark Janssens, Marc Potvin, Todd Harkins, and assistant coach Kevin McCarthy were arrested following a brawl at the Sports Grill and Network Club in Buffalo, which was owned by former Bills quarterback Jim Kelly.

You could argue about what might have happened and romanticize that the teammates were all sticking up for each other. But for a team that was one of the worst in the league the year before, was already out of the playoff race, and was in the midst of a 1-8-1 stretch, it was a miserable look. That doesn't even consider that the players involved were among the best on the team: At the time of the incident, Verbeek and Sanderson were the Whalers' top scorers and Pronger was the leader among defensemen. Verbeek, a right winger, had 33 goals and 34 assists for 67 points.

"On behalf of the Hartford Whalers, I'd like to apologize to the City of Buffalo and the Buffalo police for the unfortunate incident," Whalers director of player personnel Kevin Maxwell told reporters in a statement. "We're embarrassed. Certainly we don't condone the actions of our players."

"I will not tolerate this. I am indignant," Gordon told reporters. "There will be some announcements [today]."

"There was a twelve o'clock curfew. And we missed it. We embarrassed ourselves, our families, our organization. We let everyone down," Verbeek told the *Hartford Courant*.

Pronger was suspended the rest of the season, but when it came to the league, the Whalers did not face disciplinary action. But that was just the beginning of a godawful stretch for the franchise that showed a team in the throes of an alcohol problem. One week after the incident in Buffalo, Holmgren was arrested for drunken driving. The Whalers granted Holmgren a leave of absence to enter the Ford Clinic in Rancho Mirage, California, for evaluation and counseling. In April, Hartford defenseman Bryan Marchment was arrested for drunken driving. The twenty-four-year-old Marchment was arrested by Farmington, Connecticut, police while driving home from a charity event sponsored by the Whalers' wives.

Alcohol had always been part of hockey culture, but there seemed to be something more troubling happening. (One Whaler who was part of the team in the early 1990s said one of the unofficial mottos of the team was "Win or lose, we drink the booze.") Taken singularly, these sorts of incidents aren't necessarily indicators of something darker. But when multiple instances of alcohol-fueled trouble take place in short order, it reflected a larger problem. Marchment was the ninth member of the Whalers to be arrested on alcohol-related charges in a three-week period.

The management didn't seem to be taking the issue seriously, at least when it came to dealing with the media. Bernstein recalled one incident when she was made out to be the villain. "I was very new on the beat, and very young, and I wanted to show I'm a good, tough reporter," said Bernstein. "I found that Paul Holmgren—a really nice guy who had some issues, but he was a nice guy—was driving, and his license had been suspended because of an incident involving alcohol."

Bernstein, who shared a byline on the Holmgren story with Jacobs, said Holmgren didn't give her any grief for reporting what happened. That wasn't the case for some other members of the organization.

"They were mad at me, furious for writing that story," Bernstein recalled. "Not too long after that, I'm standing behind the glass at practice, and all of a sudden, pucks are coming at me. It was Pierre and a couple of players shooting pucks at my head. They didn't break the glass, but they were clearly trying to send a message."

Despite the clunky execution and poor decision-making, there was some occasionally compelling hockey. The Whalers added well-respected veteran Brian Propp before the 1993–94 season, and the thirty-four-year-old was on the cusp of a couple of scoring marks, including his 1,000th career point and playing in his one thousandth career game, so some believed his signing was a way to boost ticket sales. But he ended up having a bigger impact on the roster than many initially believed.

"I went to training camp with them, and they let me sign as a free agent," Propp said. "I was happy to be there—I didn't want to end my career. I wanted to keep playing, and so I was determined to make the best of it. My goal at the start of the season was to work hard and lead by example. Of course, they ended up having guys who got hurt that year, and that gave the opportunity to play more than expected."

Propp played sixty-five games during the 1993–94 season. On March 2, 1994, he played in his one thousandth career NHL game against the Kings, and on March 19, he notched the 1,000th point of his career in a win over his old team, the Flyers. It was Propp's last full season in the NHL, and with Francis and Dineen no longer around, the Whalers were happy to have his leadership.

"It meant a lot to me to be considered a leader—when I first started my career in Philly, guys like Bobby Clarke and Bill Barber were the leaders, guys who didn't say a lot but led by example," he remembered. "About five or six years in, I finally learned how to talk, and so guys started listening. That's some of what I brought to Hartford. I tell you, the fans here were so appreciative and positive, and I tried to feed off that. Hopefully, it made a difference with the younger players that were there at the time."

IN THE EARLY 1990S THE ECONOMIC LANDSCAPE OF THE NHL was changing, and a small-market team like the Whalers needed to adapt if it wanted to survive. In 1993 the team received $30 million from the state to erase the team's debt and also received the right to use the Civic Center rent-free. In return, the Whalers agreed to stay at the Civic Center twenty years and sign over the rights to luxury skybox revenue to the state. That sparked some optimism, and when tech mogul Peter Karmanos plunked down $47.5 million for the team in June 1994, it was thought that things were turning around. (The Connecticut Development Authority had to approve the sale to Karmanos after Gordon signed a lease last year that gave the state first option to buy the Whalers in exchange for Connecticut providing financial assistance.)

Karmanos, who cofounded the Detroit Compuware Hockey corporation in the late 1970s, was thought to have deep roots in the sport of hockey. At the time, the idea of him buying the team was seen as relatively positive by local fans. Anything that would put the chaos of the Gordon era in the rearview mirror and help deliver financial stability was welcome.

Gordon's exit was celebrated by many hockey fans. He later understood why. "No question," Gordon said in a 2021 interview with *Religion of Sports* when asked if he would have handled things differently. "I take total responsibility for it, because I'm the one that has to make those decisions. So you feel like it's an embarrassment really. You have an obligation to the fans and to the community. And you've let them down. And if I were to do it over again, I would do it a lot differently."

As for the new boss, things started on an optimistic enough note. "We're really good at running hockey teams," said Karmanos, who pledged that the team would remain in Hartford for at least another four years. "We know what we're doing. The CDA [Community Development Authority] was looking for someone who had commitment to Hartford but also somebody who will be successful. The difference was what we were willing to do past the price. This is absolutely wonderful."

One of the moves that endeared the new ownership to the fan base was the decision to fire McGuire after one season as head coach, reinstall Holmgren behind the bench, and name Jim Rutherford as the new GM. Many players reportedly campaigned for Holmgren's return, if only because he wasn't McGuire, and Karmanos and Rutherford happily obliged.

"I could have brought in a new coach," Rutherford said. "But there were no guarantees that it would have worked. The fact is, Paul knows the team the best, he is prepared the best to coach this team and that's why I gave him an extension on his contract. He is a better coach than his numbers show.

"I knew these questions would come up. People will say he has been here before, he gave it up, there were some problems. I feel very strong Paul is the man for the job. He had a good approach with the players. I talked to a lot of very prominent people in the NHL who think very highly of his capabilities."

"It got to a point where I didn't like coaching," Holmgren said upon his return. "I played almost 11 years in this league and I don't know if I was a good enough player to play one year. But I did play because I worked my butt off. Having watched guys not do that with a lot more talent, certain nights pushed me over the edge. To be honest, I might have strangled somebody.

"Sometimes, you don't know how much you miss something until you don't have it anymore."

But a lockout shortened the 1994–95 season—forty-eight games, as opposed to eighty-two. And while the new labor agreement was good for players across the league when it came to salaries, some of the smaller-market teams (like Hartford) felt the squeeze. The Whalers' payroll in 1988–89 was about $5 million. By 1995 it was roughly

$20 million, and that was with some brutal cost-cutting decisions, the biggest coming in March 1995 when they dealt Verbeek to the Rangers. The thirty-year-old, who had been a part of the franchise since 1989, never had the same juice as Francis, Dineen, or Liut but still moved the needle with the fan base as one of the last remaining links to the wild days of the late 1980s.

But the captain was in the last year of a $1.15 million deal and would almost certainly command more than that on the open market. (Four years later, his base salary would be $3.2 million as a member of the Dallas Stars.)

"I am going to miss Hartford tremendously," Verbeek said glumly after the deal was announced.

Without Verbeek, in a shortened season that was more like a sprint than a marathon, the Whalers were still able to hang around the fringes of the playoff race. At one point that spring, they were able to win eight of sixteen, but it wasn't enough to get them into the postseason, and it wasn't enough to satisfy the new owner. At the end of the 1994–95 season, the team announced it had lost $11.5 million. Karmanos offered a bottom-line assessment of just how far financially he was willing to go.

"If we lose $11 million for the next four years, we're outta here," Karmanos told reporters that June. "We are outta here, and I don't think anybody could blame us at that point."

To their credit, the front office was seeking a spark in the form of a trade. The Verbeek deal would theoretically give the small-market Whalers more financial flexibility, and one of the hot rumors at the time was that Hartford was going to make a pitch to reacquire Francis. After all, that had to be one of the reasons why the Whalers didn't name a new captain after the Verbeek trade. The thirty-two-year-old Francis had become one of the cornerstones of the Penguins franchise, but as far as Hartford was concerned, if there was any way to win over the fan base, it would be the return of the prodigal son.

On his way to the annual NHL Awards, Francis stopped back in Connecticut. "I went to [Bradley Airport] right before the awards ceremony in Toronto, and I picked up a *Courant*," Francis later said. "I saw the trade talk. I sat with [Penguins GM] Craig Patrick that night, and I said, 'I'm putting my house [in Unionville] up for sale. Should I take it off the market?'"

The talk continued throughout the off-season, with Pittsburgh apparently seeking a package of Andrew Cassels, Mark Janssens, and highly touted Marek Malik for Francis. But Hartford management reportedly balked at the idea of including Malik as part of the deal.

And so, with the return of Francis off the table, in the hope of trying to provide a spark, the team unleashed what was ultimately remembered as the last big trade in the history of the franchise, sending Pronger to St. Louis for Brendan Shanahan on July 27, 1995. The six-foot-three, 220-pound left winger was equally adept at scoring (in six of his seven years before he joined the Whalers, he finished with 50 points or more) and mixing it up as needed (he racked up at least 100 penalty minutes a season in each of those seven seasons). But Shanahan had been feuding with Mike Keenan, who took over the Blues prior to the start of the 1994–95 season, and Keenan was all too happy to move him for Pronger.

After expressing some doubts after the deal went down—he explained his statements by saying he was an emotional guy who had become attached to St. Louis—Shanahan sounded like a man all in at the start of camp. "I got really angry during the summer," Shanahan told reporters that September. "I hadn't met the guys here. I hadn't played for the team. But I was angered how people were so disrespectful toward Hartford, to the Whalers.

"You really don't know my personality yet, but that's a great way to make me feel like a part of this team. That's great incentive for me to stick it in their faces."

On the surface, Shanahan was a hard-nosed, well-respected vet, and the Whalers' first legit star since losing Francis in 1991. His arrival was part of an ongoing transformation around the team—Hartford was done playing finesse hockey. Inspired in no small part by some of the moves made by Burke, the Whalers would become one of the more physical, tough teams in the league through the mid-1990s, and Shanahan was going to be the sort of bruising marquee talent capable of leading Hartford back to the playoffs. But given the circumstances, more importantly, the twenty-six-year-old was the sort of guy you could put on billboards and season-ticket brochures, someone the fan base could hang their hat on.

"It's unbelievable he's here," Kelly Chase told reporters who asked about Shanahan's arrival before the start of the 1995 season. "He's going to demand respect from other teams. He's our leader. A captain. He wants guys to push themselves, because he really pushes himself. He'll grab you by the hair and kick you in the rear end when you need it. And we will need it sometimes.

"People laugh at Hartford. But just you wait and see," Chase added. "Guys here were happy just being close in the past. That's not the way it's going to be anymore. We're going into rinks and [we] will leave hated.

"When I was with other teams, when we came into Hartford, we were never really intimidated, you know? I wanted to be part of a team that tried to change that," Chase said. "We were a tough team.

"It was a big team, and we had size and toughness. Gerard Diduck . . . there were some big guys on that team, guys who could hold their own. Scotty Daniels, me, Stu Grimson, Mark Janssens, Keith Primeau. We weren't playing around. There were nights where it was miserable to play us."

That was a popular, close team that seemed to enjoy playing together, and Chase played a large role in that. He created the Hard Hat Award, meant to celebrate the more blue-collar aspects of the game.

"That was just the fact [that] we wanted to have something that wasn't all about the goal scoring," Chase said when asked about the award. "If you blocked four shots on a penalty kill and we won by a goal, you deserve some credit. It may not be recognized by the writers when it came to awarding the stars, but that's what we were about. You see another guy taking a pass through the middle of the ice, you had to figure out a way to deflect the puck. How much do you care about paying the price to win? You see a guy do that a few times, you start to think, 'Holy shit, this is a guy I want on my team. I want to play alongside this guy.'"

A lot of the team-building stuff that took place with those mid-1990s teams was about making the best of a less-than-ideal situation. "Hartford was never a real thrilling city to visit," Chase said. "I always said that the best part of playing [for] Hartford was the fact that there were no more road trips to Hartford. But the truth was that we were as close as any team in the NHL.

"I was there with some really great people, and we really bonded. Let's face it. There's nothing to do in Hartford. We had each other—that's what made it such a fun time. We had a young team with a lot of guys who just hung out, or had girlfriends or had just gotten married."

The 1995–96 team really was a fun team to watch, maybe the most fun of the mid-1990s Whalers. The dark days of the 1992–94 era were behind them, and in their place was a rambunctious, compelling bunch who could score, brawl, deliver a sharp quip, and do it all with a smile. After Holmgren was shown the gate in November—this time, for good—after a respectable 5-6-1 start, the Whalers hired twenty-eight-year-old Paul Maurice, the youngest head coach in the league. They had wild stretches—one when they won seven of eight and another when they went winless in ten of thirteen. That season, six Whalers had 100 penalty minutes or more, and only three teams had more penalty minutes per game than Hartford. They were shut out a league-high eight times but swept the Avalanche, who would win the Stanley Cup that season. And even though everyone started to come to grips with the idea that Shanahan wasn't going to be long for Hartford, it was fun getting a chance to watch him play with a bunch of scrappers like Chase every night.

Brightening things even more was the return of Dineen in a trade with the Flyers in late December. His second incarnation with the Whalers was different than the first—he wasn't the same top-level point producer he had been before he was shipped off to Philadelphia.

(In twenty games with the Whalers that year, he had 9 points and 67 penalty minutes, which meant he fit in perfectly on that roster.) But for the first time since that awful stretch where he, Francis, and Liut had all been dealt in the early part of the decade, a guy was on the roster who bled green, a rough-and-tumble presence who might as well have had Peter Good's logo tattooed across his chest. Just having that well-respected veteran presence on the roster and in the locker room meant something.

"Kevin Dineen is our town's hockey gate-keeper. He ain't Mark Messier. And he ain't the chamber of commerce. And if the Whalers do, indeed, end up moving after the 1997–98 season, he may be remembered as Davy Crockett at the Alamo," Jacobs wrote in the *Hartford Courant*. "But God bless him. If the Whalers don't kill him, he still may save them."

"When he came here at the end of last December, he brought the one element we lacked and really needed," Maurice told the *Courant* soon after Dineen was reacquired. "That was the intensity on a game-to-game basis. Physical intensity. I don't want to take away from other guys. But that's Kevin's talent. Every night. The scrap. In your face.

"He doesn't allow anybody not to go hard. Even if we struggle or he struggles or his line struggles, he doesn't quit. He never decides 'This is not the night I'm not playing well so I'll put it into neutral and wait for the next game to come along.'"

In the end, they weren't very good—Hartford failed to make the postseason again—but when compared with the rest of the mid-1990s teams, they were a lively, entertaining bunch that gave the people who showed up their money's worth. The return of Dineen was a happy bonus.

But fan support continued to be an issue, so much so that things had reached a genuine crisis point for the first time in franchise history. At the end of the season, Karmanos—who said he had already lost $31 million on the team—and the team announced a ticket drive and said he would be willing to pull the plug if more tickets weren't sold.

"If the ticket drive falls on its face, we could leave," Karmanos told reporters. "You can't say you want a major league team and average 10,000 fans a game."

To be fair, the attendance numbers had grown, with the average per game going from 10,144 during the 1992–93 season to 11,983 during the 1995–96 season. But high-end, steady revenue streams, such as sales of skyboxes and season tickets, remained an issue. That year, the team had leased just over half its skyboxes and sold 5,800 season tickets. Those numbers would have to change.

"I think that in light of our losses that the state would give us permission to leave," Karmanos said. "When you've lost as much money as we have, you have to look around and ask what we're doing here."

Against that urgent backdrop, the 1996–97 team started strongly, winning five of its first six and ten of its first eighteen. On November 22, after a 3–1 win over Montreal, the Whalers were in first place in the Northeast Division with 23 points. Maurice was clearly a good fit for the franchise (he would coach thirteen seasons, the longest tenure in the history of the team), Dineen was reinstalled as the team captain, and tickets were being sold at an impressive clip. That year marked the first since the 1989–90 season that the team averaged over 13,000 per home game: 13,680.

But storm clouds were gathering. Early in the 1996–97 season, according to *Sports Illustrated*, Shanahan had taken to driving to the rink with his suitcases because the trade he had demanded seemed imminent. Everyone could see that a deal was going to get done sooner rather than later. It was just a matter of time. The day-to-day speculation became a grind.

"Shanny had just gotten back from the World Cup, and everyone pretty much knew he wanted a trade," said Kent Manderville, who was eventually signed after a tryout following a strong preseason and training camp. "We were in Tallahassee at a preseason game against the Florida Panthers. Days before, he was playing with and against the best players in the world. Now, he was in Tallahassee, Florida. *Yeah, you look like you're thrilled to be here*, I remember thinking when I looked at him."

Rutherford had no shortage of suitors. He pulled off a deal with the Red Wings on October 9, 1996.

"We made the trade because we were at the point where we felt enough was enough," Rutherford told reporters after Shanahan was traded to Detroit along with defenseman Brian Glynn for Paul Coffey, Keith Primeau, and a first-round draft pick next year.

"When I was there, it was not a great situation because it seemed inevitable that the team was moving," Shanahan told the *New York Times* in 2009. "But they've got a lot of passionate hockey fans."

But just as soon as the Whalers had rid themselves of one veteran who didn't want to play in Hartford, they found themselves in possession of another. Coffey made it clear—in no uncertain terms—he didn't want to be sent to Hartford. He had to be talked into reporting by Karmanos, and although he didn't make as much of a public stink as Shanahan, it was soon evident his time in Hartford was going to be brief.

"Shanahan hurt his wrist and still scored 44 goals," said Hartford sportscaster Rich Coppola. "Bottom line? He went out and performed—unlike Coffey."

Coffey and Stu Grimson had been teammates in Detroit, and they had gotten along well enough with the Red Wings. But when Grimson saw Coffey turn sour when he arrived in Hartford, it was a sign bad things were on the horizon. "He was a distraction from the moment he arrived. Paul was totally disengaged," Grimson wrote in his biography, *The Grim Reaper*.

"Not everyone would have felt comfortable calling out a guy like Coffey. But right or wrong, that instinct has always been part of my DNA. Veteran Kevin Dineen—in his second tour with the Whalers—and I had been talking about Coffey and what a distraction he was becoming. If anyone on our club was going to address this it was probably going to be me."

Things came to a head during a practice drill when a lethargic Coffey missed Grimson's stick with a pass. Grimson broke ranks and started yelling at the future Hall of Famer.

"Quit dicking around, Coff," hollered Grimson. "If all you're going to do is screw off all morning, show yourself off the ice. We're trying to accomplish something here. If you're not interested in being a part of it, pack up and move on!"

The two had to be separated, and on December 15, 1996, Coffey was sent to Philly, along with a third-round selection in the 1997 draft. The Flyers sent defenseman Kevin Haller, a 1997 first-round pick, and a seventh-round pick to Hartford.

So at this point, the Whalers had dealt away Pronger, one of the better young defensemen in the league. Shanahan was gone, replaced by Coffey. And twenty games into the 1996–97 season, Coffey was gone. Hartford was able to acquire draft picks and younger players (Primeau would be an excellent addition, but his acquisition was mostly overlooked because of what the Whalers had to give up to get him), but even after the return of Dineen, the word was clearly out: Two high-profile veterans like Shanahan and Coffey wanted out, largely because of an uncertain future for the team. That spoke volumes to the rest of the league.

"The trade of Pronger for Shanny, when Shanahan came, if that had worked—if he had accepted the deal—I think everything would have fallen into place," said Forslund. "I always felt that was the one transaction that really backfired, and at the worst possible time. That was a bona fide star saying no to Hartford. If he had said yes' it might have been different. Maybe history would have changed."

Say this about Shanahan—when he was on the ice, there was no doubting his intensity. In his one season with Hartford, he led the team with 44 goals and 78 points. He didn't back down from a scrap, either—he was one of six guys on the team with 100-plus penalty minutes. Whether that can be interpreted as a sign he was playing for his teammates or showcasing his skill set for a potential trade partner depends on whom you talk to. But Shanahan and Hartford weren't a good mix.

"Brendan played his ass off that year," said one former teammate.

"He said, 'I'll come and play for a year.' And he played great," said Chase. "He wanted to be in a city and with a team where they were committed to winning. And I still believe that if it was a more stable place, he would have stayed.

"But he was just being honest. He didn't want to put anybody in a bad spot," he added. "I mean, the culture that Brendan was trying to change, trying to bring that sort of hockey mentality to Connecticut, it just wasn't going to work."

"There were some players who came to Hartford and just didn't want to be there. Paul Coffey didn't want to be there," Cassels said. "I can't speak to Brendan's experience, but I can say he played hard and played for the team when he was out there. Off the ice . . . I didn't hang around him much off the ice—I had a family and did certain things, and he was a single guy. Everyone has different lives away from the rink, and not really knowing or talking with him, I can't really comment on where his head was at.

"I know there were some guys who liked the glitz and glamour of playing in a big city—maybe that had something to do with it. Hartford was a smaller market, and it's obviously not going to offer things like bigger cities like New York and Boston and Toronto and Detroit might offer. I just know that he played hard for us. No one ever questioned his compete level on the ice. Off the ice, it was kind of on him."

IT WAS BECOMING INCREASINGLY EVIDENT THAT THE HALCYON days of the late 1980s were over. Even the most hardcore hockey fan had to admit that Hartford was a basketball town. The Huskies—both the men's and women's teams—were the number-one show in Connecticut. It wasn't like the Whalers resented the success of the Huskies. It was more a begrudging understanding that the days of hockey being the only big-time show in the state were done.

At the same time, the success of the UConn basketball teams created friction between the Whalers and some denizens. Add that to the signals that had been sent out in the wake of the departures of Shanahan and Coffey, and it was soon evident that Hartford wasn't shaping up to be a destination spot. Chase recalled an awkward encounter when he, Shanahan, and Sean Burke went out in Hartford; it spelled out just how poor of a mix Shanahan and Hartford really were. One night, the trio went out to Coach's, a downtown sports bar. The three approached the bar and were asked for ID. Shanahan forgot his wallet in his car—he didn't have his license. Despite the fact that he was arguably the most famous professional athlete in town at that point, the bouncer still wouldn't let him in.

"You have my fucking picture on the menu but you won't let me in?" Shanahan asked incredulously.

"He was the only All-Star on the team, and they didn't let him in," remembered Chase. "He said, 'Fuck it. If I can't get into the bars or restaurants, I'm not sure this is going to work.'"

The reminders they were taking a back seat to a college program were constant, remembered Carson. Chase said they organized a team boycott of a place he said was trying to get them to show up on a regular basis. The bar, which had deep roots with the UConn basketball crowd, was—at least peripherally—heavily associated with Connecticut basketball coach Jim Calhoun, much to the consternation of some players at the time. "Rebecca Lobo could show up without an ID and walk into the place with her entourage, and no one would bat an eye," said one player who was on the roster at the time. But it was just another example that basketball had long surpassed hockey as the number-one sport in Connecticut. And Shanahan was having none of it.

"He's 100 percent right," Carson said. "Every day in the paper, the front of the sports page, it was 'The Huskies Win Again.' They had top billing. We were like, 'Hey, we're a pro team.' It wasn't that way when it came to coverage, and that spilled over into our numbers, at least when I was there. You'd go to the Civic Center, and the place wouldn't be full, but you'd go to MSG or the Boston Garden, or Philly, and the crowds would be overflowing. 'Why can't we get that?' I get it—we weren't always a playoff team. But even teams that weren't doing great, they'd get better crowds than us."

The shift from the Whalers to UConn basketball could also be seen in ad revenue. "There were nights when we were getting bounced off WTIC in favor of the Huskies," said broadcaster John Forslund. "We had to find a backup station for the game because the Huskies took prominence over the Whalers. To lose a 50,000-watt station like that was a big deal. Then, your advertisers start thinking to themselves, *Should I buy more UConn and less Whalers?* That was a big part in the demise of the franchise—the shift in what Connecticut sports fans felt was truly important."

It was a difficult situation for those in the local sports media who witnessed the rise of the Whalers in the 1980s and could respect how the franchise had been run during the glory days. But UConn basketball had become a national story. The Huskies had to have top billing.

"I really think we were balanced," said former Connecticut sportscaster Rich Coppola. "We had to acknowledge that year of UConn basketball when it all went to the next level—they were putting together a season for the ages, and you also had a competitive Whalers team. It was hard to strike a balance between the two.

"But it was clear from that point on that UConn basketball had a pretty good hold on the state. Once UConn got really popular, there were a lot of the guys like Pronger who really couldn't understand why a college team was getting the exposure *over* an NHL team."

As the will-they-stay-or-will-they-go drama began to play out across Connecticut, it was a trying time for everyone connected with the team. On a regular basis, players faced questions about the state of the franchise and whether they believed the team would stick around. If they said or did the wrong thing, they'd face the consequences: Gerald Diduck put his house on the market and came home a couple of days later to find it covered in toilet paper. It was getting pretty brutal. Fiery Hartford mayor Mike Peters said that if he saw Karmanos on the street, "I'd be in jail. . . . I'd probably hit him in the back of the head." Peters later told the *New York Times* that if the team did move out of town, he'd be the one "lying down in front of the moving trucks."

But the domino effect that started with the Trade(s) and ran through the elimination of "Brass Bonanza" and the subsequent instability on and off the ice ultimately concluded with the announcement from Karmanos and Connecticut governor John Rowland in March 1997 that the team was leaving Hartford, having rejected an offer from the state for a new $147.5 million arena.

"In essence, we would build the facility and hand the Whalers the keys," Rowland told reporters. "I believe I presented the Whalers with the best offer I could reasonably expect the people of Connecticut and the legislature to support. Mr. Karmanos obviously believes that there's a better deal out there."

"The problem here is that we're in a Bermuda Triangle of markets, stuck between New York and Boston, and you need to do something special to survive," said Karmanos.

"We're done in Hartford, and there's no way we're coming back," added the owner in an interview with the *New York Times* the next month. "We gave it the old college try, but the economics just didn't work. And we lost an awful lot of money."

Karmanos didn't have a destination in mind but did eyeball a handful of other cities that were openly courting a team, including Columbus, Ohio; Nashville; Minneapolis–Saint Paul; Las Vegas; and Raleigh-Durham, North Carolina. "I remember we had a team meeting—I think it was a team dinner—and Peter Karmanos stood up in front of us and said, 'We're going to move, and we're going to move to Columbus.' I couldn't even tell you where Columbus was on the map," remembered Manderville. "*Where the hell are we going?*"

Not everyone was ready to cast Karmanos as the villain in this passion play, however. "Full disclosure—I've known him my whole life,"

Carson said of Karmanos. "He was close with my dad, and I still see him regularly now. We have lunch once or twice a year. Just an outstanding businessman, who is a big supporter of hockey in Michigan and the U.S. in general. He's a Hall of Famer.

"I think you have to remember there was a calculation when it came to Hartford. I remember the governor at the time was a guy who ended up getting in trouble, and there were always all sorts of discussions about keeping the team and splitting concessions and this and that.

"But I get it if you are a Whalers fan, and there's someone who comes in and moves the team after saying he wasn't. I think it's natural and human to want to blame that person.

"I also think you have to look at the bigger picture. We were just getting into the era of larger salaries and new stadiums, with suite revenue and concessions and TV contracts. The money was getting bigger—all that stuff," he added. "He was looking at it from a business point of view and a sustainability point of view. He believed that if we are able to compete, people will come, and we'll get the suite revenue, and that would lead to sustainability. I think he tried to get the best deal he could with the governor. In the end, he just made a business decision: I have to move the team. The NHL got behind him, and it happened."

While there were lamentations from league headquarters when it came to relocation, you could make an argument it was part of what Commissioner Gary Bettman wanted all along. The Whalers' move would be the latest in a line of northern teams moving south in search of better profits. In the previous five years, the Winnipeg Jets moved to Phoenix, the Quebec Nordiques to Denver, and the Minnesota North Stars to Dallas. (Winnipeg and Minnesota would later get new franchises.)

According to several players who were on the roster at the end, there were two distinct camps: relative newcomers or youngsters who had yet to put down roots in the community and veterans who had been with the team for the last few years and who had families. Those in the first group simply hadn't been around long enough to really understand how good they had it. It wasn't necessarily their fault, but because they were short-timers in Hartford, they simply saw it as another stop on their journey. Those in the second group took the news hard. They were losing something special.

"I think it really impacted us, to be honest, especially for the guys who had been here for a while and embraced the city and made it home," Cassels said. "I lived there a few summers, and we stayed to work out. It was home for our family . . . and now, when someone is saying you might be moving on, over an ongoing period, it does weigh on you, especially when it came to guys with families.

"I know that in our business, you can be gone any day, but when you're invested in a community, it can really sting. I felt horrible for the booster club—I had been to a bunch of their meetings, and they were diehard Whaler fans. Really, though, I think guys like us who had been there for five years or more, we were kind of feeling it. To lose a pro team, that's tough. That's a big part of peoples' lives. And for us, that last game, that was very emotional."

"The roster was pretty mixed at that point," said Adam Burt. "There were some transplants and a lot of turnover on the roster for a couple of years prior to the move. Let's just say there were guys with varying degrees of investment in the city. The homegrown guys, the lifers, they were much more serious about what was going on. There were some other guys on the roster who were just wondering what Carolina was going to be like after we all moved on."

The team was technically in the playoff hunt going into the final weekend, so any sort of special goodbye to the team at that point would have been out of place. But that was almost secondary. The circumstances dictated that, but the fact there was no countdown, no farewell sendoff, no ceremony for the fans to say goodbye to the players, the team, or the building made the last day feel so abrupt. The fan base could be pilloried for not showing up to support the team, but to not have some sort of farewell added to the overall sourness of the occasion.

The last week, there were five teams—Hartford, Montreal, Ottawa, Tampa Bay, and Washington—angling for the last two playoff spots in the Eastern Conference. Things looked good for the Whalers, as they were in the midst of a six-game stretch that included four wins and a tie. But a listless 6–4 road loss in the next-to-last game of the season to the pathetic Islanders—in which Hartford yielded a pair of short-handed goals in 1:50—left their fate up in the air. The next night, Ottawa beat Buffalo, 1–0, to officially knock Hartford out of the playoffs.

In a surreal scene, on Saturday—roughly eight hours before they were officially eliminated—the Whalers held an open practice at the Civic Center, inviting season-ticket holders who cheered their heroes. The players acknowledged the odd nature of what was going on.

"I had an awkward feeling. The fans were cheering us, and we don't deserve to be cheered," left winger Geoff Sanderson told the *Courant*.

That left the last Whalers game on the following afternoon, April 13, 1997. "When the reality had set in we would be moving, and that would be the last game, it made me sick to my stomach," said play-by-play man Chuck Kaiton. "Going to the game that day, I had an empty feeling. What will we do? Where will we go? A couple of days before that, I remember the bridge between the Civic Center and 242 Trumbull Street, and Jimmy Rutherford stopped me and asked me if I would be willing to come with the team to Carolina. I wasn't sure what he was going to ask, but my feeling was I had two years left on my deal. 'If you guys still want me, I'll go.'"

"The last game at the Civic Center was kind of like the last game for the Senators in DC," Dom Amore said, "only without the riot."

In an interview with the *New York Times*, Karmanos was asked if he would be there for the finale. "I don't think it would be a good idea for me to be there," he said.

"When you are going through a run like that, you knew the end was coming . . . but maybe not," said Forslund. "Maybe there was a playoff run? I mean, if there was a playoff run, that would have been storybook. But when we knew, the day before the last game, we handed out the team awards at the Civic Center—a nice fan event. And from that point until Sunday afternoon, a lot of thoughts ran through my head as to what I was going to say and how I would handle things.

"I finally just threw my hands in the air—I didn't really know what do to. In the end, I just [talked off] the top of my head in the open and in the close. Whatever I said, it wasn't scripted—what I said came from the heart. The only thing was I prayed it would make sense. I just had to make sure I didn't get carried away—it was hard to communicate exactly what was happening. But I did my best. I just went back and watched it a few years ago, and what we did, I was proud of it. I was proud of how we handled things, how we went on the air, how we handled the game, and how we finished the game."

The Whalers finished eighteen years of NHL play in Hartford with a sad and sorrowful end on April 13, 1997, a 2–1 victory over Tampa Bay. On an afternoon when most of the rest of the sports world was focused on youngster Tiger Woods making history with his first championship at the Masters, the Whalers were playing the last game of their existence.

The following leaflet was distributed outside the Civic Center:

Please Stay After the Game—Do Not Leave Your Seats

To show your appreciation to the players, and displeasure with the NHL and the team owner, please help us. After the game is over stay in your seats (or stand) and applaud and cheer as loud as you can for as long as you can. We will than [*sic*] peacefully refuse to leave the arena and stay as long as possible. We want to show the players how much they have meant to us, and how much we will miss them. Show the powers that be that we *want our team*. If we make national news, they have to notice.

Please read and pass along—we need the entire arena to be aware of this.

"That last day, I was just in a fog. I tried to keep my concentration, but it was tough," remembered Kaiton. "I remember, from a broadcast standpoint, I didn't break down. I did it like any other game until the end. That's when I got emotional and said my piece."

"It was an awful day," said longtime fan Dan Tapper. "During the first period they were doing a tone-deaf T-shirt-cannon thing from the ice. One came our way and my friend Rodney caught it. He held it over his head, shook it, and fired it back down to the ice—a fun act of defiance.

"But the rest of the day was just awful—people crying everywhere and most of us just not believing it was over."

In a serendipitous act, it was Dineen who delivered the game-winner. "The whole time, I was thinking I have to set up Kevin to score the final goal in Whalers history," Cassels said. "It would only be right to see him score that one. That afternoon, there were so many opportunities for him to score, and we just couldn't make it happen. Then, he goes and gets in a fight, and I'm thinking, *Jeez, Kevin, that's another few minutes you won't be on the ice to try and get that goal.* Of course, though, that just goes to show you what it meant to Kevin—I mean, we're in what is basically a meaningless game at the end of the season, and he's in a scrap. That just showed you his competitive side.

"But the fans were standing for what seemed like the entire game," he added. "They were up, and the last three or four minutes of that game, that was as loud as any building I've ever been in. That's when I started thinking, *This is coming to an end. This will be the last game I'll play in this building.* It was really emotional. After the game, I don't think many wanted to leave. I don't think they wanted to believe it was over."

They didn't. Before the game, Dineen and Maurice had a talk about the possibility of addressing the crowd after the game. Maurice said Dineen should say a few words.

"We had a quick discussion before the game," Dineen recalled, "and tossed around, you know, how will this play out? After the game, Mo, being the gracious, classy guy he is, said 'This is yours' and pointed me toward the microphone. It wasn't this big, planned thing. I thank Mo for having the recognition in that moment. I think he might have felt I was a better representative in terms of who should speak."

So Dineen addressed the fans who were left, many of whom were crying. "First, I'd like to thank the fans for their tremendous support of our charity, the UConn Children's Cancer Fund. We've raised millions of dollars, and I hope we can continue to see that support for the next number of years.

"It's been my pleasure to be associated with you, the fans, for your support," said Dineen, his voice echoing through the Civic Center. "And the enthusiasm you've shown in his building, there's none other. On behalf of all the players who have left Hartford, and for the guys sitting on this bench, we just want to say thank you from all of us. God bless, and thank you very much."

And that was that. They blew the foghorn again, and cued up "Brass Bonanza." The fans stayed and stayed and stayed, and kept cheering, hoping that something, anything, could reverse the course of what was about to happen. There were chants of "Let's Go, Whalers!" The players looked a little unsure what to do—there was no script, and other than the conversation between Maurice and Dineen, there no discussion about what to do, as the focus had been more about the chase for a possible playoff spot. After a few awkward moments, they filed into the room.

But after twenty minutes, the players, led by Burke, emerged from the tunnel. They had shed their game jerseys but were tossing pucks in the crowd, waving to those who were still hanging around, delaying the inevitable. They signed hats and T-shirts and sticks and anything else that fans, many of whom had climbed to reach over the top of the glass, could fling at them. Fans held up signs reading "I Bleed Plankton" and "Karmanos Is Satan." And a fan from Wethersfield, Connecticut, tossed a codfish on the ice.

"It was more just spur of the moment," Manderville said of the idea to return to the ice. "It does sink in—you're down there, and at the end of the season, you raise your sticks and salute the fans and, normally, you say, 'Thanks a lot for a great season.' But when I think when you are going through what we were go through, and you get back in the room and can still hear the people in the stands, you almost owe it to them to come back. And I think that's what that was. It was probably someone like Burkie or Dino who said, 'Let's go back out there.' You feel badly about what's going on, and while it's not like you did it, you want to reciprocate the appreciation with some sort of gesture."

Eventually, the players left the ice. The music ended. The fans left the building. And the Whalers were done.

"Standing in the concourse after the end of the game, seeing grown men crying their eyes out . . . seeing that, I never lost that feeling of community and how a team could bring people together, and how that was being ripped away," said Levy.

"You know, it's funny when you're younger—when you get older and your perspective changes, you probably want to just spend more time just drinking it in and enjoying the moment," Burt said of the last game. "I remember doing some of that to the point where I think we had done our final lap around the ice, and I was looking in the stands trying to find my daughter and family and friends in the stands, and I start to look around, and I realize I'm the only guy left on the ice. But I remember saying to myself that I need to remember what's going on here and remember that moment."

"It was such a terrible feeling going home," said Kaiton sadly. "I got home and had five drinks that night. I usually didn't drink like that after a game, but I had a few vodkas and just cried the rest of the night."

10

The Load Out/Stay
1997-99

For the diehards that were there, it was a real love affair. That team wasn't very good very often. They dealt with a lot of losing—and still supported the team.
—ESPN's Steve Levy

If everyone who says they were Whalers fans now actually bought a ticket back then, the team wouldn't have had to move.
—Former Whaler Kelly Chase

In the coming years, Connecticut sports fans were distracted by the men's and women's basketball teams at UConn. Geno Auriemma and Jim Calhoun were able to flip the script and make Connecticut a basketball-first state. The men's and women's teams nicely filled the void created by the Whalers' departure.

But the truth is that the state had soured on professional sports. The last straw, at least as far as Connecticut was concerned, came at the end of the century after the failed romance between Patriots owner Robert Kraft and Connecticut governor John Rowland.

Kraft was seeking a new stadium, but his attempts to find support from Massachusetts had been rebuffed by the Massachusetts legislature.

Rowland, perhaps seeing an opportunity to get back into the good graces of Connecticut sports fans, cozied up to Kraft, and in 1998 the two sides agreed on a deal that would create a new stadium along the Hartford riverfront, south of the intersection of Interstates 84 and 91, a spot that had been rebranded Adriaen's Landing. The state legislature overwhelmingly approved the plan, and on November 18, 1998, Rowland and Kraft announced to the world that the Patriots were coming to Hartford.

"This was not like it wasn't an option A and an option B. If the City of Hartford and the people of this state had not gotten together and come up with this, our family would have had to put this team up for sale," Kraft said at a press conference.

"We're disappointed that we couldn't get the deal done in our home state, but today it was like the day I bought the team. It's nice to know that there's that kind of passion in other communities about the team," Kraft told the *Courant*. "It looks like the people here are really excited about what this can mean to the City of Hartford. Believe me, we're excited too."

"The ripple effect is beyond belief," Hartford mayor Mike P. Peters told the *Courant*. "We won't just be known for finance or insurance. Now, we've got all the pieces of the pie."

Rowland and the state fundamentally bent over backward in an attempt to accommodate the Patriots, offering a $374 million deal that would be financed by state taxpayers and surcharges on stadium tickets, as well as economic concessions by Kraft. It was hailed by many as one of the best stadium deals in the league.

But delays soon started popping up. There were issues with tearing down the steam plant that was on the site, and logistical questions about just what it might take to shoehorn a stadium into the available space. There were issues with the land, the infrastructure. And Massachusetts officials—and NFL commissioner Roger Goodell—were operating behind the scenes in an attempt to keep the team in Massachusetts. Less than a week before the opt-out deadline, Kraft sent Rowland a letter: he and the Patriots were staying in Massachusetts. The steam plant delays were largely to blame.

"The scope of this project was a mountainous undertaking and much more complex than anyone anticipated when our discussions originally began," Kraft wrote in the letter.

Eventually, Kraft built the new stadium (mostly) himself. The Patriots' owner got the help of the NFL's new loan program, and the state would pay about $70 million for infrastructure improvements in Foxborough. The biggest takeaway is that although the Patriots pointed to the troubles with the steam plant that was on the site, really, in their quest to land a new venue, the Kraft family manipulated Connecticut to leverage a sweeter deal for themselves and a new stadium in Foxborough.

"It's now official," Rowland said in a press conference after it all wrapped up. "I am a New York Jets fan, now and probably forever."

Two years after the Whalers departed, the Patriots appeared to seal Hartford's fate. "It sucks," Peters told reporters.

"The idea of luring a major league team like the New England Patriots to this blighted insurance town between the lights of New York and Boston had seemed so grand, so exciting, so downright unlikely, that many Hartford boosters had feared that they would wake up from their blissful dream," Mike Allen of the *New York Times* wrote on April 29, 1999.

"Sure enough, that seemed to be happening this morning, when the breakfast television shows were dominated by shots of Gov. Paul Cellucci of Massachusetts, surrounded by legislative and business leaders, declaring shortly before midnight that his state was putting aside years of bitter negotiations with the Patriots' owner, Robert K. Kraft, and offering a package of subsidies for a new football stadium next to the one at Foxboro, just south of Boston."

IN THE FIRST YEAR AFTER THE WHALERS RELOCATED, A FAIRLY steady stream of diehards would regularly make trips to North Carolina, New York, or Boston to watch their team, which struggled to attract fans in its first year after the move. (The Hurricanes averaged a league-low 9,108 fans in Greensboro Coliseum their first season.) For many New Englanders, the Whalers were a hard habit to break. Even if they weren't really the *Whalers* anymore, there were more than enough connections to the team on a personal level that allowed them to find some small measure of satisfaction in seeing stalwarts like Dineen do well. Separating the players from the owner was a challenge, but many Whalers fans made it work.

But it was a cruel twist of the knife seeing Francis sign as a free agent with the Hurricanes in July of 1998. The legendary Whaler, whose deal with the Penguins expired, agreed to a four-year, $20.8 million deal with the guy who spirited the team out of Hartford. On one hand, the link to the Whalers, and Francis's unique spot in franchise history, provided some comfort to fans who still managed to support him, even after he was dealt to Pittsburgh. On the other hand, seeing Francis partner with Karmanos was a bitter pill to swallow for many back in Connecticut.

"Some will label [Francis] a traitor for joining forces Monday with a man who killed the NHL in Hartford," Jeff Jacobs wrote in the *Courant* after the news broke. "The fact that the greatest player in Whalers' history chose to sign with Peter Karmanos might smack romantics.

"A message to Whalers fans: forget about it. Save your heart for your sons and daughters. Save your heart for your wife and parents. Be a cold fish about this transaction," he added. "As they say on Tobacco Road, *it's bidness.*"

That the Hurricanes were bad in their first season in Carolina, finishing last in the Northeast Division at 33-41-8, was some comfort. But that quickly changed; within five years of leaving Hartford, the Hurricanes made it all the way to the Stanley Cup finals. In 2002 they lost in five games to a powerful Detroit team. And four years after that, they won it all, upending the Oilers in seven games.

Some connections to the old team remained: Glen Wesley was the last remaining holdover from the Whalers days, and he rejoiced in the chance to win a title. Equipment manager Skip Cunningham, who had been with the team since day one at Boston Arena, also got himself a ring. And Chuck Kaiton, who was the voice of so many Whalers games over the years, was suitably rewarded—and made sure to acknowledge Hartford when it was all said and done.

"Nine thousand, three hundred ninety-three days of frustration, and on the 9,394th day of NHL existence, the Carolina Hurricanes—the Whaler organization 'til '97—have won the Stanley Cup!" he exulted when it was all over.

But the image of Karmanos enjoying the spoils of victory so soon after leaving Hartford was difficult to watch. "Maybe you're happy for the old Whale," Jacobs wrote in the *Courant* after the Hurricanes beat the Oilers in Game Seven. "Or maybe you would rather burn in hell before seeing Karmanos' name engraved on the Stanley Cup.

"It really doesn't matter.

"It's about Mayberry. It's about their tailgaters.

"It's about Ronnie [Francis] and [Kristi] Yamaguchi cheering on the Hurricanes.

"There is joy in Mayberry.

"Even if Hartford shrugs."

There was still hockey in Hartford. The year the Whalers left, the Rangers' minor-league affiliate moved in, and right out of the gate, the Wolf Pack was competitive and relatively popular—12,934 fans showed for their first-ever home game October 4, 1997, and they finished that season with 99 points under GM Don Maloney and coach E. J. McGuire. They made the playoffs in the first twelve years of their existence and won the Calder Cup in 2000, beating the Rochester Americans in the finals. This was a consistently competitive team that, in any other market, would have been a fan favorite.

But it wasn't the same. They won, sure, but they were a Rangers affiliate, which meant the same fans who would come to town to taunt Hartford fans during Rangers-Whalers games now fundamentally owned the building. Some fans said they didn't want to be perceived as settling for an inferior product. And even though they worked to establish roots in the community, there was little local emotional investment.

There was some turnaround when Howard Baldwin came back in 2010. He entered into a business agreement with the Rangers that year and became the face of the franchise, leading a charge to rebrand the team the Connecticut Whale and returning the color scheme to the old green and white combination. Initially, the return of Baldwin provided a jolt to local hockey fans. There was a sense that after many years, the guy who had helped deliver professional hockey to the people of Hartford had come home. If anyone could help show their viability as a legitimate NHL market, it would be Baldwin.

But that initial spark never seemed to catch fire, at least with the fan base. Although the team remained competitive, the attendance numbers never took off as anticipated. That was in spite of memorable events that helped bring fans together, including a team reunion in 2010 that drew more than a thousand fans.

"We came up with the idea for Whalers' Fan Fest," Mark Willand said of the first reunion, held in 2010. "We got Rentschler Field, opened it up, and invited the players back. We got Dineen and Quenneville and Francis to come back. But nobody—not me, not Howard, not the facility manager, not anyone—knew how many people would show. We thought if we got eight hundred to one thousand people, we'd consider ourselves fortunate. I mean, we didn't have any money to promote it, and we were really sweating it out.

"So, we got it all set up, and I went upstairs to the press box to catch my breath before we opened the gates. I looked out the window, and the line of people started at the entrance and wound all around the stadium. As far as I could see, it was a sea of green and white and blue. We had five thousand posters, and we gave them all away. It was a beautiful moment."

Then, there was the Whale Bowl, a massive outdoor hockey event played February 19, 2011, also at UConn's Rentschler Field. It was a tripleheader played on a freezing cold afternoon, featuring a game between the Whale and Providence Bruins, a Whalers-Bruins alumni game, and Army and American International game. Attendance numbers were all over the map—the team announced that 21,673 tickets were sold, and roughly 7,000 had been distributed as freebies, while just over 15,000 were scanned. The windchill was in the single digits by the time the day wrapped up (which may have kept some fans away), but in the end, it was the nostalgic event the organizers had hoped for.

A few years later, the rise of women's hockey sparked the creation of the National Women's Hockey League. After the Rangers cut ties with Baldwin's group in 2012—and the team was branded as the Wolf Pack again—the NWHL's version of the Connecticut Whale was born. The franchise has played home games in Stanford, Northford, and Danbury, and as of 2021, it's one of the most competitive teams in the newly renamed Premier Hockey Federation.

THEN THERE'RE THE UNIFORMS. IN 2009 THE NHL ALLOWED companies to start using and producing the Whalers' logo once again, and a number of brands—including Mitchell & Ness, Old Time Hockey, New Era, Reebok, CCM Hockey (a division of Reebok), Original Retro Brand, Majestic, '47 Brand, and Zephyr—all jumped in, helping spark a boom on the nostalgia market and creating a sizable resurgence in Hartford's popularity. It was no surprise that Whalers gear became Reebok's top selling paraphernalia that year among noncurrent, or defunct, NHL hockey teams.

The legacy of the logo continues to amaze Good. "I've been doing this now for fifty years, and so when you complete a design, you end it, and you go on to the next project," he said. "I remember once when I was going down the highway and I saw three trucks with logos on them that I had designed. That was pretty much as far as it went. With this, it was just different—I know a lot of people are still quite fanatical about it."

In an era where teams are routinely going to three and four alternate jerseys, it was only a matter of time before the Hurricanes decided to try to cash in. In 2018 the Hurricanes indulged in some of their past by wearing old-school Whalers throwback sweaters. Some dismissed it as a naked money grab designed by a team without history, while others engaged in a sweet reverie that came with seeing the old logo and the green-and-white sweater on the ice again.

The one thing that most Whalers fans could agree upon? At the bare minimum, it was good to see someone connected with the Carolina franchise acknowledge its roots—under Karmanos's control, that never would have happened. With new owner Tom Dundon at the controls, at least it was a little more palatable.

"It's ours, right? I mean, it's who we were. It's part of the history," Dundon told reporters when asked about using the logo. "To me, it makes a lot of sense. . . . This was too easy. 'How could I not?' was probably the better question.

"I think it's really good-looking stuff, so for me it was like, this is great gear, and this is where we've come from, and you know, I think it's fun," Dundon added. "And so for me, this is supposed to be fun, it's entertainment, and we're supposed to care about the team, and you see something like that that looks good and creates something to talk about and something to enjoy."

Connecticut governor Dannel Malloy took notice and fired off a letter hoping to get the Hurricanes to take things a step further and play a game in Hartford. "As you are no doubt aware, Whalers fandom remains strong in Connecticut and throughout the region," Malloy wrote to Dundon, in a letter obtained by the *Courant*. "Nearly 20 years after the team left, Whalers gear remains the top-seller among non-current NHL teams, and the Whalers Brigade continues to host a successful radio program.

"In short, the Whalers spirit is alive and well in Hartford."

One hockey traditionalist who wasn't crazy about it was Bruins play-by-play man Jack Edwards. Edwards—who had been an occasional critic of Hartford's hockey history—had a beef with the Hurricanes using the jerseys without acknowledging the old retired numbers, including Johnny McKenzie's number 19.

"A lot of New Englanders, who were hardcore John McKenzie fans and a few New Englanders who were dear friends of the man, take great umbrage that even for a day . . . [Carolina] would have a number that is retired, which used to be a sacred thing, worn by another player, and a much lesser one at that," Edwards said during the third period of the Bruins' 5–3 road loss. "It shows the disconnect between the Carolina marketing department and hockey history."

But some believe the idea of the Hurricanes wearing the throwbacks is a good thing, especially when it comes to the long-term possibility of hockey returning to Hartford. "One of the reasons Washington got baseball back long after people thought it was possible was because there was a group of people who kept them in the public eye," *Courant* sportswriter Dom Amore said. "The Rangers wore Senators jerseys. The Twins wore Senators jerseys. They did their part to keep the team and the city in the public consciousness. That wasn't the only reason it happened, but it played a role. That's one of the potential upshots of what the Hurricanes are doing with those jerseys—keeping the Whalers in the public consciousness."

And when it comes to "Brass Bonanza," the song remains the same. A timeless tune that still resonates throughout the region, it pops up on ringtones and at high school and college hockey games in New England. That enduring charm still makes former Whalers chuckle.

"You know what? It was unique. And after a while, because of it, it started to grow on me. I liked it because if you heard it, that meant we had scored. But it was . . . unique," said Dave Tippett with a laugh. "Maybe something different would have been better? But it was there when I got there, and there when I left. But it really is amazing how many people still instantly know and recognize the song and where it comes from. I used to appear on a radio show in Seattle—I had a segment called "Tuesdays with Tipp"—and every time I'd come on, they'd play the song. It was fun—only good memories."

"I always loved it," Kevin Dineen said. "I mean, I love the fact you still hear it at games today. I heard it at a Harvard hockey game a few years ago. I know they play it at the Red Sox games. It rarely doesn't come up when I talk with people about the Whalers.

"I was in Switzerland recently coaching in Davos, and we were on top of one of the mountains, and there was a restaurant there, and a guy with a Hartford sweater on. We went over to talk to him, and you could tell right off the bat he didn't understand a word of English. But I started humming 'Brass Bonanza,' and he instantly knew what I was talking about. He laughed. You don't need a translator when it comes to 'Brass Bonanza.'"

"When I had a young family, we used to have the 45s, and my oldest son, Travis, who was born when we were in Connecticut, every time the Whalers would be playing he'd grab his stick and be playing ball hockey in the living room. And he'd score and play it all the time," said Mark Howe. "It's a catchy tune—as a Whalers player, you love to hear it all the time. It meant you were doing well. But I heard it a lot more at home than I did at the rink."

THESE DAYS, SOME OF THE ONLY TANGIBLE EVIDENCE THE Whalers existed lies in the rafters of Hartford's XL Center, where the retired numbers of the former franchise greats still hang, alongside the 1986–87 Adams Division Championship banner and a WHA banner listing their accomplishments.

But more evidence can be found around the league; ex-Whalers are in some powerful positions across the NHL, including working in the league office, running teams, coaching, and scouting. The heart of the best teams in franchise history lives on in an extended cast of prominent alums: Joel Quenneville won two Stanley Cups as coach of the Blackhawks. Tippett has been a head coach in Dallas, Phoenix, and Edmonton. Dean Evason is the head coach in Minnesota. At one point, there were twelve NHL head coaches who played in Hartford from 1982–83 to 1989–90, including Quenneville, Tippett, Dineen, Evason, John Anderson, Randy Cunneyworth, and Brad Shaw. In addition, Ron Francis is one of several current or former GMs who played in Hartford. In all, more than a half dozen members of the 1986–87 Adams Division Champions have gone on to serve as coaches in the NHL, not to mention players like Ray Ferraro who have carved out a reputation as excellent TV and radio analysts.

Dineen and Tippett say two people should get the credit for spurring so many of those mid-to-late 1980s Whalers into coaching and front-office jobs. "I think it was a testament to the type of players that Emile [Francis] brought together," said Dineen. "He was drafting guys that had the ability to play but also had a good hockey IQ. I think you realized that when we were going out to dinner after games on the road. You'd be out with your teammates, and the topic of conversation wasn't what nightclub you were going to hit up later but more about hockey and playing the game and how the game should be played. That was a testament to the veterans we had, guys like John Anderson and Joel Quenneville and Doug Jarvis and Mike Liut. We were pretty young, but we were focused."

"It was a unique situation, because we had such good people. I think the key behind it all was Emile Francis, the general manager," Tippett said. "He had a collection of players—there was a good group of players there, kind of the core of the group. We were there a long time—we made Hartford our home. It's kind of different now when everybody scatters in the summer. We were all living there in the summer. We were all members of different golf courses so we played each other's golf courses all the time—just a real good group of great people.

"I think we were always studying, always preparing," he added. "You have to remember, the game was different then—we talked a lot more before games. Now, there's a lot of video, and while that's great, we did it a different way. For example, the conversations we would have at the whiteboard—or the blackboard, back then—were about things like when we faced the Stastnys in Quebec. They were great on the power play, and before every game, we'd talk as a group about what we needed to do and what our assignments were and what we had to look for. Guys like me and Joel and Dougie and Mike and Kevin and the rest of us, we'd be there and communicate. 'Here's what we'll see tonight. Here's where Peter likes to set up. Here's where Anton is going to be. Let's be aware of all the scenarios.' It was more of a collaborative process than it is today, and I think some of that played into all of us becoming coaches. It was necessary to do back then."

Tippett says the legacy of Evans and Francis lies in every one of the former Whalers who holds a position of power in the NHL. "Our first coach there was Jack Evans. He was a great guy, not a real vocal guy, but he was a very honest coach. He wasn't all about Xs and Os. The players talked a lot about strategy and things like that, but Jack was a real honest man and treated us with great respect.

"I think the biggest factor of all was Emile Francis and his leadership. He was the general manager, and he brought all of us there and really empowered our group. He was very supportive of our group and wanted to build something in a small market like Hartford, but he wanted to build something special," Tippett added.

"He had a great relationship with the community, and he wanted our team to play and act like a team. All of us look back with very fond memories of Emile and the focus he had. He was never just adding players. He was building a team.

"We had a team that we knew we had to work very hard and play well as a team. We had some skill. Francis was our superstar, and Liut was in his heyday as a goalie. But we knew we were going to have to play well as a team if we were going to have success.

"We had a lot of role players. Quenneville was a shutdown defenseman. Jarvis, Peterson, and myself were penalty killers. Then we had real good two-way players like Evason and Dineen. But we were playing in an era where there were some great teams that we couldn't get by."

"If you look back at it now, it was a lot of really good players that came through there that became good coaches and management," said Sean Burke, who's now goaltending coach of the Canadiens. "The list goes on and on of guys who played there that are still having an impact on the NHL as coaches and management."

"They were good leaders then and it translates into coaching," goaltender Jean-Sébastien Giguère told the Associated Press in 2020. Giguère was one of the last NHL players to have worn a Whalers uniform—he was a nineteen-year-old rookie in Hartford during the 1996–97 season and retired in 2014.

"I played with Kevin Dineen and Sean Burke, and those guys were good with the young guys[,] at talking to them and making them feel welcome, teaching them the ropes of the game, and stuff like that. Those are the guys I remember from when I played there. I think that's a quality you need to be a coach."

ALTHOUGH THEY'RE GONE, THE WHALERS REMAIN A POP-culture touchstone for many, hardcore hockey fans or not. There's a quirkiness to their history—the logo, "Brass Bonanza," the what-might-have-been element of the team through the late 1980s and early 1990s—that makes them endearing, not to mention fashionable, among hockey intelligentsia. The whole package is catnip for hockey hipsters who still rally to the memory of the NHL's most dearly departed team.

In the 1994 Kevin Smith movie *Mallrats,* Jason Lee's character, Brodie, is about to break up with his girlfriend, Rene, played by Shannen Doherty. Locked into *NHL94,* he won't leave his gaming console:

> RENE: What are you doing? You promised me breakfast.
> BRODIE: Breakfast, shmreakfast. Look at the score, for Christ's sake. It's only the second period and I'm up 12–2. Breakfasts come and go, Rene, but Hartford—the Whale—they only beat Vancouver once, maybe twice in a lifetime.

In an interview with the *Hartford Courant* after the movie was released, Smith—a hockey fan who has referenced the Whalers in multiple movies—lamented the loss of the team. "When we played hockey on Sega, we used to go for the Whalers all the time. You have to love those jerseys. I'm going to have to go out and buy one before they all disappear. It's a shame they left. What else is there to do in

Hartford? What are they now, the Carolina Hurricanes? That's not a hockey team. It's like one day I woke up, and all of a sudden there was an NHL team in Dallas. Does ice even freeze there?"

"You don't get the same level of snark you get with other teams," recalled Sam Kennedy, a Whalers intern who later became CEO and president of the Red Sox. "I mean, when it comes to the Red Sox, we get a lot of praise, but there are also a lot of critics. I get it at Dunkin' Donuts every morning from Red Sox Nation. It's 50 percent positive and 50 percent negative. But I haven't had anyone since 1992 or 1993 that hasn't had a positive feeling or memory from the Whalers. It's really amazing. You don't really appreciate it when you're in the middle of it every day, but when something like that gets taken away, it causes you to realize how much you really love it. You have to take a step back. New England is arguably one of the greatest hockey regions in America—there's such a passion for hockey. And Connecticut has such a passion for the game, from youth hockey to high school hockey to college hockey. You're talking about a region that's hockey crazy, and when a team leaves, that's going to create a void."

"They had a devoted, devoted following that, in the end, was just too small," said former *Courant* hockey writer Viv Bernstein. "If somehow, they had a Glen Sather type to build a team like the Edmonton Oilers, they could have pulled it off. I mean, Edmonton was just as much of a hockey outpost as anywhere else in the league, but it became the center of the NHL universe because Glen and that team put together one of the greatest teams in the history of sports. It would have taken something like that to make Hartford matter, especially in a market with New York and Boston a hundred miles away."

"A lot of the guys still keep in touch from those years in the 1980s, even if it's at a great distance now," said Paul MacDermid. "And when we get together, it's like we never left Hartford."

"The nice thing is, when you have such a tight-knit team like we had in Hartford, when you see those guys at different times now, it's like that old feeling returns," said Stew Gavin, who now runs the Gavin Management Group, which helps athletes manage their cash flow.

"If I see [Paul Lawless] or [Evason], it's like no time has passed," continued Gavin. "There's still that same feeling of respect and admiration. I mean, it ebbs and flows—there are guys who are around hockey that I see, like Joel Quenneville, Kevin Dineen, and John Anderson, guys who I played with in Toronto and Hartford—I still them quite a lot. And it's nice to touch base. Some guys go off and do their own thing, but it is nice to see the guys when we get back together."

"It's amazing how close this group was," Tippett said. "I've been in pro hockey almost twenty-five years, and I've never seen anything like the bond we had and probably never will again. There's a group of ten to twelve guys who are still best friends. We all live all over the place, but when we run into each other, it's like the way the game should be.

"Nowadays, the athletes play one place and live in another, but when we were here, we all lived here. We were from Hartford, and I remember my wife [Wendy] going to games and saying, 'I know three thousand people.' Where else can you say that in a major sports town now?"

Will professional hockey ever return to Hartford? Can Connecticut's capital city ever regain that magic that it enjoyed with the Whalers in the mid-1980s? Right now, it's a long shot. When the league announced the most recent round of expansion, Hartford was passed over for Seattle. (There is small satisfaction in knowing the Kraken is run by Francis and the organization is staffed by many ex-Whalers.) Ultimately, however, the hopes for a new team would seem to hinge on the possibility of a new building, and given Connecticut's current financial climate, that might best be classified as unlikely.

One semi-feasible answer? Work with either Mohegan Sun or Foxwoods to get an eighteen-thousand-seat venue at one of the state's two major casinos. Gambling is no longer the taboo subject it has been—there's a team just off the strip in Vegas, for goodness sake—which removes one potential roadblock. As for location, well, the San Francisco 49ers play in a stadium that's an hour away from downtown

San Francisco. If a Hartford hockey team ends up playing in Mashantucket or Uncasville, there's nothing wrong with still referring to the team as the Hartford Whalers.

However, the biggest obstacle in that scenario is geography. Putting a new team along that eastern corridor, sandwiched between Boston and New York, is still a pipe dream, at least in the eyes of NHL officials.

Relocation is a possibility. In a 2013 story, *FiveThirtyEight* weighed the possibility of the financially troubled Islanders making the move from Brooklyn to Hartford. Nate Silver estimated that roughly 175,000 avid NHL fans live in the Hartford–New Haven metro area, which was "comparable to or slightly better than some of the lower-tier American NHL markets, including Columbus, Raleigh-Durham, Miami and Nashville (and better than Las Vegas, where the NHL is expanding)." Silver also noted there was room for growth.

"According to our estimates, 7 percent of adults in the Hartford metro area were avid NHL fans in 2013. But the percentage is 13 percent in the New York metro area and 17 percent in the Boston metro area," he wrote. "If the Islanders or another team were to relocate to Hartford, the numbers would probably improve. The Hartford–New Haven media market is the largest in the U.S. without a 'big four' sports franchise. But it's only about one-eighth the size of New York's media market (which includes Long Island and Northern New Jersey)."

In 2017 the governor of Connecticut and the mayor of Hartford sent a letter to Islanders ownership. "It has come to our attention that the Islanders may be in the need for a new home after the 2017–18 season. Recognizing that many issues will complicate your decision making, we would nonetheless like to offer Hartford's XL Center as an option for your interim use," said the letter, penned by Governor Dannel Malloy and Mayor Luke Bronin. "Of course, as we pursue the transformation of the building into today's NHL standards, we would suggest the building as a long-term solution to your needs as well. We are certainly willing to work with private partners to develop the building you would be proud to call home and to adjust our development plans to the needs of your clubs and fans."

But in the end, the Islanders spent time in Brooklyn before heading back to Nassau Coliseum. That, combined with the establishment of the Kraken, was another sign that the NHL no longer considers Hartford a feasible market.

Former Whalers like Sean Burke understand that it'll be a sizable challenge to bring an NHL team to Hartford because of how it all ended last time. "Quebec City might not be in a lot of ways any better of a market than Hartford on the surface, but it's Canada," Burke said. "When you speak of Hartford, people are going to remember that the team failed ultimately; at the end of the day, it couldn't make it. That's really, really hard unless there's somebody out there that can convince you that it's definitely going to make it this time around."

FOR NOW, HARTFORD IS PART OF A GROUP OF NORTH AMERICAN cities that have seen their professional franchises leave and never return. It happened in Seattle with the SuperSonics, in St. Louis with the Rams, and in Montreal with the Expos.

In Seattle, Sonics fans have the same simmering resentment for NBA leadership—specifically, former NBA commissioner David Stern—that Hartford holds for Bettman and Karmanos. There are many striking similarities between the Sonics and the Whalers. Both had a sizable grip on the local sporting population but needed some help—financial or otherwise—to survive. And both were done wrong by a league that ultimately wanted them elsewhere and a commissioner who was only too happy to engineer a move. After forty-one years in Seattle, the SuperSonics moved to Oklahoma City to become the Thunder in 2008. Like Hartford watching the Hurricanes, Seattle fans saw the Thunder go on an extended run of success almost immediately after leaving town following the 2007–8 season—in a six-year run from 2010 to 2015, Oklahoma City got as far as the Western Conference finals on four occasions, reaching the NBA finals in 2011–12. No wonder that a decade later, like in Hartford, the bitterness and depth of feeling that Seattle basketball fans have for NBA leadership is still present.

"With Stern, there is an overwhelming amount of good that's reflected in the robust nature of NBA basketball, nearly five years after his resignation," wrote *Seattle Times* columnist Larry Stone on the occasion of Stern's passing in 2020. "But any honest assessment of Stern's tenure as NBA commissioner must include his unsparing treatment of the Sonics, and the devastating impact that will outlive him."

Replace "Stern" with "Bettman," "NBA" with "NHL," and "the Sonics" with "the Whalers," and you'd have a fairly spot-on assessment of where Hartford hockey fans stand when it comes to Bettman's role in the removal of the Whalers from Hartford. "If Bettman had put in a scintilla of the effort that [he] has done to keep the Coyotes in Arizona, the Whalers would still be in Hartford," said longtime Whalers fan Gabriel Serrano.

But the people of Seattle haven't given up hope. Seattle sports radio personality Dave "Softy" Mahler is part of a charge trying to get the Sonics back to Seattle, a movement that continues to gain momentum. "It's been pretty impressive," he said. "People here have not just stayed on the wagon, but the wagon has gotten bigger. Now, it's a personal thing for a lot of people, almost like a mission to get a basketball team back in Seattle. I've been pretty impressed how fans have dialed it up."

The sports fans of Seattle have seen the Seahawks and Mariners rush in to fill the void left by the Sonics, but Seattle's beloved basketball team, like Hartford's Whalers, has carved out a retro niche that appeals to young and old alike. "It is a status symbol, in some ways, to show your Sonics colors. It shows you represent Seattle," Mahler said. "There's a store downtown called Simply Seattle that sells Sonics gear, and they have a website that's popular. You go to the golf course or the mall and you can see people walking around with Sonics gear. It still resonates with people in the community. I don't know if thirteen years after the Clippers left San Diego, you could go to a mall in Southern California and get a San Diego Clippers shirt."

For the people in Hartford, Mahler has a simple message: "Tell them to not ever let that fire die," Mahler said. "It doesn't cost you anything to have hope. It doesn't cost anything to wear your gear in public, post on social media, and keep that fire. The more people see it, the more likely other people will be motivated to do the same. [Hedge fund manager] Chris Hansen saw the Golden State Warriors championship parade and really realized that there was this growing group of Sonics fans, and he said he'd like to help out and jump on the bandwagon. The more passion people have, the greater the likelihood there is that someone with the financial wherewithal would be inclined to help out and work with you. If you are willing to be disappointed—which we have, again and again and again—if you are willing to fight and be a part of a cause to bring hockey back to Hartford like we're trying to do here back in Seattle, then keep that fire alive."

In the end, whether with a new team or relocated franchise, the hope is that one day, the league will smarten up and have a team in Hartford. One day, politicians will come to their senses. A hockey-mad billionaire will see an opportunity. And one day, in the not-too-distant future, "Brass Bonanza" will ring out once again, signaling the return of professional hockey to Connecticut. Until then, a series of indelible green-and-white memories will help nurture and sustain the diehards who—for now—are left to root for a team that no longer exists.

"Wise people always say that when a friend or family [member] you care about dies, their soul lives on in your heart," said longtime fan Jeff Bamberger. "Diehard Whalers fans like us feel that way about their team."